**SECOND EDITION**

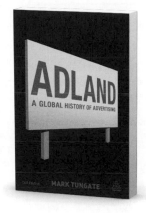

# Adland
# A global history of advertising

Mark Tungate

**KoganPage**

LONDON  PHILADELPHIA  NEW DELHI

First published in Great Britain and the United States in 2007 by Kogan Page Limited
Second edition 2013

120 Pentonville Road
London N1 9JN
United Kingdom
www.koganpage.com

1518 Walnut Street, Suite 1100
Philadelphia PA 19102
USA

4737/23 Ansari Road
Daryaganj
New Delhi 110002
India

© Mark Tungate 2007, 2013

The right of Mark Tungate to be identified as the author of this work has been asserted by him in accordance with the Copyright, Designs and Patents Act 1988.

ISBN      978 0 7494 6431 8
E-ISBN   978 0 7494 6432 5

**British Library Cataloguing-in-Publication Data**

A CIP record for this book is available from the British Library.

**Library of Congress Cataloging-in-Publication Data**

Tungate, Mark, 1967-
  Adland : a global history of advertising / Mark Tungate.
    pages cm
  Revised edition of the author's Adland published in 2007.
  Includes bibliographical references and index.
  ISBN 978-0-7494-6431-8 – ISBN (invalid) 978-0-7494-6432-5   1. Advertising–History.   I. Title.
  HF5823.T83 2013
  659.109–dc23

                                                                                  2013014332

Typeset by Graphicraft Limited, Hong Kong
Print production managed by Jellyfish
Printed and bound in Great Britain by CPI Group (UK) Ltd, Croydon, CR0 4YY

# CONTENTS

# PREFACE TO
# THE SECOND EDITION

When this book first came out, in 2007, I was surprised by how many people said something along the lines of: 'That's all very well – but what happens next? What's the future of advertising?'

While I devote a short chapter to the future of the industry, for me the response is in the subtitle: 'A Global *History* of Advertising'. This, then, is a history book. Pure and simple.

There's a problem, however, which is that history doesn't stand still. When *Adland* was published, Facebook was barely on the radar (it had been opened to the general public a year earlier). The iPhone came out in June that year, after I had finished writing. The iPad was still three years away. All these things and more would radically change the structure of the industry, accelerating an audience fragmentation process that had begun with satellite TV and continued with the growth of the internet.

In other words, just sticking your product on a major TV channel wasn't necessarily the best way of plugging it any more. Your public might be elsewhere, enjoying a new kind of entertainment on a different sort of screen. Confusing times for advertising agencies. Not only that, but the rate at which history is made seems to have accelerated. A new app can rocket from obscurity to worldwide renown in a matter of weeks. Advertising people often tell me they feel as though they're constantly running to keep up.

I address some of these problems in a revised chapter about the future, as well as in the short introduction. Other chapters have been adjusted and updated here and there, but largely left intact.

I fully admit that my real passion is for the history of the industry. During the original writing process, I took great pleasure in evoking the lives and times of people such as Leo Burnett, Bill Bernbach and David Ogilvy. I imagined walking into Ogilvy's office, perhaps to find him testily tapping a pencil on his desk as he examined my attempts to write a pithy phrase. And I was delighted to interview people who had experienced just that.

I also relished listening to experienced ad men and women as they recounted their early careers and recent successes. It's not every day you get to sit down with Alan Parker and listen to his stories about the London adland of the 1970s. Or visit the Greenwich Village apartment of George Lois and hear about his days at Bernbach's DDB.

If you already know these people, you'll realize why researching this book was such a blast.

And if you've never met them before – well, you're in for a treat.

## Author's note

As far as contemporary agencies are concerned, all job titles were correct at the time of writing. If I have missed out any advertising luminaries due to lack of space or simple misjudgement, I apologize. Your egos will recover, I'm sure.

# Introduction

*'Advertising is show business'*

The adman sits on the glassed-in terrace of a Parisian café and gazes out over the rapidly darkening square. People are hurrying home with baguettes and bottles of wine; maybe even some of the pungent cheese he loves. In the café there is chatter and warmth as apéritifs are served and the city tunes up for another evening of pleasure – an act it has been polishing for centuries. The spindly old streetlamps across the street have just come on, as have the tiny spotlights above an advertising billboard. It exhorts him to buy a new Peugeot.

The adman is pensive. The billboard he is staring at seems to belong to a bygone era. In just a few short years, the landscape of his industry has shifted around him. Not so long ago, the 1960s advertising execs depicted in the hit TV show *Mad Men* would have slotted in to his agency without anybody noticing. But not now. Today they'd look out of place quicker than you can say 'anachronism'.

The world has gone digital. A creative idea – the seed of any good advertising campaign – can now be expressed in myriad ways, across numerous media platforms. Posters still exist, certainly. So do newspapers, magazines, TV and radio. But there are also apps and online videos and social networks and all the rest of it. Clients are demanding more for less, and their procurement people are screwing the lid down tight on budgets. Greedy management consultants are nibbling away at his territory.

The adman isn't disheartened by any of this. Faintly anxious, perhaps. There's a lot to think about. But it's exciting. In the *Mad Men* era there were a finite number of solutions to any advertising problem. But now the answer can come from anywhere. It might be a gadget, an event, an art installation. He'd design a car for a client if he had to. There's a reason why the annual advertising festival in Cannes is now called the Festival of *Creativity*.

That's the difference, he thinks, between his agency and a management consultancy. His people actually create things. They *make* them. And the things they make create success for their clients.

The adman smiles and sips his glass of Bordeaux. Despite everything, he thinks, an advertising agency remains a very cool place to work.

## Servants and masters

Sir Martin Sorrell, the chairman of marketing group WPP, commented during an interview that 'advertising is considered an extension of show business'. Agencies are by no means court jesters, but the industry's glitz does tend to detract from its vital contribution to the global economy. It may also explain why many agencies have struggled to raise their status from suppliers to strategic advisers in the eyes of their clients.

One of the things that surprised me most during the research for this book was the sheer power that clients wield over their agencies. I was left with the impression that an advertising executive will stop at nothing to gain or retain a client. Certainly, when a client summons them they do not hesitate to cancel a meeting with a journalist, even if he has arranged to fly thousands of miles to interview them. This happened to me not once, but several times. The fashion industry, the subject of my last book, has a reputation for rudeness and inaccessibility. But nobody in the fashion business treated me with the lack of courtesy afforded me by some advertising agencies. And the client always got the blame. Perhaps this is only to be expected in a business where the clients hold all the cards. As one agency boss said, 'We know we're only three phone calls away from disaster.'

We consumers don't have the luxury of worrying about where the power lies in the partnership. We only know that, between them, advertising agencies and their clients have an immense impact on our lives. As digital media challenge the ability of TV to disseminate advertising effectively, brands are forcing their messages onto every blank space, into every crack in the urban landscape. More than wallpaper, advertising is the stuff that surrounds us.

Yet, even today, there is debate about how much of this advertising is really effective. Retail tycoon John Wanamaker stated over a century ago that half of all advertising works, but nobody knows which half. (The quote is occasionally attributed to adland legend David Ogilvy, which seems unlikely, for reasons we'll discover later.) In 2006, a book called *What Sticks: Why Most Advertising Fails and How to Guarantee Yours Succeeds*, by Rex Briggs and Greg Stuart, suggested that 37 per cent of advertising budgets are wasted.

Most clients continue to spend, however, despite the certainty that many of their advertising dollars end up down the toilet. In a world over-supplied with brands, they can't afford to stop trying to imprint their names on our minds. Worldwide spend on advertising currently stands at over US$500 billion a year and rising (according to media agency ZenithOptimedia). Agencies may be required to spread budgets over a wider number of media, but their relentless pursuit of consumers continues unabated.

# Learning to love advertising

While I allow myself to express an occasional burst of cynicism about the advertising industry, I can't help feeling that it's too much of an easy target. At a casual, dinner-party level, most people are pretty contemptuous about advertising. 'Sheer manipulation,' they mutter, darkly. The jargon, psychobabble and doubletalk of advertising have been spoofed in print, film and television since at least the 1950s. And yet, there are several reasons to like – even admire – the advertising industry.

I put Jean-Marie Dru, president and CEO of TBWA Worldwide, on the spot and asked him why we should love advertising. 'First of all,' he said, 'there will always be an intermediary between a product and a potential customer. You may say, "On the internet, that isn't the case", but in that environment the web itself is the intermediary. Sellers naturally want to reach out to buyers. Second, advertising is a catalyst for innovation. It stimulates competition, creates demand and encourages the development of new products. It is the accelerator at the heart of a liberal economy.

'Another advantage of advertising – although I'm not saying that this is its primary role – is that we have yet to find a more effective means of financing a free, varied and democratic media.'

Like many of his colleagues, Dru is convinced that consumers enjoy 'good' advertising: 'Nobody likes a bad product, but a well-made product will always find an appreciative audience. Furthermore, the agencies I know and admire have a great deal of respect for consumers. It is, after all, our job to understand consumers. In fact, advertising has far more respect for consumers than many other industries I could mention.'

Do advertising agencies provoke avarice, obesity and lung cancer? It's debatable. Do they interrupt our favourite TV shows with garbage that we don't want to watch? Thanks to today's ad-skipping technology, less and less. Do they create tiny gems of popular culture? Occasionally – yes.

One could also argue that advertising is a springboard for creative talent. The list of writers and film directors who have worked in advertising is long and illustrious: Salman Rushdie, Fay Weldon, Len Deighton, Peter Carey,

Sir Alan Parker, Sir Ridley Scott, David Fincher, Spike Jonze, Michel Gondry… I could go on… and on. The French creative director Olivier Altmann, of the agency Publicis Conseil, once told me, 'Working in advertising is one of the few ways you can be creative and make money at the same time.'

Another reason to respect advertising people is that they work hard. The image of young creatives playing table football in the agency bar is not exactly false, but it is taken out of context. Agency people work long hours, and they rarely switch off. Coming up with 'the big idea' to sell a product in a memorable way is not easy. And then, of course, there are those demanding clients.

In his book *Ogilvy On Advertising*, David Ogilvy wrote: 'The copy-writer lives with fear. Will he have a big idea before Tuesday morning? Will the client buy it? Will it get a high test score? Will it sell the product? I never sit down to write an advertisement without thinking THIS TIME I AM GOING TO FAIL.'

Ogilvy went on to claim that the account executive and the head of the agency lived in perpetual fear, too – mostly of their clients.

Having said all that, there's something enviable about a job in advertising. It seems to be a lot of fun, despite the pressure. Advertising people are often dynamic and charming. At the more senior level, they get to dine in expensive restaurants and travel to interesting places.

Let's face it: advertising is simply one of those industries that make you itch to pull back the curtain and take a good look behind the scenes.

## An impossible brief

Strangely enough, this book was inspired by a conversation outside a bar in Tbilisi, Georgia. I was covering a conference about advertising in Central Europe when I found myself chatting with a war correspondent. I observed that my specialist subject seemed pretty trivial compared to his. 'Not at all,' he protested, kindly, 'I find advertising fascinating. You'd be amazed how deeply engrained the trading mentality is – even in the harshest of circumstances. And advertising is part of that.'

After a brief pause, he asked me, 'Come to think of it, can you recommend a book about the history of advertising?'

I thought for a moment. And then I went on thinking. Finally I said to him, 'You know what? I don't think I've ever read one.' 'Well, there you go!' He slapped the table. 'There's your next project.'

There have of course been hundreds of books about advertising. Most of them have been written by agency bosses selling their own soup. Others have covered the industries of the United States or the United Kingdom. Few have taken a broader perspective.

Perhaps this is not surprising. Attempting to write a global history of advertising is a vast – if not impossible – task. For a long time I wondered whether it was even worth embarking on such an insane project. Then I stumbled across a line in the book *Paris: Biography of a City*, by Colin Jones. 'No history of anything,' writes Jones reassuringly, 'will ever include more than it leaves out.'

I was also greatly encouraged by Cilla Snowball, the wonderfully named boss of leading UK agency AMV BBDO, who said, 'It's definitely a story that needs telling. There is an archive [The History of Advertising Trust], but who sits down to read an archive?'

'Read' is a key word here. Although I've put together a small and rather eclectic selection of images, this is clearly not a picture book. Many such coffee table tomes are already on the market, and TV commercials are widely available on the web. A quick search for *1984* or *Launderette* on YouTube will provide access to those classic spots. What you'll find here are the stories behind the ads.

Neither did I wish to write an encyclopaedia. In order to provide something manageable for the author and digestible for the reader, the book takes a satellite view of the industry. In roughly chronological order, it endeavours to cover the most famous agencies, the best-known personalities, and the most compelling themes. And as the advertising industry is full of fascinating characters, all of them brimming over with insights and anecdotes, I tried to interview as many industry veterans and leading practitioners as I could get hold of. If any of the big names are missing, that's either because they declined to speak to me, or were unable to fit me in between client meetings.

You may also note that this book has a faintly European slant. This is only to be expected, given that I am a Brit who lives in France. And it's worth pointing out that, of the six biggest agency groups, no fewer than four are based outside the United States: WPP, Publicis, Dentsu and Havas. Two of them – Publicis and Havas – are based right here in Paris.

# Pioneers of persuasion

## 01

*'The duly authorized agent'*

**W**hen exactly did advertising begin? It's doubtful that the ancient Egyptians and Greeks were insensible to the benefits of product promotion. The Romans certainly knew how to make a convincing sales pitch, and early examples of advertising were found in the ruins of Pompeii. A roguish adman told me that one of these was a sign promoting a brothel, which is an appealing idea: the two oldest professions benefiting from one another. Others claim that prehistoric cave paintings were a form of advertising, which seems altogether more fanciful. But it's safe to say that advertising has been around for as long as there have been goods to sell and a medium to talk them up – from the crier in the street to the handbill tacked to a tree.

Advertising took a leap forward, of course, with the appearance of the printing press and movable type – an invention generally credited to German former goldsmith Johannes Gutenberg in 1447. Other important names loom out of the murk of early advertising history: notably that of 17th-century French doctor, journalist and unlikely adman Théophraste Renaudot.

Born in Loudon in 1586 to a wealthy protestant family, Renaudot studied medicine in Paris and Montpellier. A doctor by the age of 20, he was considered too young to practise medicine, so he travelled instead to Switzerland, England, Germany and Italy. On his return, through a family connection, he met and befriended the future Cardinal Richelieu. This fortuitous encounter led to Renaudot's eventual appointment as official doctor to Louis XIII.

But Renaudot was a writer and a thinker as well as a physician. His reflections on the Parisian poor led him to create, on the Île de la Cité, what he called a *'bureau des addresses et des rencontres'* – a recruitment office and notice board for the jobless. This establishment soon became a veritable information clearinghouse for those seeking and offering work, buying and selling goods, and making public announcements of all kinds. To disseminate this information more widely, Renaudot created in 1631 the first French newspaper, which he called *La Gazette* (inspired by the unit of currency he'd discovered in Italy, the *gazetta*). Thus he became the first French journalist – and the inventor of the personal ad.

## An industry takes shape

However, most histories of advertising start later, in the mid 19th century. When the advertising group Publicis published a book of ground-breaking ads from throughout history, it was called *Born in 1842*. A hunt for the earliest ad in *The Creative Director's Source Book* (compiled in 1988 by Nick Souter and Stuart Newman) unearths a newspaper advertisement from 1849. (Bizarrely, it is for a new method of measuring your head, thus accurately determining your hat size.)

Everyone agrees, then, that advertising got into its stride with the industrial revolution – aided and abetted by the rise of the newspaper as a mass medium. Advances in technology meant consumer goods could be produced and packaged on a previously undreamed-of scale. This glut of food, clothing, soap, and so forth, encouraged manufacturers who had previously been confined to doing business in their backyards to seek far-flung new markets. Some of them established chains of retail outlets. Others distributed their wares through wholesalers and inter-mediary retailers. In order to blaze the names and virtues of their products into the memories of consumers, they branded their goods – and began to advertise them.

In Britain, one of the most prominent clients of the day was A&F Pears, makers of Pears' Soap. The company's success was assured by prototype adman Thomas J Barrett, who joined the firm in 1862. As well as securing one of the first celebrity endorsements – from Lillie Langtry, actress, courtesan and mistress of the Prince of Wales – Barrett convinced the popular artist Sir John Everett Millais to sell him a painting of a young boy gazing at rising soap bubbles. Not only that, but he persuaded Millais to add a bar of Pears' soap to the scene. Queasily sentimental, 'Bubbles' became one of the earliest advertising icons, and set the tone for a highly successful campaign.

In his 1984 book *The Complete Guide to Advertising*, Torin Douglas recounts: 'Firms such as Cadbury and Fry started packaging their products, not simply to protect them and preserve their quality, but also to *establish* their quality by the use of the company's own name. Instead of leaving it to the retailer to determine which company's products a customer would buy, they began to build their own relationship with the customer.'

As Douglas points out, the essential argument for advertising was established right here. By advertising their products to the public, manufacturers were able to boost sales dramatically: 'Since that also increased the retailers' turnover, both sides of the business benefited. So too did the customers, since they had a wider choice of brands and a stronger guarantee of the quality of the goods.'

Meanwhile, the same technology that had powered the industrial revolution was overhauling the printing industry, making newspapers far cheaper to produce – and to buy. From being precious items gingerly passed from reader to reader, they became suddenly accessible to everyone. Magazines, particularly those aimed at women, also became more commonplace and affordable.

In France, the poster was about to enter a golden age. (*The Creative Director's Source Book*, by the way, tells us that the word 'poster' derives from the wooden roadside posts to which advertising messages were often attached.) In 1870s Paris the printing house Chaix and the artist Jules Chéret were taking advantage of the development of lithography – which allowed for richer colours and larger print-runs – to produce groundbreaking posters for the Folies Bergère cabaret. These bright, vivacious advertisements were so popular that the high-kicking girls depicted on them became known as 'Chérettes'.

Chéret's images were complemented by Henri de Toulouse Lautrec's equally vibrant work for the rival Moulin Rouge nightspot. Known as 'The Spirit of Montmartre', the nocturnal painter was the natural choice for capturing the debauched appeal of a Parisian cabaret. Simple yet evocative, the posters took their unlikely cue from Japanese art, which Lautrec admired.

Another towering talent of the era was the inimitable Alphonse Mucha. Born in Moravia (in the modern-day Czech Republic), Mucha was the archetypal struggling artist in Paris until he was commissioned to come up with a poster for Sarah Bernhardt's play, *Gismonda*, over the Christmas holidays. (Legend has it that he got the commission because he was the only painter left in town.) The result was the first of the gloriously intricate images – not only for the theatre, but for brands such as Moët & Chandon champagne and Lefèvre Utile biscuits – that brought the Art Nouveau style to advertising and fame and fortune to Mucha. Throughout history, art and advertising have often dovetailed in the French capital.

On the other side of the Atlantic, advertising was off to a more rambunctious start. Among the earliest goods advertised on a national scale in the United States were 'patent medicines'. Familiar today via a stock character in Western movies – the quack doctor who stands on a crate in a dusty frontier town, extolling the virtues of his dubious potions – they generated profit margins that left plenty of room for advertising expenditure. As Stephen Fox recounts in his book *The Mirror Makers* (1984) – a superlative account of American advertising history up until the 1970s – these were the first products 'to aim directly at the consumer with vivid, psychologically clever sales pitches, the first to show – for better or for worse – the latent power of advertising'.

Unfortunately, the American public began to associate patent medicines with advertising, to the detriment of both.

## Early advertising agencies

It is generally accepted that the first advertising agency in the United States was opened by one Volney B Palmer in 1842. Located at the 'NW Corner of Third and Chestnut Street, Philadelphia,' Palmer's office was an unlikely precursor of today's agency monoliths. Nevertheless, there he is in a local directory, describing himself as 'the duly authorized agent of most of the best newspapers of all the cities and provincial towns in the United States and Canada, for which he is daily receiving advertisements and subscriptions...'

The earliest advertising agents worked for newspapers rather than for advertisers. Acting as intermediaries, they sold space and took a commission out of the fee. As well as offering endless opportunities for corruption, this arrangement meant that they had nothing to do with creating ads. In *The Mirror Makers*, Stephen Fox cites this juicy morsel dished out by a client to another early advertising agent, Daniel M Lord, who had dared to criticize his ad: 'Young man, you may know a lot about advertising, but you know very little about the furniture business.'

Along with the negative image engendered by the hollow claims of the patent medicine pushers, the lowly status of these early admen suggested that advertising was barely an honest trade, let alone a profession.

The next figure to move the industry on was George P Rowell, a Boston-based advertising agent who, at the prompting of a client, had compiled a directory of advertising rates covering almost every newspaper in New England. His main income, however, came from buying newspaper space in bulk and selling it, piecemeal, at a profit. In 1869 – by which time his business had expanded considerably – Rowell came out with the first media directory: a guide to more than 5,000 newspapers across America, including their circulations and advertising rates.

If Rowell's directory nudged advertising towards respectability, the industry was given a further shove in the right direction by Francis Wayland Ayer, founder of NW Ayer & Son. (He named the operation after his father, an instinctive marketing ploy that provided the agency with a reassuring family background.) Ayer brought transparency to the business of buying and selling space, charging advertisers a fixed commission of 12.5 per cent. This later rose to 15 per cent, which remained the standard commission fee for advertising agencies for many years to come.

But while these people were prototypes for today's media buyers, where were the creatives? The first such creatures to emerge from the primordial swamp of advertising were freelance copywriters. And the most influential of them all was John E Powers, described by *Advertising Age* as 'the father of creative advertising' (The Advertising Century: adage.com/century/people). Little is known about this intriguing character's early career, although he seems to have been an insurance agent and then a publisher of *The Nation* (he apparently started out in the subscriptions department) before finally turning to commercial writing. The department store tycoon John Wanamaker snapped him up in 1880 after seeing one of his ads for a rival store. By the late 1890s he was earning more than US $100 a day writing copy.

Powers was stern and reticent, with a neatly cropped beard and piercing eyes emphasized by round, steel-framed spectacles. It was the face of a man who believed in honesty and plain speaking. Indeed, Powers once claimed that 'fine writing is offensive'. He concentrated on facts and regarded hyperbole as anathema. He was once hired by a Pittsburgh clothing company that was on the verge of bankruptcy: 'There is only one way out,' Powers told his client, 'tell the truth... The only way to salvation lies in large and immediate sales.' The resulting ad read: 'We are bankrupt. This announcement will bring our creditors down on our necks. But if you come and buy tomorrow we shall have the money to meet them. If not we will go to the wall.' Impressed by the directness of the ad, customers rushed to save the store.

The success of Powers inspired another notable copywriter, Charles Austin Bates, who went on to found his own agency. Positioning himself as an 'ad-smith', the outspoken Bates flaunted his expertise by becoming the first professional advertising critic, establishing a weekly column in the trade journal *Printer's Ink*. Arch self-promoter though he may have been, Bates was a crucial figure in the history of advertising, as his agency became a cradle of creativity.

Central to this development was a man called Earnest Elmo Calkins, who started out as a copywriter, yet did more than most of his peers to take advertising design away from the client and into the agency. Deaf due to childhood measles, but blessed with a heightened visual sense, Calkins was recruited by the Bates agency in 1897 when he won a copy-writing competition, of which Charles Austin Bates had been a judge. Initially shining in his new role, Calkins soon clashed with the agency's art department – one of the few in the industry at the time. Frustrated that he could not improve the look of the ads that bore his copy, Calkins took evening classes in industrial design. He had come to the conclusion that fancy copy was no longer enough: consumers needed to be assailed by visuals that stopped them in their tracks.

With Bates unwilling to let him explore this potentially costly theory, Calkins set up his own agency with Ralph Holden, the firm's former head of new business. Designing ads for clients rather than merely placing them, Calkins & Holden effectively became adland's first creative hot shop.

## Arrow to the future

While European advertisers often commissioned established artists to design posters for their brands, in the United States at the beginning of the 20th century a new generation of illustrators working on a commercial basis began to emerge. The images they created were accessible yet compelling. For the first time, advertising was to have a major impact on popular culture.

The most dramatic examples of this were the 'Arrow Collars & Shirts' advertisements. The owners of the Arrow brand hired Calkins & Holden, who in turn commissioned illustrator Joseph Christian Leyendecker to create a suave 'Arrow man'. They hit the jackpot: Leyendecker's illustrations resonated with consumers to an extent that they could hardly have dared imagine.

Leyendecker was a German-born émigré whose parents had moved to the United States in 1882. He'd had his first brush with the world of advertising in his teens, when he was apprenticed to a Chicago printing house, while at the same time taking evening classes at the Art Institute of Chicago. In 1896 he moved to Paris (along with his brother Frank, a talented artist in his own right) to study for two years at the city's best schools. By the time C&H commissioned Leyendecker, in 1905, he'd carved out a solid reputation working for magazines such as *Collier's* and *The Saturday Evening Post*.

But Leyendecker's Arrow saga was an altogether different phenomenon. The men he painted actually generated fan mail. They were tall, rakish, impeccably dressed and yet forever nonchalant, their cheekbones gleaming above pristine shirt collars. To use a phrase that had not yet become hackneyed, men wanted to be them and women wanted to be with them. Perhaps Leyendecker's own enthusiasms shone through in his art: his first Arrow model was Charles Beach, his companion in life as well as work. He illustrated other campaigns – for Kellogg's and Ivory Soap, among others – but none of them had the same impact as his Arrow men, who firmly established the brand's values and sauntered elegantly across its advertising for the next 25 years.

As Calkins & Holden and their collaborators were bringing a new sensibility to the art department, copywriting skills were also evolving. No-nonsense, 'reason why' advertising was competing with a more poetic, atmospheric style, as practised by Theodore MacManus at General Motors. MacManus favoured an approach that dispensed with the hard sell and instead gently wooed potential buyers, convincing them in melting prose that the Cadillac – for which MacManus wrote his best copy – was an irreproachable luxury purchase.

At the Chicago agency Lord & Thomas, a dynamic young executive named Albert Lasker had developed a 'copywriting school' in association with an irascible yet talented Canadian-born writer called John E Kennedy. With a few years of experience under his belt, Kennedy had simply presented himself at the agency one day claiming that it desperately needed his help. Flipping through Kennedy's work, Lasker was persuaded. Unfortunately, it transpired that the socially awkward Kennedy felt unable to teach the firm's nascent copywriters. 'So he taught Lasker,' writes Stephen Fox in *The Mirror Makers*, 'who passed the message along...'

The Kennedy method combined Powers-style plain speaking with striking typographical eccentricities, including a liberal sprinkling of capital letters and italics, 'that caught the eye despite a jerky rhythm that reminded one reader of riding in a wagon with one lopsided wheel'.

Opinionated, unpredictable and unmanageable, after two years Kennedy left Lord & Thomas to go freelance, a situation in which he flourished. He was replaced at the agency by Claude C Hopkins – who went on to become an advertising legend.

## The Hopkins approach

Claude Hopkins never denied – in fact he overtly stated – that the sole purpose of advertising was to sell. He spent his entire career honing the techniques that would best serve this end, describing his style as 'dramatized salesmanship' in his autobiography, *My Life in Advertising*, first published in 1927. He believed in research, both before and after the event, and insisted that advertising was worthless unless it could demonstrate a tangible effect on sales.

In photographs Hopkins looks dour and aloof, with his clipped moustache, round spectacles and balding pate. And yet he was a populist, believing that a good adman should retain a common touch. His utter devotion to the advertising business, which he admitted to reading, writing and thinking about 'night and day', could perhaps be explained by the diametrical rejection of his oppressively Christian upbringing.

Claude was born in Detroit in 1866. His journalist father died when he was just 10 years old, placing him entirely in the shadow of his deeply religious mother. Although she hoped he would become a preacher, he broke with the church at the age of 18 and made his bid for freedom. In Grand Rapids, he got a job with a company called Bissell, a maker of mechanical carpet sweepers. Here he tentatively began preaching an entirely different gospel.

Initially a bookkeeper, Hopkins took it upon himself to rewrite the company's brochure, which he felt showed limited knowledge of the product. Ironically, it was written by that other copywriting pioneer, John E Powers, then at the height of his fame. But Hopkins was not daunted by Powers' reputation. 'He knew nothing about carpet sweepers. He had given no study to our trade situation. He knew nothing of our problems. He never gave one moment to studying a woman's possible wish for a carpet sweeper.' Hopkins considered that only with a thorough understanding of the product, its benefits and its potential customers could a copywriter pen a convincing ad.

The success of Hopkins' early promotional efforts for Bissell led him to the Chicago offices of Swift & Company, a marketer of meat products and derivatives. In his book, Hopkins describes how he applied for the job of advertising manager, only to be told during an interview that he was 106th on a list of 106 applicants. Undaunted, he asked all the advertising agencies that had approached him with job offers to send references to Swift confirming his talents as a copywriter. Next, he convinced his local newspaper to let him write a column about advertising, free of charge, in return for a byline with his photograph above it. Each time the article appeared he clipped it out and sent it to Swift. Finally, the man who had interviewed him – a Mr I H Rich – called him back and offered him the post.

One of his greatest triumphs at Swift was the promotion of a beef suet brand called Cotosuet, used in baking as a substitute for butter. To demonstrate the product's effectiveness, Hopkins ordered that a giant cake be baked and displayed in the window of a department store. His newspaper ads pulled in customers while emphasizing the colossal cake's key ingredient. The stunt was a perfect example of dramatized selling.

It was while he was freelancing in Chicago that Hopkins honed another of the techniques that was to leave its mark on advertising history. Hired to promote the beer brand Schlitz, he discovered that its bottles were steam-cleaned – just as they were in every other brewery. But no other brewery had thought of including this nugget of information in its advertising. When an ad penned by Hopkins pointed out that Schlitz bottles were 'washed with live steam', it gave the impression that the brand cared more about purity and hygiene than any of its competitors.

This was the essence of the Hopkins approach. For each product, he would find the unique factor that set it apart from its rivals. 'You cannot go into a well-occupied field on the simple appeal "buy my brand",' he wrote. 'That is repugnant to all. One must offer exceptional service to induce people to change from favourite brands to yours.' Hopkins called this the 'pre-emptive claim'. Later, in the hands of Rosser Reeves, who worked for Ted Bates & Co in the 1950s, it became the Unique Selling Proposition. Reeves pushed the idea to an extreme, turning each USP into a simple slogan that he punched home with repetitive ads.

For the time being, though, it was Hopkins who attracted attention with his quasi-scientific methods of advertising. His work for Schlitz caught the eye of magazine publisher Cyrus Curtis – a teetotaller. Bumping into Albert Lasker of the Lord & Thomas agency on a train, Curtis advised him to hire the copywriter who could turn the thoughts of abstemious men towards beer.

Lasker took Curtis at his word and lured Hopkins to Lord & Thomas in 1907. This was not an easy task, as Hopkins was happy freelancing and had no intention of returning to 'serfdom', as he called it. Lasker initially lured Hopkins with an unusual freelance contract: 'Give me three ads... and your wife may... select any car on the street and charge it to me.' Finally, Hopkins agreed to work for Lasker at the remarkably high salary of one thousand dollars a week, later rising to US$185,000 a year.

This comfortable new position did nothing to slow the workaholic copywriter's output. He experimented with direct response advertising, becoming a sorcerer of cut-outs and coupons, realizing that it was an invaluable way of assessing readership of an ad. While researching dental hygiene for a product called Pepsodent, he 'discovered' plaque, and wrote the first advertisement offering a means of combating it. Clearly convinced of the power of his imagery, he bought a stake in Pepsodent and made a fortune when it took off – thanks to his own copywriting skills.

But although Hopkins was an advertising genius, for the rest of his career he always deferred to his boss: Albert Davis Lasker.

## Lasker's second choice

There were other contenders for the title, but few historians would disagree that Albert Lasker was the true father of modern advertising. Ironically, it was not his first choice of profession. He originally wanted to be a journalist – and continued hankering after that trade throughout his career, despite (or perhaps because of) his seemingly effortless ability to sell things to people. 'So far as I know, no ordinary human being has ever resisted Albert Lasker,' wrote Claude Hopkins. 'He has commanded what he would in this world. Presidents have made him their pal. Nothing he desired has ever been forbidden to him.'

Lasker's father had emigrated from Germany and, after years of struggle, built up a prosperous grocery business in Galveston, Texas. Albert, then, was born into a wealthy family on 1 May 1880, the third of eight children. Showing a journalistic bent early on, he launched a weekly newspaper when he was only 12 years old, and worked for the local Galveston title while still in high school. His dream was to work on a big city paper, preferably in New York.

In a series of reminiscences published by *American Heritage* magazine in December 1954 (and more recently unearthed by a business website), Lasker describes his unlikely entry into the advertising business. 'My father had a dread of my becoming a newspaperman, because in those days (and this is no exaggeration) almost every newspaperman was a heavy drinker... I was very devoted to my father, and he proposed instead that I go to a firm in what he considered a kindred field – Lord & Thomas in Chicago, an advertising agency... He wrote to Lord & Thomas, and they wrote back that they would give me a three months trial. Then they would see whether they could keep me on' ('Wall Street History', StocksandNews.com, 4–18 February 2005).

Established by Daniel M Lord and Ambrose L Thomas in 1881, the agency had moved with the times, graduating from placing ads to creating them. Among its biggest clients was the brewer Anheuser Busch. But the young Lasker was given menial tasks that would make even the most mundane modern internship seem thrilling, such as sweeping floors and emptying ashtrays. Unable to take the job seriously, he turned his attention to big-city living. Perhaps in order to augment his meagre 10 dollars a week salary, he started gambling, and lost several hundred dollars in a crap game.

'Then I had to think, and think fast, so I went to Mr Thomas, who was a very sympathetic man... and I told him what I'd done. I had never before sold anything to anybody, but I did a salesmanship job that day. I talked Mr Thomas into advancing me five hundred dollars – which was a fortune in those days. He went with me, and we settled with the gambler. I had to stay with Lord & Thomas to work out the five hundred dollars. I never got back to reporting.'

In fact, in order to speed the repayment of his debt, he convinced Lord & Thomas to give him the sales territory of Indiana, Ohio and Michigan, which had just become free following the departure of a colleague. Encouraged by the fact that Lasker offered to continue working for 10 dollars a week unless he brought in business, Ambrose Thomas accepted the proposal. Now Lasker had to go out and literally prospect for clients.

In the interview with *American Heritage*, he recounts: 'I had three assets: energy, dedication, and luck. I was a success from the first – from the time I was nineteen... The first town I covered, after Mr Thomas gave me a territory, was Battle Creek. There was a prospect there who was going to spend $3,000... a big account... I was lucky. I was full of energy and determination. I was a young boy – and that intrigued people. The first day I was out... I was awarded this order of US $3,000... which my predecessor could have landed any time before. He was a fine man, but he wasn't a "closer".'

Albert certainly was, and he continued to bring in business, despite his later modest protestation that this was 'largely as a result of the good work done by my predecessor'. Helped by a gift for spotting talents like John Kennedy and Claude Hopkins, Lasker rose smoothly to the top of the agency. Along the way, he began to change the advertising business. While most advertising firms still had only two copywriters, Lasker created a department of 10. He closely monitored the efficiency of the agency's campaigns, tracking his clients' sales curves against media placements to determine which mix of newspapers and magazines was the most successful. In 1904, Lord & Thomas made him a partner. Immaculately dressed, fast-talking and sparking with ideas, Lasker seemed to sweep aside all in his path like a snowplough. By 1912, he had bought out his former employers and become head of his own agency. With Lasker at the helm, advertising was well on its way to modernization.

In Europe, however, events were taking shape that would cast the advertising industry in a new and sinister role.

# From propaganda to soap

## 02

*'We sold the war to youth'*

With the outbreak of the First World War, advertising was used to attract volunteers. In 1914, Lord Kitchener, the British Minister of War, appeared on a poster urging young men to 'join your country's army', with a steely gaze and a pointing finger. In 1917, the US army adopted an almost identical approach, with a stern Uncle Sam pointing the finger: 'I want YOU for U.S. army'. Everywhere, it seemed, the same guilt trip was required: 'You too should enlist in the army of the Reich', said a German soldier, with the inevitable accusatory digit. On Italian posters, it jabbed out yet again.

The US propaganda machine was cruelly efficient, with the establishment of a Committee on Public Information and its 'four minute men', who would deliver encouraging speeches to potential volunteers. In *The Mirror Makers*, Stephen Fox writes that the committee's advertising division placed US $1.5 million worth of advertising.

After the war, though, some of those who had fuelled the propaganda machine were stricken with remorse. James Montgomery Flagg, the artist behind the Uncle Sam 'I want YOU' poster, said: 'A number of us who were too old or too scared to fight prostituted our talents by making posters inciting a large mob of young men who had never done anything to us to hop over and get shot at... We sold the war to youth.'

A hint of light in the darkness: in neutral Switzerland, Zurich became known as 'the grand sanatorium' – a gathering place for pacifists, deserters, iconoclasts and of course artists, who often combined all of the above. This loose band collected around the paternal figure of German poet Hugo Ball. He created the Cabaret Voltaire, a nightly event held in the back room of a tavern. It comprised art exhibitions, readings, dance and amateur theatricals in a liberating and faintly anarchic environment. These soirées spawned the artistic movement that became known as Dada, a word supposedly chosen at random by Hugo Ball from a French–German dictionary. (It means either 'wooden horse' or 'see you later', depending on whether you are French or German.)

But wait a moment: other sources suggest that the name may have been lifted from an ad for a product called Dada, the name of a popular hair tonic made by Bergmann & Company of Zurich. After all, it was suitably absurd – not to mention a sly indictment of vanity at a time of human suffering. An advertising campaign inspires one of the most influential art movements of the 20th century? The jury is still out – but it's an attractive idea.

## The legacy of J Walter Thompson

After the First World War, society on both sides of the Atlantic had been twisted and broken – and the structure that emerged to take its place was radically different. This did not mean that advertising had lost any of its momentum. On the contrary, the admen seemed determined to improve on the techniques of persuasion they had deployed so successfully during the war, and to put them once again at the service of brands.

The agency that rose to dominate this era in the United States was J Walter Thompson. Although its achievements in the twenties overshadowed everything that had gone before, it had its roots in the 19th century.

James Walter Thompson was born in Pittsfield, Massachusetts in 1847 and grew up in Ohio. After serving in the navy at the end of the Civil War, he strode down a gangplank in New York determined to carve out a career in the big city. In 1868 he was hired by a tiny advertising agency run by William J Carlton, at that point still involved in the primitive business of placing advertisements in newspapers and magazines. It was the latter that interested Thompson, who noticed that they ran few advertisements while staying longer in the family home than newspapers, thus making them potentially a more effective medium. He began to specialize in magazine advertising, gradually building up an exclusive stable of publications available only to his clients. Ten years after joining the agency, he bought it for a total of US$1,300 (US$500 for the company and US$800 for the furniture) and put his own name above the door.

Mild-mannered and good-looking – with blue eyes and a trim brown beard – 'The Commodore', as he became known, charmed clients. He hired staff specifically to look after clients' needs, creating the account executive role. Soon he began to offer a 'full service', designing as well as placing ads. He opened offices in Chicago, Boston, Cincinnati and even London – the first US agency to expand abroad. In these ways and others, J Walter Thompson created the first modern advertising agency.

In 1916, after 48 years in the business, with both his health and his enthusiasm failing, Thompson handed over the reigns to the man who would take the agency to even greater heights: Stanley Resor.

Cincinnati-born Resor had tried his hands at a number of jobs – from banking to selling machine tools – before he stumbled into advertising thanks to his brother Walter, who worked at Procter & Gamble's in-house agency. It was here that Stanley met Helen Lansdowne, a young copywriter who was to have an enormous impact on his professional and personal life. Meanwhile, Resor took to his new milieu like a natural, soon becoming respected for his drive, his keenness to innovate and his way with clients. At a certain point he attracted the attention of J Walter Thompson, who hired him in 1908 to open the Cincinnati branch of the agency. Helen Lansdowne was taken on as copywriter.

Lansdowne was the first woman to make an impact in a profession that remains overwhelmingly male-dominated to this day. In a previously unheard-of development, she presented campaigns to major clients, notably Procter & Gamble. Working for an agency whose clients made a great many products aimed at women, she possessed market insight as well as natural copywriting flair. Stephen Fox reports that, for Wood-bury's Soap, 'which came to JWT in 1910, she made ads that increased sales by 1,000 per cent in eight years'. These were among the first to refer obliquely to sex, promising to deliver 'the skin that you love to touch' alongside a picture of a young couple. Helen married Stanley Resor in New York in 1917 – one year after the pair had effectively taken control of the agency.

JWT was a modern environment in many other respects. It has often been noted that Resor was the first agency boss with a college degree (from Yale, at that) and as such he did not accept the view that advertising had to 'talk down' to consumers. His kind of advertising was aimed at a wealthy, educated target audience. He hired researchers and psychologists with the aim of creating a 'university of advertising', which would ensure that the agency's sales pitches worked with scientific precision. In JWT's ads, doctors and scientists testified to the efficacy of products along with the usual movie stars.

The hierarchy of the agency was also a break with what had gone before. Resor was literally the kind of boss whose door was always open. At the same time, he consciously resisted meddling in the day-to-day work of the agency, assuming that people would come to him if there was a problem. Instead, account handlers were overseen by a core of high-ranking executives known as 'backstoppers'. Any urgent matters that arose during the week were discussed with senior management at an informal Thursday lunch.

With Stanley Resor's administrative skills perfectly balanced by Helen's creative genius, JWT became the most successful advertising agency to date (although it was some years before it became the first to pass the US $100 million billings mark, in 1947). Thanks to the General Motors account, of which it held a chunk until the Depression, the agency followed the example of its founder by opening branches around the world: Europe, Africa, Asia, Latin America... a pioneering network that would fuel future growth.

Symbolic of its status was its move in 1927 to the monolithic Graybar Building, next to Grand Central Station – the largest office building in the world at the time. This daunting Art Deco skyscraper, with vaguely nautical embellishments, features gargoyles in the form of steel rats scurrying up the 'mooring ropes' that support the canopy above the front entrance.

The interior design of JWT's offices was overseen by Helen Resor. Work spaces were divided by wrought iron grilles, instead of walls, so the entire staff could admire the view from the 11th-floor windows. The walls that remained were adorned by a growing art collection, and Helen established her own department among an all-female team of copywriters. Meanwhile, the quietly authoritarian Stanley Resor ruled over the agency from a baronial panelled office. But the executive dining room was modelled on the kitchen of an 18th-century Massachusetts farmhouse, suggesting that, despite everything, the couple had rather provincial tastes.

# An onomatopoeic agency

The comedian Fred Allen famously observed that the name BBDO sounded like 'a steamer trunk falling down a flight of stairs'. By then the agency had entered the 1940s. Its original name was even more of a mouthful: Batten, Barton, Durstine & Osborn. But that's rushing things a bit. Before BBDO, there was BDO. Still with me?

The simple fact is that Bruce Barton became the most famous adman of his day. The son of a church minister, in 1924 he wrote a 'modern' biography of Jesus Christ, called *The Man Nobody Knows*, which was the bestselling book in America for two years in a row. In it he described Jesus as the ultimate adman, who had 'picked 12 men from the bottom ranks of business and transformed them into a world-conquering organization'. Barton advised his clients to get in touch with the 'souls' of their companies before they began communicating to the public. After all, if they didn't have faith in their own organization, how could they preach it to others? 'Barton had a regard for business that crossed the border from respect to reverence,' notes an article in *Advertising Age* ('Advertising's true believer', 3 August 1999).

Barton had started out as a journalist on the magazine *Collier's Weekly*, where he occasionally turned his hand to writing copy for advertisers such as Harvard Classics, with its series of educational books. Later, he was involved in First World War sloganeering, which is how he met advertising men Alex Osborn and Roy Durstine. The trio served together on a panel planning the United War Work campaign. In 1918, Osborn and Durstine invited Barton to join their start-up agency. Although he thought of himself as a writer, Barton agreed – figuring he could still be a man of letters in his spare time.

In its early years BDO won a succession of cornerstone accounts, such as General Electric, General Motors and Dunlop. It moved to spacious new offices at 383 Madison Avenue, where it was not the only advertising agency: the other was the George Batten Company.

Like many advertising pioneers, George Batten had started a one-man agency towards the end of the 19th century. However, his was the first operation to offer in-house printing, as he believed in the use of plain, simple type to attract the attention of readers. Batten died in 1918, having built an agency to reckon with. By the time it shared a headquarters with BDO, in 1923, the Batten Company had 246 employees. It merged with BDO in 1928 to form one of the industry's largest players, with billings of US$32 million.

The unprecedented success of agencies like JWT and BBDO demonstrates the extent to which the 1920s were boom years for advertising. In London, the decade had kicked off with an International Advertising Exhibition at White City. The poster for the event showed a London Underground platform crammed with cross-track advertising, while the waiting passengers included many familiar advertising characters: Monsieur Bibendum (better known in Britain as The Michelin Man), the Bisto Kids, Nipper the HMV dog and the red-coated striding man found on bottles of Johnnie Walker Black Label (he was first drawn in 1909 by the cartoonist Tom Browne). Brands had definitively entered the public consciousness.

Back in the States, the introduction of hire purchase made costly goods available to a raft of new consumers. Sales of radio sets rose from US$60 million in 1922 to US$850 million by the end of the decade, while the number of cars on the road rose from 6 million to 23 million in 10 years. In 1928 Ford replaced its Model T with the Model A, with the NW Ayer agency handling advertising for the launch. Just as JWT's overseas expansion had been accelerated by General Motors, so Ayer's was driven by Ford, with the agency opening offices in London, São Paulo and Buenos Aires. Slowly, the big agencies were going global.

This period also saw the strengthening of an industry that was to remain a reliable source of income for advertising agencies for years to come: tobacco. In the United States, rival firms RJ Reynolds (Camel), Liggett & Myers (Chesterfield) and American Tobacco (Lucky Strike) had been fiercely competing for the traditionally male market of cigarette smokers. But now they noticed that a new generation of young, liberated women was starting to smoke – even though this was still considered socially unacceptable. The tobacco companies made contorted efforts to target women: a poster showing a woman gazing at a Camel poster was a typical example; or a woman saying to her Chesterfield-puffing guy, 'Blow some my way.' Despite this oblique approach, the number of women smokers in the United States rose from 5 per cent of the total in 1923 to 18 per cent 10 years later.

But the profits that the advertising agencies reaped from this new market were not enough to protect them from the approaching financial maelstrom.

# Rubicam versus the Depression

An image provided by the ad agency D'Arcy, of Santa Claus dressed in the red and white livery of Coca-Cola (his traditional attire from then on), was one of the only cheerful sights on the wintry streets of America in 1931. Unemployment had risen to 8 million, having doubled in a year. The Wall Street Crash of October 1929 had ripped the floor out of the US economy and sent a shudder through the entire Western world (with the shockwave hitting debt-ridden Germany particularly hard). By 1932 the Dow Jones Index had lost 89 per cent of its value – and would not fully recover until 1954.

As one might have expected, the advertising agencies adopted fixed grins and preached optimism. Things would get better soon, they said. But, as Stephen Fox reports, Albert Lasker was forced to cut salaries at Lord & Thomas by 25 per cent, 'and then later had to fire over 50 employees... BBDO tried to carry its people through the hard times and so consequently was overstaffed'. The hard sell got harder; more sex appeared in advertising. The bitter public glanced disdainfully at ads for products they could no longer afford. With the glory days of the 1920s at an end, advertising would never regain its coquettish charm.

And yet, a couple of famous agencies rose from this mire. One of them was Leo Burnett, which opened in 1935 with a bowl of apples on its reception desk (see Chapter 5, The Chicago way). Another was Young & Rubicam. Although the agency had been around since 1923, it was one of the few to wrench a profit from the Depression, when it also developed the techniques that would have a lasting impact on the industry.

Raymond Rubicam was another frustrated writer in a sector littered with them. Born in Brooklyn in 1892, the youngest of eight children, he was just five years old when his father died of tuberculosis. With his mother unable to look after him, he was shuffled around surrogate parents in Ohio, Denver and Texas. A bright yet undisciplined child, he left school at 15 to work in a diverse variety of positions – from salesman to hotel porter – hitching illegal rides on the railroad as he made his way slowly east. Finally he pitched up in Philadelphia, where his family had its original roots. Here, aided by relatives, he made ends meet with short stories and journalism.

Then he fell in love, and realized that his finances would need a boost if he was to become a family man. After a short, unsatisfactory period as an automobile salesman, he turned his attention to the nascent advertising industry. He wrote some sample tobacco ads and took them along to the offices of F Wallis Armstrong, the first agency in the phone book and, unbeknown to Rubicam, a notoriously cantankerous adman. Initially agreeing to see the budding copywriter, Armstrong then let him 'warm a bench' in the lobby for nine days in a row. On the final day, Rubicam went home and wrote an angry letter explaining exactly what he thought of such treatment. It was, he recalled, 'designed to produce an immediate interview or a couple of black eyes for the writer' ('Leaders in Marketing', *Journal of Marketing*, April 1962). Rubicam's talent must have blazed off the page: Armstrong called him back into the office and hired him.

Even so, Rubicam was unlikely to shine at the antediluvian Armstrong operation, and stayed just long enough to learn the rudiments of copywriting before moving on – this time to NW Ayer. Here, for the Steinway piano account, Rubicam hit the right note, with an ad describing the piano as 'The Instrument of the Immortals'. Later, he wrote another winning line for the pharmaceutical company ER Squibb: 'The priceless ingredient of every product is the honour and integrity of its maker.'

Rubicam's closest friend at Ayer was James Orr Young, an amiable account man seven years his senior who had also moved over from the Armstrong agency. At a certain point they began to feel that there wasn't enough room for manoeuvre at Ayer, which had grown stuffy and complacent. While taking a stroll across Independence Square one afternoon, they decided to launch their own agency.

At its peak, Y&R was the closest adland had so far seen to the kind of freewheeling agency that would later spark 'the creative revolution' of the 1950s. Reflecting his own lack of a formal education, Rubicam recruited talented oddballs and rebels rather than intellectuals. Hardly anyone turned up before 10 in the morning, but the agency specialized in late-night creative sessions, fuelled by coffee and cigarettes, known as 'gang-ups'.

Ironically, the agency's first successful campaign was for a caffeine-free coffee substitute called Postum. Previous campaigns for the product had taken a vaguely medicinal approach, placing coffee in a negative light and talking up Postum as a solution for anxiety, insomnia and poor digestion. But the ads had never caught on, so Rubicam commissioned research to find out what consumers really thought of the beverage. It turned out that many of them were attracted by a factor nobody could have guessed – Postum's flavour. So Y&R's new magazine campaign threw that in to the mix too, portraying the drink as a soothing and tasty bedtime beverage. Postum's sales took off. The brand's owner, General Foods, promised the agency more work if it could relocate to New York – which it did.

Y&R had got itself a reputation as a creative agency, but Rubicam was keen to stress that even its wildest flights of fancy were based on solid research. 'Ideas founded on facts' became his mantra. He said the aim of every advertiser should be to 'try to know more than your competitors do about the market, and put that knowledge into the hands of writers and artists with imagination and broad human sympathies'.

To help develop this idea, Rubicam hired an academic with a research background. George Gallup was a professor of advertising and journalism at Northwestern University. He had become something of a star in the advertising world after publishing his research into magazine readership habits and – crucially – the aspects of magazine advertising that had the greatest impact on readers. He discovered that while the largest percentage of ads focused on the economy and efficiency of products, those that pushed the right buttons with readers concerned quality, vanity and sex-appeal. Other agencies tried to poach the researcher, but Rubicam convinced him by promising greater room for experimentation and freedom from financial constraints.

Once established at Y&R, Gallup built up a marketing research department that was the envy of other agencies. At one point, no fewer than 400 people around the country were involved in field research work for Y&R, all sending back information about which ads were working and why. Later, Gallup and Rubicam devised a procedure for monitoring reactions to radio shows, recruiting listening panels from 'churches and women's clubs'. At the beginning, listeners' likes and dislikes were recorded with the aid of a notepad, a pencil and a questionnaire – but later General Electric provided Y&R with a machine adapted to the agency's needs. In 1935, while still at Y&R, Gallup established the American Institute of Public Opinion. This later broke away to become the Gallup Organization, in 1958.

Meanwhile, in 1934, Young had left the agency, effectively acknowledging Rubicam's dominance over the firm. Somewhat older than his partner, Young had always been less passionate about the advertising business, preferring to spend time with his family.

Rubicam, however, continued building the agency for another decade. His winning formula of strong creative ideas driven by solid research seemed impervious to recession and war. Billings continued to climb: US $6 million in 1927, US $12 million in 1935, US $22 million in 1937. By 1944, when Rubicam began contemplating an early retirement, the agency was billing US $50 million a year. He left without remorse, hoping to finally write that book. But after toying with journalism, he came to the conclusion that writing was 'a life of drudgery', and that years of working in the exciting surroundings of an advertising agency had spoiled him for such a solitary existence.

## New sights, new sounds

European artists were occasionally embraced by the United States. In 1938, NW Ayer commissioned the French poster artist Adolphe Mouron – better known as 'Cassandre' – to come up with an image for the new Ford V8. Cassandre was already a legend, having transformed poster advertising in France with his bold, minimalist Art Deco designs. By 1936, he merited his own exhibition at the Museum of Modern Art in New York. Solicited after this event by Ford, he provided a surrealistic eye with 'V8' imprinted on the pupil. Staring down at the scurrying pedestrians, the giant eye might have been the inspiration for Big Brother. It was also a plea in defence of illustration, which was slowly being superseded by the glaring eye of photography.

Some of the most groundbreaking work in that field was done by J Stirling Getchell. An influential figure in the thirties who barely survived the decade, Getchell died at the age of 41 when his chronically weak heart finally succumbed to his frantic lifestyle.

After stints at Lord & Thomas and JWT, among others, the restless Getchell started his own agency in 1931. His method was to hire the most talented photographers and create ads around their images, favouring a high-impact, tabloid approach, with staccato copy and blazing headlines. Probably his best-known ad was for the 1932 launch of the Chrysler Plymouth. It featured a photograph of Walter P Chrysler, foot resting firmly on the car's fender, above the bold statement: 'Look at ALL THREE.' Chrysler appeared to be encouraging readers to compare his automobile to two rival vehicles – from Ford and General Motors – before making a well-informed decision. This unorthodox 'honesty' appealed to consumers, with a positive result for sales of the Plymouth.

Getchell even briefly launched a magazine called *Picture*. 'Widely reputed as a pioneer user of news-style pictures in advertisements… Mr Getchell… goes in for illustrated expositions of topics like the life of a chorus girl, the dangers of lightning, 'Strange Animal Diets' or what happens to you in a Turkish bath…', sniffed the rival *Time* magazine ('Getchell's *Picture*', 27 December 1937). It was typical of Getchell that he promised to run the magazine *in his spare time* in order to continue serving his clients at the agency. Three years later he was gone – leaving behind a bold new style of ad for a harsher era.

But if photography was an evolution, the industry was also dealing with a technological revolution. In a few short years it had mastered an entirely new method of diffusing its messages. This was to be joined in short order by another, even more powerful medium. And, as is the case today, the biggest rewards went to the agencies that were the quickest to adapt.

In the United States, radio was a commercial business almost from the start. As early as 1922, a New York radio station called WEAF, owned by American Telephone & Telegraph, had begun offering 10-minute advertising slots for US$100. By 1926, WEAF had evolved into the National Broadcasting Company (NBC). The Columbia Broadcasting System (CBS) launched the following year. While in the United Kingdom the BBC, launched in 1922, remained ad-free, in the United States radio became the almost exclusive domain of advertisers, who sponsored and produced shows. Dark mutterings about advertising 'intruding on the family circle' were drowned out by the sound of the Lucky Strike Dance Orchestra.

The new medium also made a couple of agencies' reputations. Radio men were considered unconventional and modern, the dotcom pioneers of their day. An agency called Benton & Bowles, which had been teetering on the brink of bankruptcy, became known for its radio expertise when it launched a variety show called *The Maxwell House Showboat*, which spurred an 85 per cent rise in sales in a single year.

But the leading name in radio was Frank Hummert, creator of 'soap operas' (so called, as if you didn't know, because they were frequently sponsored by detergent brands). Though ironically reticent and uncommunicative in person, Hummert had a genius for radio advertising.

He'd begun creating campaigns for the medium at Lord & Thomas before joining Blackett & Sample (soon to become Blackett-Sample-Hummert) in 1927. At that point, the standard format for a sponsored radio show – particularly if it was aimed at women – was a selection of chatty household hints. But Hummert decided to experiment with something more like the cliff-hanging serials in newspapers. Along with his co-worker and eventual wife Anne Ashenhurst, he created, wrote and produced 'serial dramas'. Some of these stayed on the air for years. The *Jack Armstrong* adventure series, sponsored by the breakfast cereal Wheaties, started its run in 1931 and continued airing in one form or another until the early 1950s. Even more impressively, a soap opera called *Ma Perkins*, for Oxydol detergent, ran for no fewer than 37 years. Thanks to his radio royalties, by 1937 Hummert was the richest man in advertising.

## The end of the beginning

Advertising went back to war. As well as being deployed for the purposes of boosting morale, advertising agencies rushed to give the impression that brands were in the thick of the fighting. In a manner that seems even more distasteful today than it did at the time, products were linked to the war effort. For instance, Cadillac claimed to be 'in the vanguard of the invasion', as Cadillac-built parts could be found in the engines of fighter planes. Texaco assured motorists that the gasoline they were forced to do without was 'being turned into war products to speed our forces to victory'. The tasteful accompanying image was the bright flash of a bomb exploding, with Germans running for cover.

In the UK as elsewhere, the government's voice was heard through advertising. Familiar slogans on the British home front concerned fears of espionage ('Careless talk costs lives') and the need to grow vegetables for ration-starved citizens ('Dig for victory'). Britons were warned to take care in the blackout and keep gas masks close at hand.

Stephen Fox estimates in *The Mirror Makers* that the US advertising industry donated about a billion dollars' worth of space to the war effort. He quotes Bruce Barton, who said: 'We did not tell the truth, of course. We simply set forth in pictures and copy the Administration's argument... This was sound and patriotic and moral while the war lasted.'

Conversely, Leo Burnett felt that the Second World War was a demonstration of the power of modern advertising. '[The] government got an entirely new idea of advertising as an effective means of communication to the people of this big country of ours, and as a tool for getting people to do things on a voluntary rather than compulsory basis. This in itself was not bad public relations for advertising.' During the war, he argued, 'advertising revealed itself to itself'. He added, 'A lot of people... discovered for the first time that they had a moral obligation to society and could use their techniques just as effectively in selling ideas as in peddling goods.'

NBC affiliate WNBT had begun commercial TV broadcasts in 1941. A year later, the minimum programme time required of TV stations was cut from 15 hours to 4 hours a week for the war period. After the war agencies hovered around the medium, still unsure what to make of it. 'Television is the strongest drug we've ever had to dish out,' Leo Burnett told the National Television Council in 1949. 'Maybe that's why our hands shake a little when we take the cork out of the bottle, but we'll get over that.'

Some were steelier than others. At BBDO, the charismatic Irishman Ben Duffy – who had taken over at the head of the agency from Bruce Barton in 1946 – was particularly keen on TV. By 1949, according to Stephen Fox, Duffy was spending US$4 million on the new medium, and the agency's TV department had grown from 12 to 150 people. Total US advertising spend on television rose from US$12 million in 1949 to US$158 million just three years later. Having successfully occupied the radio landscape, brands were now firmly established on television.

# Madison Avenue aristocracy

## 03

*'Creative organizations are led by formidable individuals'*

I flew in to New York clutching two books: *The Hidden Persuaders*, by Vance Packard (1957) and *Madison Avenue, USA*, by Martin Mayer (1958). The thing I liked most about them was that I had managed to get hold of the original editions – tattered ex-library copies with yellowing paper – so I was effectively taking them back to the street that inspired them. One April afternoon I strode half the length of Madison Avenue, stopping occasionally to grab a coffee and leaf through their pages. At the beginning of the Packard book there was a note scrawled in blue ink: *New York, Xmas 1960*. It may have been the perfect time and place to work in advertising.

Mayer's book informs us that Madison Avenue is 'the only major New York street named after a president of the United States'. The author concedes that 'the stretch that has made the street famous takes up one-fifth of its length, beginning at about 200 Madison and ending at about 650... forming what the vulgar call ad alley or ulcer gulch...'. At the time that Mayer wrote his book, the agencies on Madison Avenue controlled half of the total expenditure on advertising in the United States – while most of the rest was handled by their branch offices. Madison Avenue had been the unofficial home of the advertising business since before the war, but in the past few years an unprecedented building boom had turned it into a glistening canyon of communications firms. 'Madison Avenue as it appears today is impressively new,' writes Mayer in 1958. 'More than a dozen new office buildings, each more than 20 stories high, have been built since the war...'

And what was it like inside these monolithic agencies? Having done the tour, Mayer could tell us that the offices of Young & Rubicam were predominantly decorated in green. McCann-Erickson featured 'restful pastels', but J Walter Thompson was 'a class in itself'. The agency's stylishness had clearly not waned since the 1930s, and we rediscover with a sense of warm familiarity the dining suite 'decorated like a New England colonial farmhouse'. The stylish Barcelona chairs by Mies van der Rohe may have been a more recent touch, however.

Madison Avenue symbolized the US advertising industry. When I interviewed him in 2006 (sadly, he passed away the following year), Phil Dusenberry, the former vice-chairman of BBDO, who came to work on the street as a young copywriter in the early 1960s, confirmed: 'Like Hollywood, it became an idea rather than a physical place. You could say that Madison Avenue *was* advertising.'

By the 1950s, advertising was considered a glamorous – if still not exactly honourable – profession. Attitudes to the industry at the time are personified by the Cary Grant character in Hitchcock's *North by Northwest* (1959), a dapper Madison Avenue man who is mistaken for a spy. Towards the beginning of the film, Grant says to his secretary, 'In the world of advertising there's no such thing as a lie. There's only the expedient exaggeration.'

An entire mythology formed around the advertising business during this period. The standard template for a New York advertising executive was *The Man in the Gray Flannel Suit*, the titular figure of Sloan Wilson's 1955 novel, who actually worked in public relations. If admen had ever worn flannel suits before the book became a bestseller, they certainly avoided them afterwards – although they were paid handsomely enough to be well dressed. They were also known to work hard – often ridiculously so, until the early hours of the morning – hence all the talk of ulcers and heart disease in the profession. They fought stress with alcohol, giving rise to the 'three martini lunch'. This actually existed, according to Phil Dusenberry: 'Taking a break for lunch, particularly if you were with a client, wasn't a big deal in those days.'

One figure we might have seen strolling down Madison Avenue on his way to lunch – perhaps with a young colleague hanging onto his every word – was a lanky Englishman, dressed in tweeds for winter or in a lightweight suit brightened with a pocket square in summer. Good-looking, charming and (on the surface, at least) irrepressibly self-confident, David Ogilvy was one of the stars of the Manhattan advertising scene. And he was British.

# A British advertising agency in New York

David Ogilvy played such a large part in the creation of his own myth that it is often hard to tell where the truth ended and the branding began. There are a few things we know for certain, however. He was born in 1911 in West Horsley, England and educated at Fettes College, Edinburgh – a school renowned for its 'Spartan disciplines', according to Ogilvy. Apparently destined to become a historian, he won a scholarship to Christ Church, Oxford – but by his own admission he 'screwed that up'. The reasons for this are unclear. In his book *Confessions of an Advertising Man* (1963) he writes glibly that he was 'too preoccupied to do any work, and was duly expelled'. Later he revealed that he had two serious operations on his head, for double mastoids, which contributed to his lack of concentration ('David Ogilvy at 75', *Viewpoint*, September/October 1986). In any event, what Ogilvy forever described as 'the great failure of my life' helped to shape his paradoxical personality: that of the scholarly entrepreneur; the daydreaming pragmatist.

Having been a keen reader of Mark Twain as a schoolboy, Ogilvy was stricken with wanderlust. Although the eventual goal was America, his first destination was France, where he got a job in the kitchen of the Hotel Majestic in Paris. 'I have always believed that if I could under-stand how Monsieur Pitard, the head chef, inspired such white-hot morale, I could apply the same kind of leadership to the management of my advertising agency,' he wrote later. He came to the conclusion that 'no creative organization... will produce a great body of work unless it is led by a formidable individual'.

Ogilvy would become that individual – but not for a while yet. In the meantime he was lured back to England to sell Aga cooking stoves, because the company needed somebody who could pitch to French chefs in London restaurants. Ogilvy maintained throughout his career that advertising was no more or less than a sophisticated form of selling, and closing a sale was something at which he turned out to be adept. His admiring boss asked him to write a sales manual for other Aga employees: it later became a standard text for aspiring sales people, eliciting admiration from *Fortune* magazine journalists some 30 years later. Ogilvy's older brother, Francis, was an account executive at the advertising agency Mather & Crowther, where he showed the crisply written sales manual to management. Sure enough, David was duly asked to join the agency too.

With the combination of charm and chutzpah that was to aid his rise in advertising, in 1938 David convinced the agency to send him to New York to study transatlantic advertising techniques. The boy who had revelled in *Huckleberry Finn* was off to America at last. 'When he saw the Manhattan skyline he wept for joy,' claims Stephen Fox in *The Mirror Makers*.

Needless to say, Ogilvy did not return home. Instead, he sought the advice of established New York admen like Rosser Reeves, at that time a copywriter at Blackett-Sample-Hummert. Although Ogilvy admired Reeves, he could never fully accept his new mentor's coldly scientific approach to advertising, believing like Raymond Rubicam (another of Ogilvy's heroes) that effective advertising had to be entertaining as well as persuasive. In essence, Ogilvy's style of advertising was a synthesis of everything that had gone before: the science of Claude Hopkins, the sophistication of JWT under Stanley Resor, and the research-based creativity of Young & Rubicam.

As if to continue his advertising education, Ogilvy got a job with researcher George Gallup, and spent the best part of three years travelling across America learning about the hopes, dreams and habits of his adopted homeland's citizens. Perhaps what he saw disturbed him, because after wartime military intelligence service he took an unlikely sidestep into rural life, buying an Amish farm in Pennsylvania. Fortunately for the advertising industry, his efforts to farm tobacco were as unsuccessful as his attempts to become a history scholar, and he realized that he would have to go back into business. He also realized that he was unlikely to get a job at an advertising agency.

In the book *The Unpublished David Ogilvy*, an internal agency document compiled in 1986, a short autobiographical note captures his predicament at the time. 'Will any agency hire this man? He is 38, and unemployed. He has been a cook, a salesman, a diplomatist and a farmer. He knows nothing about marketing, and has never written any copy. He professes to be interested in advertising as a career (at the age of 38!) and is willing to go to work for US$5000 a year. I doubt if any American agency will hire him. However, a London agency *did* hire him.'

The facts are a little more complicated. Convinced that he would never find employment at a US agency, Ogilvy decided to start one of his own. His capital amounted to US$6,000, but fortunately by that stage his brother Francis was managing director of Mather & Crowther, which agreed to lend him money and its name. David also persuaded another well-known British agency, SH Benson, to invest. At the same time, he convinced the American branch of Wedgwood China to take a risk on a new agency, if only for strategic space-buying purposes.

At first, Ogilvy's backers assumed that the agency needed an American (and presumably more experienced) front man. And so Anderson Hewitt was persuaded to leave the Chicago office of J Walter Thompson, where he was an account man, and become president of the new agency. Hewitt, Ogilvy, Benson & Mather, 'a British advertising agency in New York', was born in September 1948. Ogilvy was named vice-president in charge of research. Although the partnership toddled along for four years, it became quite clear that Ogilvy yearned to stand on his own two feet, and Hewitt eventually left.

In the meantime, Ogilvy had been busy making a name for himself as one of the industry's emerging stars. If his backers in London had imagined that his archetypal 'Britishness' would be a drawback in New York, they were quite wrong. As he later recalled in the interview with *Viewpoint*, Ogilvy knew how to brand himself: 'I had a terrific advantage when I started an agency in New York. I had a British accent. With so many agencies, so much competition, I'd got a gimmick – my English accent, which helped to differentiate me from the ordinary. There are an awful lot of English over there in advertising now, but in those days there were only about two of us. That was very helpful.'

Of course, two of the campaigns that made Ogilvy famous were based on exactly this kind of 'branding by personality'. The first was 'the man in the Hathaway shirt'. In 1951 Ogilvy was hired by Hathaway, a small Maine-based clothing firm, to create a national advertising campaign for a line of mid-priced shirts. As Ogilvy himself explained in *Confessions*, the modest size of the account did not prevent him from having grandiose ambitions. He was determined to come up with a campaign that would surpass even that of Arrow Shirts. 'But Hathaway could spend only US$30,000 against Arrow's US$2,000,000. A miracle was required.'

The miracle turned out to be an eye patch. Ogilvy wanted the ads to exude class and sophistication, so he recruited a dashing, moustached model named George Wrangell. Early on, he had the idea of accessorizing George with a piratical eye patch, but this was rejected as too unorthodox. Finally the day of the shoot came, and on the way to the studio, Ogilvy 'ducked into a drugstore and bought an eye patch for US$1.50... Exactly why it turned out to be so successful, I shall never know.'

But Ogilvy knew very well why the campaign worked. He called it 'story appeal'. The rakish eye patch was unusual and caught readers' attention. '[The reader] glances at the photograph and says to himself: "What goes on there?" Then he reads your copy to find out. The trap is set.'

Ever the practical daydreamer, Ogilvy used the Hathaway campaign to re-create 'a series of situations in which I would have liked to find myself: conducting the New York Philharmonic at Carnegie Hall, playing the oboe, copying a Goya at the Metropolitan Museum, driving a tractor, sailing, fencing, buying a Renoir, and so forth.'

At the same time, Ogilvy had a cost-effective and strategically sound approach to buying advertising space for Hathaway. The ads ran only in the literary, upmarket *New Yorker* magazine, thus adding a further touch of class. As Stephen Fox notes in *The Mirror Makers*, after four years 'the campaign was so familiar that Ogilvy could run an ad without copy, without even the name of the product – just a photograph of the man and his eye patch. Customers were buying an image, not a sales pitch.'

Ogilvy repeated the process for Schweppes tonic water, this time recruiting the company's luxuriantly bearded advertising manager, Commander Edward Whitehead, as the star of the campaign. This nautical-looking figure captured the imagination of the public exactly as the man in the Hathaway shirt had done, with a commensurate rise in sales.

But image was not the only key to a successful ad. Ogilvy was also a crack copywriter, often working until the early hours of the morning to polish the perfect pitch. The result was invariably compelling. Joel Raphaelson, a copywriter who joined Ogilvy's agency in 1958, recalls: 'Despite his air of breeding and sophistication, David never used complicated words when simple ones would do. I remember him leaning over some copy I'd written that read, "Choice seats are still available", and asking, "Why don't you just say '*good* seats'?" And the ads for Hathaway shirts always used words like "made" or "sewn" – never "handcrafted".'

When he won the Rolls Royce account in 1957, Ogilvy produced 26 different headlines for the first advertisement. The client chose: 'At 60 miles an hour, the loudest noise in this new Rolls Royce comes from the electric clock.' It was probably a coincidence that a BBDO ad for Pierce Arrow cars had used more or less the same slogan 25 years earlier. Ogilvy later insisted that he had spent three weeks researching his new client before starting on the copy, and that his headline had been inspired by a magazine article.

Nobody, in any case, could have doubted his dedication. When he won an account, he believed in learning everything he could about the company, believing like Claude Hopkins that this was the best route to sales insights. He worked all the hours that God sent, including weekends. 'Nobody ever died from hard work,' he was fond of saying, quoting his father.

Fortunately, he also knew how to motivate staff. Joel Raphaelson recalls: 'When I joined the agency, David must have been about 46 or 47, and he cut a dashing figure. After about a week, he asked me to speak with him about an ad for the New York Philharmonic – he was on the board and we ran ads promoting fundraising subscriptions. He said, "Let's talk about it over lunch", and asked his secretary to call the Pavillon, which was *the* fanciest restaurant in New York at the time.'

But, like Monsieur Pitard in the kitchen of the Majestic, Ogilvy never forgot that an effective manager should be formidable. 'He scared the hell out of me a couple of times,' says Raphaelson. 'He was temperamental and he didn't pull punches. Once he sent me a note that read: "Joel, I thought you promised to show me the Sears ads last Tuesday. You have now been working on them for three months – longer than the gestation period in PIGS."'

Ogilvy could appear arrogant, although his arrogance seems to have been a cloak for lurking insecurity. He was intelligent enough to be aware of this, and even to have a sense of humour about it. 'I am a miserable duffer in everything *except* advertising,' he wrote in *Confessions*. But a few lines down, he added: 'When *Fortune* wrote an article about me and titled it "Is David Ogilvy a genius?" I asked my lawyer to sue the editor for the question mark.' Many years later, he gave a speech at the Bombay Advertising Club. Afterwards he was asked: 'Mr Ogilvy, Indian advertising draws its inspiration from Madison Avenue. What about Madison Avenue? What is *its* source?' Ogilvy replied: 'Modesty forbids.'

The film-maker and former adman Sir Alan Parker skewers Ogilvy's faintly caricature-like image in the preface to the 1983 re-edition of *Confessions*. 'I suspect that Ogilvy's Turnbull & Asser shirts and puffing pipe were as much an egregious concoction as the man in the eye patch he had made famous, but who could fail to be seduced by a little British narcissism fused with hard-nosed American, self-serving salesmanship?'

Although he is sometimes associated with the period revered in advertising circles as 'the creative revolution', Ogilvy was suspicious of the idea of creativity. His terse summary of the adman's role was: 'Sell – or else.' He claimed that he had 'a reasonably original mind, but not too much so. I thought as clients think.' In a later book, *Ogilvy on Advertising* (1985), he wrote: 'I occasionally use the hideous word *creative* myself, for lack of a better.' But he also said that 'if you ask which of my advertisements was the most successful, I will answer it was the first I wrote for industrial development in Puerto Rico. It won no awards for "creativity", but it persuaded scores of manufacturers to start factories on that poverty-stricken island.' He quoted his old friend Rosser Reeves: 'Do you want fine writing? Do you want masterpieces? Or do you want to see the goddamned sales curve start moving up?'

Joel Raphaelson says, 'David did little to correct the misconception that he was overly scientific about advertising. He simply didn't like advertising that sold the creative more than it sold the product. He thought the things that some of the younger guys were doing were a little nutty. He knew the history of advertising and he understood what worked most of the time – and he felt that any professional should know that.'

Rather than trying to turn advertising into an art form, Ogilvy strived to raise its professional status: 'I think he failed in that effort, but it is one of the reasons he remains an honoured figure in the industry, even if others had a greater influence on the development of advertising.'

Ogilvy played on his gentlemanly appearance – something his upscale clients liked. Yet he remained a salesman at heart, constantly promoting his agency in speeches, in books, and socially. Although he disliked cocktail parties, he forced himself to go to them, because he claimed he could 'smell billings'. In the 75th-birthday interview with *Viewpoint* (the agency's internal magazine) he recalled, 'I once went to a... thing called the Scottish Council. They had a lunch in New York... And from that lunch I eventually got Shell, because Max Burns, then president of Shell, was at the lunch.'

In fact it took another lunch, this time in London – where Ogilvy had flown to doorstep Burns after hearing that he'd sacked his existing agency – to secure the account. But the story does justice to the Ogilvy charm: and he claimed he got three other clients from the same event.

Practically from day one, Ogilvy was approached by rival agencies with offers to buy him out. Over the years he fended off overtures from almost every big name in the business: Interpublic, J Walter Thompson,

BBDO, Leo Burnett... 'I guess the real fundamental reason was a rather personal one,' he told *Viewpoint*. 'I liked Ogilvy & Mather. I thought it was in the process of becoming the best damn agency in the history of the world. And I didn't want to muddle it up with any other agency.'

When WPP finally acquired the agency in 1989, Ogilvy took it as a personal affront. Yet he calmed down enough to accept the post of non-executive chairman, still unable to let go. He died in 1999, an advertising legend who began his career when he was almost 40.

## The science of selling

In the process of establishing his agency, Ogilvy often spoke of the need to 'reform' advertising, well aware that people were as repelled by the business as they were fascinated by it. This was hardly surprising, given that thanks to TV they were being bombarded by more advertising messages than ever before.

It also explained the success of Vance Packard's *The Hidden Persuaders*, which became a bestseller when it exposed the 'motivational research' techniques agencies were using to probe the minds of consumers. 'Large-scale efforts are being made', Packard warned, 'to channel our unthinking habits, our purchasing decisions, and our thought processes.' He claimed that scientists were furnishing advertising agencies with 'awesome tools', with the result that 'many of us are being influenced and manipulated, far more than we realize, in the patterns of our everyday lives'.

One can almost hear the eerie wail of the Theremin on the soundtrack. Indeed, in retrospect the book makes amusing reading – rather like one of those paranoid 1950s B-movies in which white-coated scientists do battle with unconvincing aliens. ('It was clearly all crap,' chuckles John Hegarty, the British creative and co-founder of Bartle Bogle Hegarty. 'If everything in the book was true, we'd be able to sell anything to anybody.') Yet *The Hidden Persuaders* was by no means pure fantasy. The father of motivational research was Ernest Dichter who, in the late 1930s, pioneered the use of 'depth interviews' to explore consumers' attitudes to products. (Dichter's work is said to have directly inspired a slogan for Ivory Soap, 'Wash your troubles away'. Dirt, guilt, anxiety... you get the idea.) By the 1950s a number of agencies – McCann Erickson, Foote, Cone & Belding and Leo Burnett among them – were using motivational research techniques to hone their campaigns.

McCann Erickson is thought to have been the first to hire psychological research staff. The agency developed a reputation for data-driven efficiency rather than creative flair under its post-war boss, Marion Harper Jr. This somewhat straight-laced man (don't be fooled by the 'Marion') had joined the agency in 1939 as an office boy and worked his way up to head of research in just six years. Two years later, at the age of 32, he was placed at the helm of the agency by its founder, Harrison King McCann, who became chairman.

McCann had started the agency – then called HK McCann – in 1911 when Standard Oil broke itself up at the behest of the US government, thus robbing him of his position as the company's ad manager. His agency was effectively Standard Oil's spun-off advertising department. Servicing companies formed from the scattered units of Standard, as well as important new clients like General Motors and Coca-Cola, McCann was able to expand rapidly into overseas markets, soon rivalling J Walter Thompson for global reach.

McCann proclaimed himself a believer in 'total marketing', moving the agency into disciplines such as public relations and sales promotion. In 1930, the Depression pushed him to merge with the AW Erickson agency. Albert Erickson had gone into business in 1902 after leaving his job in the advertising office of a department store. Although his agency was a limited success, he made a fortune investing in other concerns – including the company that invented Technicolor film. Erickson died four years after the merger (The Advertising Century: adage.com/century/people).

With McCann now in a largely symbolic role, Marion Harper could get stuck in to his mission to turn the agency into a super-efficient selling machine. He is said to have hung a Mexican painting of a cockfight in his office as a metaphor for the advertising business. He pushed for a greater emphasis on consumer psychology and buying motives, as well as carefully studying the effect of media placements on sales. As quoted by Stephen Fox in *The Mirror Makers*, Harper felt that advertising people should base their work on statistics rather than 'skipping around the Maypole of creativity'. 'Advertisers are not spending billions to decorate media,' he said. 'Their messages are not meant as ornaments.'

This viewpoint gave Harper something in common with another notable 1950's ad man – Rosser Reeves, David Ogilvy's former mentor, now working at the Ted Bates agency. But Reeves had little time for motivational research or any other highfalutin' theories about consumer behaviour. His overriding concern was getting his brands noticed amid the deluge of advertising that now swamped consumers. A strong proponent of Claude Hopkins' theory that advertising was merely an embodiment of the hard sell, he developed the Unique Selling Proposition (USP): the single claim that separated a brand from its competitors. His ads were stripped down to this one message, with no creative frills, and repeated again and again. Indeed, he described elements that distracted the audience from the key message of an ad as 'vampires'. At the end of each campaign, he would audit thousands of consumers across the country to see if they remembered the claim. More often than not, they did.

In this manner, Reeves drove the success of the Ted Bates agency, which had been established in 1940 by the quietly spoken account executive whose name was on the door. They ran the agency together, but nobody was in any doubt about who possessed the most energy and charisma. Reeves published his theories in 1961 in a book called *Reality in Advertising*, which was the anti-*Hidden Persuaders*, crammed with common sense. 'Advertising began as an art, and many advertising men want it to remain that way,' he wrote, 'a never-never land where they can say: this is right, because we feel it's right.'

But Reeves' insistence on using advertising like a blunt instrument was at odds with his hidden, sensitive side. A chess fanatic with a huge library of books and a wide range of hobbies – including sailing and flying – he was another in the long line of copywriters who harboured dreams of writing the Great American Novel. Indeed, when he retired he wrote a book set in bohemian Greenwich Village – and he wrote poetry throughout his life. An acquaintance described this hobby with considerable understatement as 'surprising'.

If the history of advertising has one overriding theme, it is this constant tug of war between two schools: the creatives, who believe art inspires consumers to buy; and the pragmatists, who sell based on facts and come armed with reams of research. In the 1950s, the antithesis of Rosser Reeves (and even of the gentlemanly David Ogilvy) was Bill Bernbach. His brash new agency, Doyle Dane Bernbach, sparked the creative revolution.

# Creative revolutionaries

'Let us blaze new trails'

'In the late fifties in New York if you talked about "Bill" you meant Bill Bernbach,' writes Mary Wells Lawrence, recalling her days as a DDB employee before she set up her own agency (*A Big Life in Advertising*, 2002). Bernbach was a big noise in town because he'd set out to challenge the monolithic pre-war agencies that now dominated Madison Avenue. According to Wells, Bernbach felt that their ads had become 'dishonest, boring, insulting – even insane'. He argued that the repetitive tactics of people like Rosser Reeves had reduced the industry to 'one poor tired ad' and that the giant agencies were 'turning their creative people into mimeograph machines'. Unless advertising shook up its ideas, he warned, it would become invisible, with zero impact on consumers. And Bernbach wasn't about to let that happen.

Bernbach had left Grey Advertising to found his own agency with a clutch of fellow revolutionaries: Ned Doyle (an account man), Maxwell 'Mac' Dane (a promotions wizard), Bob Gage (an art director) and Phyllis Robinson (a copywriter). Bernbach himself was essentially a copywriter with a strong visual sense – but above all he was an ideas machine. In 1949, Doyle Dane Bernbach set up shop in the shadow of the big Madison Avenue agencies. It wouldn't stay there for long.

Not that Bernbach looked like somebody who was about to light a fire under an entire industry. Mary Wells Lawrence writes that he was 'shorter than he sounded' with 'a wary half-smile, cow's milk eyes, pale skin [and] soft shoulders'. But she confirms that his appearance was deceptive. 'He communicated such a powerful inner presence that he mowed everyone around him down and out of sight. There was something volcanic; something unsettling going on... In his peak years many people were afraid of him.'

Bernbach was born in The Bronx, New York, on 13 August 1911, to Rebecca and Jacob Bernbach. Although he liked to hint that he came from an underprivileged background – saying, for instance, that he had no middle name because his parents couldn't afford one – in fact his family was solid and respectable. In the 1987 *Bill Bernbach's Book*, written by his friend and ace DDB copywriter Bob Levenson, he is quoted as describing his father, a designer of women's clothing, as 'austere but elegant'.

After attending public schools, Bill went to New York University, where he studied an unusual trio of subjects: music, business administration and philosophy. (Advertising is perhaps the only profession in which one might be expected to draw on knowledge of all three.) He also played the piano. Despite being 'physically unprepossessing', he was 'bright, observant, articulate and could reasonably feel that he was a cut above many of the people around him'. This outsized ego – not uncommon among those with impressive minds lodged in inconvenient bodies – never deserted him. An oft-repeated joke about Bernbach has a colleague commenting on the day's beautiful weather. 'Thank you,' says Bernbach.

Bernbach got a job as a mail boy at the Schenley Distillers Company, where he wrote an impromptu ad for a brand called Schenley's American Cream Whiskey, and personally delivered it to the firm's advertising department. The ad ran, and Bernbach ensured that the company's president, Lewis Rosenstiel, knew who had written it. Young Bernbach was promptly promoted to the advertising department. In 1939, he went to work as a copywriter for the New York World's Fair. But he was far more influenced by his subsequent job, at the William H Weintraub agency, where he worked as a copywriter alongside the legendary graphic designer Paul Rand.

Both the Weintraub agency and Rand himself were templates for the Doyle Dane Bernbach method. In 1941, William H Weintraub had created New York's first 'ethnic' agency as an alternative to the overwhelmingly WASP (white Anglo-Saxon protestant) Madison Avenue culture. Its accounts included Dubonnet, Revlon and Schenley Liquors – which probably explains how Bernbach ended up working there. Rand was the agency's firebrand art director, who'd arrived at the age of 27 demanding (and getting) exclusive control of the art department. Influenced by cubism, constructivism and De Stijl, Rand bought a European sensibility to US graphic design. His images were crisp and uncluttered – in fact, disturbingly spartan by the standards of the day. (Much later he went on to design the IBM logo, among hundreds of other iconic images.) 'Paul was the creative revolution,' insists a fellow Weintraub designer in Steven Heller's (2000) biography, *Paul Rand*. 'It's like Cezanne. After Cezanne came Braque and Picasso and they invented cubism. But everything started with Cezanne.'

Highly unusually for the day, Bernbach worked in tandem with Rand, his lively copy rendering the art director's images doubly effective. This was the birth of the 'creative team'. At the lumbering traditional agencies, copywriters and art directors still worked in separate departments – often on different floors – trying gamely to crunch their words and images together with little or no discussion. But Rand and Bernbach developed concepts together from the beginning. When Bernbach opened his own agency, it was on this basis: copywriters and art directors working side by side.

Although Bernbach and Rand were close friends at Weintraub, Madison Avenue legend has it that Bernbach's mentor never forgave him for favouring photography in his ads over illustration. Rand was interested in aesthetics, while Bernbach was after impact.

In the meantime, Bernbach had left Weintraub for military service. When he returned, he was hired by Grey Advertising, which had a similarly non-WASP, multi-ethnic makeup to that of Weintraub. Here he moved up from copy chief to vice-president and creative director 'in a matter of months', according to Bob Levenson, who explains Bernbach's rise thus: 'He was a visionary, with a visionary's zeal. And he was a worrier. It was a killer combination.'

At Grey he met art director Bob Gage, with whom he enjoyed the same meeting of minds and talents that he had experienced with Paul Rand. Gage felt it too, telling his wife that one day he expected to go into business with Bernbach. That moment came closer in May 1947, when Bernbach wrote a famous letter to his bosses at Grey: 'I'm worried that we're going to fall into the trap of bigness,' he warned, 'that we're going to worship techniques instead of substance... There are a lot of great technicians in advertising... But there's one little rub. Advertising is fundamentally persuasion and persuasion happens to be not a science, but an art... Let us blaze new trails. Let us prove to the world that good taste, good art, good writing can be good selling.'

As an ideology, it was sound enough. But not sound enough for Bernbach's bosses, who appear to have ignored the letter. And so

Bernbach decided to 'blaze new trails' with his own agency. He took with him a founding account – the department store Ohrbach's – and a colleague, a Grey vice-president and account executive named Ned Doyle, with whom he had formed 'a mutuality of respect', in Doyle's words. Later, Doyle was among the first people the aspiring young copywriter Mary Wells met when she arrived at DDB. She describes him as 'as Irish as could be... a slender, older man with white-and-grey hair, cool eyes and a carved face'.

Doyle brought in Maxwell Dane, at that point running a small agency of his own. Mac Dane had started his career as a secretary to the advertising manager of a New York retailer called Stern Brothers. After stints as retail promotion manager of the *New York Evening Post* and account executive and copywriter at the Dorland International agency, he became advertising and promotion manager of *Look* magazine, where he met Doyle. He then headed advertising and promotion at the radio station WMCA (where he introduced the concept of news bulletins every hour on the hour, an innovation at the time), before starting his own agency in 1944. He now joined forces with his old friend without regret, and his cramped, walk-up premises on Madison Avenue became the new agency's first home.

And so Doyle Dane Bernbach was born. The lack of commas was another departure from the norm. 'Nothing will ever come between us,' Bernbach explained. 'Not even punctuation.'

The agency caught the rhythm of the time – it was more like a hip jazz combo than an advertising agency. Indeed, Bernbach once compared its work to that of the great jazz pianist Thelonius Monk. Calling the tune at the beginning was the department store boss NM Ohrbach: 'uneducated, insecure and big', as Bernbach described him. And yet it was Ohrbach, previously a Grey client, who had encouraged Bill to set up his own agency. He also agreed to pay for the store's first campaigns up front so Doyle Dane Bernbach could cover its overheads. 'Ohrbach was a brute of an entrepreneur, and Bernbach made Ohrbach's cash registers ring,' observes Bob Levenson. But the relationship was not without friction: 'At least some of the steel in Bill's blue eyes was hammered in the Ohrbach forge.'

Nevertheless, Doyle Dane Bernbach turned out a series of arresting images for Ohrbach's, all serving the store's brand positioning of high fashion at accessible prices. One of the most famous features was a man carrying a cardboard cut-out of his wife under his arm; 'Bring in your wife, and for just a few dollars we'll give you a new woman,' says the copy. A slam-bang image and witty text in perfect equilibrium – that was the DDB style. It was powered by the snappy writing of Phyllis Robinson and the spacious design of Bob Gage, arguably the first modern art director in advertising.

The agency's next major account, Levy's Bakery, confirmed its talents. Levy's made rye bread, a quintessentially Jewish product. Knowing that the pre-packaged bread was unlikely to taste as good as a fresh loaf 'from the Jewish bakery on the corner', Bernbach suggested targeting a non-Jewish audience, which would be less likely to make the comparison. Hence the first campaign: 'You don't have to be Jewish to love Levy's.' And that was the only text, below big portrait photos of an Irish cop or a cute black kid, among others. Once again, the ads were spare and sharp and sold the product in a few seconds. An even simpler execution featured three shots of the same slice of bread. The first slice had a bite taken out of it – by the third shot only the crust and some crumbs remained. 'New York is eating it up!' said the text.

The agency's skilful use of photography came into play again with its campaign for Polaroid, a strange new camera that produced instant snaps. The product's previous print ads had been cluttered and gimmicky, the cheapness of their execution belying the fairly hefty pricepoint of the camera. Doyle Dane Bernbach junked the text. In the words of Bob Levenson: 'Polaroid was selling pictures, so the advertising showed big, beautiful pictures in unadorned, totally straightforward ads.'

The headline on a print ad for Avis, 'We try harder', led to copy explaining that the car rental agency was number two in the market, so it couldn't afford to be complacent. The copy was so effective that Avis bosses allegedly complained to Bernbach, worrying that they wouldn't be able to live up to the high standards that the ad promised.

But Doyle Dane Bernbach's most famous campaign was also its biggest challenge. It was for Volkswagen.

## Thinking small

'They wanted us to sell a Nazi car in a Jewish town,' is the typically caustic summary of art director George Lois, who joined Doyle Dane Bernbach around the time it won the Volkswagen account. Lois (from whom we'll hear much more) worked on VW van campaigns and collaborated on the Beetle work. But the task of selling this small, oddly shaped German vehicle to the America of the late 1950s initially fell to art director Helmut Krone and copywriter Julian Koenig, overseen by Bernbach himself.

It's no coincidence that Krone was a first generation German American. 'I got on Volkswagen because I was the only one who had ever heard of the car,' he is quoted as saying in *Helmut Krone. The Book*, by Clive Challis (2005). 'I had one of the first Volkswagens in the States, probably one of the first hundred, long before I ever worked [at DDB].'

Influenced by Paul Rand and Alexey Brodovitch – the pioneering art director of *Harper's Bazaar* – Krone was more interested in design than in advertising. He'd worked at *Esquire* magazine before joining Doyle Dane Bernbach in 1954, at the age of 29. Stubborn and exacting, he focused on the beauty and impact of the image above and beyond any selling concerns. Forever 'looking for a new page', he laboured steadily towards perfection. One story recounted by Challis has Krone working on a label for a brand of wine called Thunderbird. Entering his office, Ned Doyle tells him, 'We resigned that account months ago.' Krone replies, 'It doesn't matter. It isn't right yet.'

Julian Koenig was something of a hipster. He wore stylishly rumpled dark suits, narrow ties, and oxford shirts with button-down collars. According to Challis, he had dropped out of law school to write a novel and hang out at the Metropolitan Museum of Art, before 'falling into advertising'. At the Herschon Garfield agency, he wrote the Timex 'torture test' commercials.

This mismatched pair came up with the most influential advertising campaign of all time. Krone went against the DDB grain by selecting what was thought of as 'the Ogilvy layout' for a print ad: headline, picture, and text, as neatly arranged as a suburban lawn. 'In adopting it Krone would have put Bernbach's nose out of joint,' Challis writes. 'But it was also absolutely right: cool, unassuming, restrained.'

And while Ogilvy's pictures were always spiced with intriguing details, Krone used stark, raw, images. He also chose a brutally simple sans serif typeface. The accompanying copy was deadpan yet self-deprecating, tacitly assuming the reader's intelligence.

One of the earliest ads focused on the Beetle's air-cooled engine. It showed the car, shot from above, covered in soap suds. The headline read: 'The only water a Volkswagen needs is the water you wash it with.' Here, already, was a tiny revolution – if one that passed unnoticed by the vast majority of the public. The headline ended in a full stop. Clive Challis explains: 'Putting a full point in a headline was an act of sedition. It broke the pace and invited inspection – maybe even circumspection – of the statement. Of course this is exactly why Krone used one: he had statements to make which he wanted to be examined.'

All of these elements – the stark simplicity, the dramatic effect of the full point, the factual yet entertaining copy – came together in the most iconic ad of the series. It started out as a corporate ad for the trade press, the longish copy ending in the lines: 'Volkswagen has become the world's fifth largest automotive maker by thinking small. More and more people are doing the same.'

For the headline, Julian Koenig plucked out the words 'Think small.'

Krone is said to have been fairly unimpressed by the idea at first, although the visual interpretation was obvious: 'I suppose you want me to make the car small?' Almost everyone in the art department – including George Lois and Bob Gage – seems to have offered advice on the matter, but Krone finally placed a little Beetle on the upper left corner of a blank page, at a slight angle. The ad was so well received that a slightly tweaked version – this time with even tighter copy by Bob Levenson – ran in the consumer press a few months later. Encouraging consumers to 'think small' in the land of the large, where the automobiles were the size of buses, was subversive.

Another celebrated ad in the series shows a straightforward picture of a gleaming new Beetle, above the word 'Lemon'. The copy, by Julian Koenig, explains: 'This Volkswagen missed the boat. The chrome strip on the glove compartment is blemished and must be replaced.' It concludes: 'We pluck the lemons; you get the plums.' In her book, Mary Wells claims that the ad got past the German client because he didn't understand the play on words – and was too embarrassed to say so. Bernbach later recognized that the daring one-word headline changed the fortunes of the agency: 'Suppose we had merely said, "Every VW must pass rigid inspection?"'

Bob Levenson writes that DDB's Volkswagen advertising has been 'imitated, mimicked, swiped, copied, misunderstood and admired more than any other campaign before or since'. But its secret lay in Bernbach's unwavering focus on the product. 'He saw the Volkswagen car for what it was: honest, simple, reliable, sensible, different. And he wanted the advertising to be that way too.' The imitators were therefore doomed 'because they weren't selling Volkswagens and he was'.

Advertising people tend to get a little over-excited about DDB's VW ads. But there's no denying that their iconoclastic wit and (let's face it) Teutonic precision have stood the test of time. When the New Beetle was launched in 1998, the advertising paid homage to the 1959 original, with only minor changes to Helmut Krone's classic layout. It speaks volumes that the older campaign still looked far superior.

## Murderers' row

George Lois was one of the street fighters of the creative revolution. A Greek florist's kid from The Bronx, he was the archetype of the band of fast-talking, self-confident New Yorkers who wanted to upset the protestant applecart of Madison Avenue. When I met Lois in his Greenwich Village apartment, his opening line was this: 'At Doyle Dane Bernbach [in the late fifties] you had the four best art directors anywhere in the world: Bob Gage, Bill Taubin, Helmut Krone – and me. It was a killer line-up. It was murderers' row.'

Lois admits that he was 'very aggressive and passionate'. He had learned the value of hard work from his florist father, who would finish each day with his fingers lacerated with scratches. And as a Greek kid growing up in an Irish neighbourhood, George got used to fighting his corner. Talented from day one ('I was always sketching and drawing 3D lettering on everything'), with the encouragement of a teacher he put a portfolio together and gained entrance to the prestigious High School of Music and Art (a public school founded in 1936 by New York City mayor Fiorello H LaGuardia for students who excelled in the arts). 'The greatest school in the world, influenced by Bauhaus,' says Lois.

When he emerged, although he knew he wanted to be a designer, advertising was 'still a wasteland' in the late 1940s. 'The stuff they were doing was awful. You were taught six basic layouts.' After being drafted for the Korean War and getting back in one piece, he worked at CBS for its creative director Bill Golden, designing advertising and graphics for the network.

'But I still had this idea that there were things to do in advertising. Bill warned me not to go. He said: "Don't do it George – advertising is a world of schlock." He thought I was crazy.'

Fortunately, Lois got a job at Sudler & Hennessy, where the art director was Herb Lubalin, the highly influential graphic designer. 'But even then it was clear that the place for me was Doyle Dane Bernbach. In fact Bob Gage had already tried to hire me once, for the agency's promotions department, but I turned him down – I told him I wanted to do my own advertising. When I went back there two years later, it was as an art director.'

Lois says DDB was 'the only creative agency in the world' at the time. 'The industry was very WASPy. There were some ethnic kids doing edgy things in design, but apart from that it was pure bullshit. Ogilvy was creative, but in a different way – it had a traditional look, there was no room for an art director to breathe. There were a million rules; I had no rules.'

Even in the hothouse environment of Doyle Dane Bernbach, Lois stood out. 'When I joined Doyle Dane in around 1958, I got an immediate reputation as a very different kind of art director. My stuff was edgy, tough, with a sort of street sensibility. It was pretty striking even by Doyle Dane standards.'

Plus, Lois was a livewire. His colourful language and incendiary temperament are legend. George recounts the time at Sudler & Hennessy when his boss and some clients entered his office at the very moment he was embroiled in a brawl with an account man. 'I literally had the guy off the floor by the scruff of his neck. Sudler turns to the client and says: "All our art directors are very passionate individuals."'

Another of his favourite anecdotes concerns the fact that at Doyle Dane Bernbach art directors weren't allowed to talk to clients. 'I changed that single-handedly. During my first couple of weeks I produced a subway poster for Goodman's Matzo [snacks]. It was basically a giant matzo... really striking-looking image. The account guy took it over to the client, Mr Goodman. When he came back he said, "He doesn't like it, do another one." I said, "F**k you!" and I took the poster and went over there myself.

'So Goodman is sitting there in a big glass office, surrounded by his grandchildren. And they're all looking at the poster and saying, "You know, that's kind of fun, we ought to run with that", and the old man keeps barking, "I don't like it!" Finally I lose my temper and stride over to the big casement window. I open it and lean out with the poster, as if I'm about to throw myself out. "See what you make me feel like doing?" I shout. "You make the matzos – I'll make the ads!" He yells at me to come back in, practically having a heart attack. His people are fanning him; they give him a pill and a glass of water. When he can finally breathe again he says: "All right, kid, all right: run the goddamned ad. And if you ever get fired, come back and see me. I'll give you a job as a matzo salesman."'

After a few weeks at DDB, a small delegation of art directors and copywriters did indeed go to Bernbach with the intention of getting Lois fired. 'They thought I wasn't right for Doyle Dane. But it was the wrong move, because Bernbach had liked me since the first day, when he came to say hello to me in my office. I'd painted the place over the weekend and brought in this great Mies van der Rohe chair. And I was working on an ad for a liquid ear wax remover – I'd made a huge photograph of an ear about to be attacked by pencils and paperclips, which Bernbach absolutely loved. So when they tried to get me fired, Bernbach paid me the greatest compliment of my life. He said: "Are you kidding? This guy's a combination of Paul Rand and Bob Gage!"'

As it transpired, even Doyle Dane Bernbach wasn't big enough to contain the Lois persona. In late 1959, he approached DDB copywriter Julian Koenig with the idea of setting up 'the world's second creative agency'. They would join forces with Fred Papert, who had left an agency called Kenyon & Eckhardt. 'When I told Bernbach that I was leaving, he was beyond stunned,' recalls Lois. 'It was like I'd punched him in the mouth. He said to me very seriously, "But George, you don't understand, *there can't be two creative agencies.*"'

Undaunted by this challenge, Papert Koenig Lois set up shop in the new Seagram building in January 1960. The agency drew on the ethos of DDB, with the same disregard for research and emphasis on raw talent. 'It was the first time the art director had assumed the most prominent role in an agency,' says Lois. 'From that moment on, every hip young kid wanted to work in advertising as an art director. We were like rock stars.'

Immediately successful, PKL won work from Peugeot and Xerox. Its Xerox TV campaign zeroed in on the simplicity of the machine, showing a chimpanzee making copies. 'We were really the start of the creative revolution,' contends Lois. 'One agency is not a revolution. Doyle Dane Bernbach was the trunk, but we were the first branch.'

## The revolution will be televised

Further branches soon emerged. Another renegade, Carl Ally, broke out of PKL in 1962 to set up his own agency with the US$1 million Volvo account. A fighter pilot during the Korean War, the pugnacious Ally wanted to make advertising that grabbed people by the throat. On his wall he hung an exhortation: 'Comfort the afflicted; afflict the comfortable.' Ally won the Hertz rental car business and turned DDB's advertising back against it. 'For years Avis has been telling you that Hertz is number one,' read the lashing copy. 'Now we're going to tell you why.' Later, for Volvo, his agency came up with the line: 'Drive it like you hate it.'

The new generation revelled in their irreverence. The copywriter Jerry Della Femina summed up the attitude a few years later, when he wrote a book that took its title from a slogan he had wickedly suggested to a Japanese electronics firm: *From Those Wonderful Folks Who Brought You Pearl Harbour*.

In 1967, copywriter Ed McCabe teamed up with Sam Scali and Marvin Sloves to form Scali McCabe Sloves. McCabe had started working in the mailroom of McCann Erickson when he was just 15 years old, and he went on to become one of the most respected wordsmiths in the business. Creativity, in other words, was breaking out all over. As Lois puts it, 'Even the traditional agencies became creative around the edges.'

At the centre was one of the most important women in the history of advertising: Mary Wells, co-founder of Wells Rich Greene. In its Advertising Century round-up, *Advertising Age* calls her 'advertising's first international superstar'. If Lois thought of television advertising in terms of moving art, Mary Wells considered it a form of theatre. Arguably, she was the first advertising executive to unlock the potential of TV advertising as spectacle.

Born in Youngstown, Ohio, Wells could have easily become an actress. As she reveals in her biography, her mother – who clearly wanted her to get ahead – found her an elocution teacher at the age of five. At the age of 10, again encouraged by her mother, she played her first roles at the Youngstown Playhouse. Later, she enrolled at the Neighbourhood Playhouse School of Theatre in New York, followed by further theatre studies at the Carnegie Institute of Technology in Pittsburgh. But here she suddenly realized with a shock that 'I not only didn't care about becoming an actress... I didn't know what I wanted to study or be or who I was.'

During this period she met and married Bert Wells, an industrial design student at Carnegie Tech. She left the school and returned to

Ohio determined 'to make money Bert and I would need for life in New York'. She fell into a copywriting job at a department store called McKelvey's, where she had sold hats as a teenager. Vera Friedman, who headed the store's advertising department, hired Wells 'because I had theatre training and I could type – the perfect combination of resources, she thought, for a trainee copywriter'.

Friedman would soon discover how right she was. Energized by the idea that her words could induce people to buy clothes, Mary discovered her metier. By 1952 she was back in New York with Bert, where she got a job in the advertising department of Macy's. She had a gift for romanticizing the world that was perfect for marketing clothes. 'Fashion is about... wearing your dreams,' she writes. Her next stop was McCann Erickson – but her career locked into gear in 1957, when she went to work at Doyle Dane Bernbach.

At first, neither Wells nor Bernbach were sure that the agency was the right place for her. For a start, she didn't trade in snappy puns. 'My strong suit, theatricalizing life with dreams, irritated him.' Later, though, Bernbach referred to her as 'the agency's dream merchant' and would bring clients around to get a look at her customized office, with its orange vinyl floor and tropical rattan furniture. This oasis was a sight to behold in the notoriously ramshackle agency, which prided itself on scruffy normality as a contrast to the slicker Madison Avenue monoliths.

Wells spent seven years at DDB, working on accounts such as Max Factor, General Mills and the French tourist office. (For the latter, Wells commissioned photographer Elliot Erwitt, who shot a classic image of a father and his little boy, both in berets, on a bicycle gliding down a tree-lined French road, with a baguette strapped to the bike. It romanticized the simple pleasures of the French countryside for a generation – and when I saw a print at a photography exhibition in Paris recently, the image still leapt out at me.)

In 1964, Wells was lured away from DDB by Marion Harper, then busy building the Interpublic marketing empire (see Chapter 11, Consolidation incorporated). Harper had set up an 'advertising think tank' called Jack Tinker & Partners, which he hoped to turn into a genuinely creative agency. Wells would help him do it.

She struck gold early on with a series of TV vignettes for Alka-Seltzer, the indigestion relief tablet. Wells reckoned that anybody with a truly sixties lifestyle couldn't avoid an upset stomach: it was an inevitable consequence of all that hard work, all that partying, all those new, exotic and spicy foods. In other words, everyone needed Alka-Seltzer. The first ad showed a cheeky montage of different-sized stomachs over a jingle that became a chart hit. 'No matter what shape your stomach's in,' was the tagline. A short while later, the agency added the iconic shot of two tablets being dropped into a glass of water: 'plop, plop, fizz, fizz'.

The Alka-Seltzer story also reveals another of Wells' contributions to the creative revolution: as well as injecting razzmatazz into TV commercials, she was a natural branding consultant, able to persuade clients to change their entire marketing strategy so that it chimed in with her advertising. When she repositioned Alka-Seltzer as a lifestyle product, brand owner Miles Laboratories created 'portable foil packs that held two Alka-Seltzers each and sold them in new places, magazine stands, bars, restaurants... and, naturally, Miles began selling twice as much Alka-Seltzer'.

This feel for integrated marketing was further highlighted by the agency's next hit campaign, for Braniff Airlines. At that stage, Wells recalls, all aeroplanes were either 'metallic or white with a stripe painted down the middle of them'. Terminals were grey and soulless. Flying, which should have been a thrilling experience, was actually miserable.

Standing in a grim terminal building one day, Wells pictured Braniff 'in a wash of beautiful colour'. So she had Braniff's fleet of aircraft painted bright pastel colours. Red-hot Italian fashion designer Emilio Pucci was hired to redesign the hostess's uniforms. (Parts of the uniform could be removed as the plane flew into warmer climes; Wells later ran a provocative commercial dramatizing this as 'The Air Strip', which proved a huge hit when shown during the Super Bowl.) Interior designer Alexander Girard, who had styled one of Wells' favourite restaurants – 'in a high-octane colour montage of Mexican and modern' – gave the inside of the planes a new look. 'The end of the plain plane,' said the print advertising. Wells and her team had created the coolest, the sexiest – the most *sixties* – airline around.

There was plenty of steel beneath her romantic nature. When Marion Harper refused to make her president of Jack Tinker & Partners, she resigned. She took with her the art directors Stewart Greene and Dick Rich – the first calm and reassuring, the second edgy and contemporary – and the Braniff account. Wells Rich Greene opened its doors on 4 April 1967.

After moving out of its temporary base in the Gotham Hotel, the agency found cramped office space on Madison Avenue. 'We didn't have time for decorating,' writes Wells, 'although we did plaster the walls with Love posters and tossed psychedelic pillows around and we allowed Mick Jagger to sing "Have You Seen Your Mother, Baby?" in the waiting room.' More importantly, Wells Rich Greene set out to hire young men and women 'who had a gift for cinematic use of television'.

And this was the simple, complex secret of Wells Rich Greene. The Technicolor imaginations of Wells and her loyal creative director Charlie Moss spawned highly engaging advertising for the likes of Benson & Hedges, American Motors, Procter & Gamble and Ford. Wells' early success for Braniff attracted a string of airline accounts: TWA, Continental and Pan Am. By the mid-1970s, she was the highest-paid woman in advertising, earning more than US$300,000 a year. During that same decade, she was able to help out the city that had witnessed her climb to the top. Her agency popularized a slogan that no visitor to New York can escape, even today.

'I lost count of the amount of people who claimed to have invented the line "I love New York",' writes Wells, of her 1970s campaign to bring tourists back to the city. 'Nobody created the expression; it is what people have been saying since I can remember...'

At the time, though, New York was distinctly unlovable: bankrupt, crime-ridden, and still reeking after a strike by garbage workers. Perhaps only Mary Wells could have envisioned an advertising campaign that played like a Broadway musical, with everyone from Gregory Peck (impressively) to Henry Kissinger (surprisingly) and Frank Sinatra (inevitably) appearing on screen to glow about how much they adored the city.

The finishing touch came courtesy of the designer Milton Glaser, who showed up at Wells Rich Greene with a selection of posters. While the team was examining them, 'he pulled a crumpled piece of paper out of his pocket and said, "I like this, what do you think?" It was the "I Love New York" logo with a heart in the place of the word "Love".'

Next time you see a coffee mug or a T-shirt bearing the words 'I ♥ New York', spare a thought for Milton Glaser.

The agency went on to other triumphs, and it was not until the very end of the acquisitive 1980s that Wells began to consider selling up and moving on. The industry had become consolidated, global reach was the key to success, and – for Wells, at least – some of the romance had leached from the industry. She'd had earlier conversations with DDB and Saatchi & Saatchi, but now she became attracted by BDDP, a French agency with 'a cool, young, sophisticated style', that had approached her with tentative talk of a partnership deal. The discussions grew more serious, and after much soul-searching and hesitation, she sold Wells Rich Greene to BDDP in 1990, for US $160 million ('Queen of advertising tells all', *USA Today*, 2 May 2002).

The newly baptized Wells BDDP was about to get off to a rocky start. By then, adland was a very different place.

# The Chicago way

## 05

*'The advertiser wants ideas, needs ideas and is paying for ideas'*

**M**aybe it was just good advertising, but Chicago immediately struck me as a friendly city. On a breezy autumn morning, as I stood in the middle of the street with an unfolded map trying to wrap itself around my face, three different people came up to ask me if I needed directions. After twice insisting that I would be OK, I finally gave up and admitted to the third person that I was hopelessly lost. 'Leo Burnett?', the man repeated. 'It's on West Wacker Drive. You're on East Wacker. Just go back in the direction you came and keep walking: you can't miss it.'

As I walked on, I realized that I hadn't asked the man if he worked in advertising – I'd just accepted the fact that he knew all about Leo Burnett. While Ogilvy and Bernbach are not part of the mythology of New York City, Burnett has entered Chicago folklore. He remains as larger-than-life as the characters his agency created, from the Jolly Green Giant to Tony the Tiger – not to mention the Marlboro cowboy.

The Leo Burnett Building at 35 West Wacker drive is a 50-storey sky-scraper with a lobby big enough to provoke agoraphobia. An elevator whisks visitors up to a crescent-shaped reception area featuring banks of television screens, a battery of black-clad receptionists, a bowl of rosy red apples and – suspended from the ceiling – a giant black pencil. The significance of these last two items will be discussed shortly. Beyond the reception area is the usual maze of offices, including the lair of Tom Bernardin, the agency's chairman and CEO.

Leo Burnett Worldwide has always been considered a solid, reliable, unpretentious agency. Under Bernardin's leadership, its brand position-ing is a curious blend of the homely and the cutting edge: a multinational with a family atmosphere. Bernardin says, 'My intent since I arrived [in

2004] has been to emphasize our unique heritage and the core values of our company, while demonstrating that these very qualities, properly applied, can be utterly modern, relevant values.'

Perhaps Leo Burnett owes some of its corporate culture to the city itself. Is there a Chicago school of advertising?

'I think there is – which can be both a good and bad thing. Being headquartered here arguably takes us out of the mainstream New York advertising community. On the other hand, we leverage that as a point of difference from the mainstream. But Chicago and New York aside, one of the things I've been working on is reinforcing the fact that we're a global company, rather than a company based in Chicago with offices around the world.'

And perhaps it's slightly unfair to link Leo Burnett inextricably with Chicago. After all, the man himself wasn't born in the city. 'I snuck up on her slowly by way of outlying cities,' he once said. 'When I finally got there, I was 40 years old and stuck in my colloquial ways.'

## An unhurried start

Leo Noble Burnett, the first of four children, was born in St Johns, Michigan, on 21 October 1891, to Noble and Rose Clark Burnett. Noble Burnett owned a dry goods store, and Leo grew up watching his father lay out ads for the store on the dining room table. The shopkeeper would use 'big pieces of wrapping paper... a big black pencil and a yardstick,' Burnett recalled. In her 1995 book *Leo Burnett, Star Reacher*, the agency's former corporate communications director Joan Kufrin explains that this was how Leo discovered the big black Alpha 245 pencils he used throughout his career – and which the agency has adopted as part of its brand identity.

Leo eventually laid out some of the ads for his dad's store, although working there didn't appeal to him, so he got a job as a 'printer's devil' on the local newspaper – at first cleaning the presses and later setting type and running the machines. After that he became a reporter. 'Rarely a week passed that I did not scoop the rival paper with a hot obituary,' he said dryly.

In 1914 he was offered a job on the *Peoria Journal* – but after a year, like so many budding journalists, he was lured away by the prospect of a better-paid job writing advertising copy, in this case for the Cadillac

Motor Car Company. Burnett had the good fortune to arrive at the moment that the celebrated copywriter Theodore F MacManus was turning out groundbreaking ads for the company. 'MacManus... taught me the power of the truth, simply told,' Leo said. Inspired, he realized that advertising was the business for him.

Burnett rose to become advertising manager of Cadillac, which kept his job open for him even while he served for six months as a seaman second class during the Great War (he spent it building a breakwater in Lake Michigan, which 'undoubtedly caused a great deal of agitation among the German High Command', as he observed).

In 1919, Burnett moved to Indianapolis to work for a new auto company called LaFayette Motors, founded by a former Cadillac executive. Although LaFayette went out of business in 1924, Burnett stayed in Indianapolis, landing his first agency job at an outfit called Homer McKee. While it's fair to say that McKee has not had the same impact on advertising history as Theodore MacManus, he was an important Burnett mentor. Leo was undoubtedly influenced by some of McKee's basic rules of advertising, which included 'Don't try and sell manure spreaders with a Harvard accent', and 'If a kid can't understand it, it's no good.'

Burnett could have coasted through his career in Indianapolis, but the Wall Street Crash of 1929 seems to have jolted him out of complacency. One of Homer McKee's biggest clients, Marmon automobiles, was in trouble and Leo guessed that his time at the agency was coming to an end. 'At my age... I thought I'd better get the hell out of Indianapolis if I was ever going to amount to anything in the ad business.'

Burnett had kept in touch with Art Kudner, a copywriter who had worked on the LaFayette account at the Chicago arm of the advertising agency Erwin, Wasey & Company. Now, following up an earlier offer, Leo put a call in to Art and asked if there were any jobs going at the agency. And so, in late 1930, his wife Naomi pregnant with their third child, Leo Burnett found himself moving to Chicago in the middle of the Depression.

A seething morass of jazz, mobsters, prohibition and poverty, Chicago must have presented a dramatic contrast to Indianapolis. In *Star Reacher*, Joan Kufrin says that there were 750,000 unemployed in the city. 'During the fall of 1930, the International Apple Shippers Association, faced with an oversupply of apples, hit on the bright idea of wholesaling them to out-of-work men who could resell them for a nickel apiece. There was an apple seller on every corner.' As Naomi Burnett told Kufrin, 'Everybody we knew had suffered financially and many men had no jobs at all. I thought [Leo] was a miracle worker.'

Burnett moved his family to the comfortable suburb of Glencoe and set to work as chief copy editor at Erwin, Wasey & Company, based in the splendid Union Carbide Building. Busying himself with accounts such as Minnesota Valley Canning Co. (which later became Green Giant), Real Silk lingerie and Hoover, Burnett couldn't have known that one of the world's biggest agencies was about to begin a slow decline. One executive even referred to it as 'advertising's fall of the Roman empire'. In late 1931, the agency lost radio manufacturer Philco as a client. This was followed in the spring of the next year by General Foods and Camel cigarettes.

At around this time, Burnett's clients quietly began suggesting that he set up his own agency. A colleague, Jack O'Kieffe (whom Burnett had originally hired as a 21-year-old copywriter back at Homer McKee), also urged him to go it alone. But given the state of the world, Burnett reckoned he had too much to lose. 'Although I thought I knew something about advertising, I knew practically nothing about business administration and all of the other things that go into running an agency, small or large.'

In 1935, however, he changed his mind. Later he wrote to a friend: 'What really pushed me into a decision was the fact that I just plain couldn't stand the ads coming out of Chicago agencies... I knew damned well I could make them better and had a couple of close associates... who felt the same way about it.'

In unconscious imitation of his father, Burnett drafted the plan for his new agency on the ping-pong table of his home. Prefiguring the revolution that was to sweep through Madison Avenue some 10 years later, this document emphasized the importance of risk-taking creativity. 'The advertiser wants ideas, needs ideas and is paying for ideas,' Burnett wrote. 'We are going on the principle that every possible cent of income from an account should go into creative and productive efforts on that account.'

Burnett started his agency with US$50,000. He took with him a handful of Erwin, Wasey people, including copywriter and 'ideas man' Jack O'Kieffe. The agency officially opened for business at 360 North Michigan Avenue on Monday, 5 August 1935, with a bowl of red apples on the reception desk. Today, a bowl of apples sits on the reception desk of every Leo Burnett agency around the world.

## Quite a character

To say that Leo Burnett did not look like a thrusting agency chief is something of an understatement. While Ogilvy looked donnish and Bernbach simply resembled the guy next door, Leo was beyond plain. Rumpled, pillow-shaped, balding and jowly, his heavy horn-rimmed glasses perched on his spud-like nose, he was the very opposite of dapper. His suits were invariably navy or grey, with the jacket often buttoned askew. A famous picture of Burnett shows him setting off for a meeting clutching his trusty black leather portfolio, clad in a raincoat that even Columbo might have raised an eyebrow at. Neither was he a great orator – although he could make the written word soar from the page, a colleague once described his speaking voice as 'a medium-low rumble with a slight gurgling overtone'.

Stubborn and indefatigable, he built an agency based on family values while working so hard that he was rarely at home. To the exasperation of colleagues, he did not flinch at impossible deadlines or overnight turnarounds. The only time he ever entirely forgot about advertising was when he was at the racetrack, one of his few diversions. Asked to sum himself up for a journalist, he wrote that he was 'naively respectful of the simple verities and virtues, but venturesome in the pursuit of fresh ideas... Direct and outspoken, but mumbles his words'. Indeed, he preferred to fire off telegrams and memos. In person, he mostly limited his praise to 'damn good'. He disliked confrontation and hated firing people. During meetings, staff measured his opinion of the ads they showed him by the LPI – or the 'Lip Protrusion Index'. The more Leo's jutting lower lip stuck out, the bigger trouble they were in.

Yet there is no doubt that Leo was capable of inspiring immense affection: his wife Naomi, recalling when they first met at her mother's restaurant, summed up his appeal. 'He wasn't tall, handsome or that type... but there was something about his personality and bearing that intrigued me... He was a charmer: the *darlingest* sense of humour.'

He believed in loyalty and repaid it – even as far as clients were concerned. When he collapsed due to low blood sugar before a meeting, a colleague rushed off to get a chocolate bar. Leo croaked from the floor: 'Make sure it's a Nestlé's.'

In a sense, the contrast between Burnett's apparent disadvantages – humble origins, unlovely appearance – and his achievements is summed up by the agency's original logo, which depicts a hand reaching for the stars. Jack O'Kieffe came up with the idea just after the founding of the agency. It was inspired by a line in Virgil's *Aeneid*: 'So man scales the stars.'

Some years later, Leo asked the agency's copy director, John Crawford, what he thought the logo meant. Crawford blurted, 'Why, Leo, when you reach for the stars you may not quite get one, but you won't come up with a handful of mud either.' Burnett wrote down the explanation and used it from then on – but he never forgot who said it first.

Even today, Leo Burnett staffers occasionally refer to themselves as 'star reachers'. 'And we don't consider it corny,' one of them says.

Always a distance man rather than a sprinter, Burnett saw the agency carefully through the lean years of the 1930s. 'Even the person who ducked out at midnight to get coffee for the crew knew he was helping to hold the place together,' he later recalled, unwittingly confirming the agency's reputation for hard slog. It's difficult to believe there was enough work to merit such agonizingly long hours: new clients came and went, but the place was hardly a roaring success. Net income for the agency in 1937 was only US$5,889, according to agency records sourced by Kufrin. By the end of 1938 the agency had gained a handful of new accounts – including the Pure Oil Company, the Brown Shoe Company and the Standard Milling Company – and billings stood at US$1.3 million.

Although the war years were hardly less difficult for the agency – particularly as some of its younger men went off to fight – there were some highlights in the gloom. In 1942 Leo Burnett won the Santa Fe railroad account. But it was not until 1949 that the agency received the two phone calls that would change its fortunes, propelling it into the big league at last. They were from Procter & Gamble and Kellogg.

## Cornflakes and cowboys

The call from P&G concerned only a project, but any contact from the Cincinnati, Ohio, company had to be taken seriously. P&G was the largest advertiser in the United States, with sales of US$696 million from some 18 household products. Indeed, at that very moment a congressional committee was looking into the impact of big corporations on business competition, a development that understandably made P&G nervous. It hired Leo Burnett to examine the ways it might defend itself against potential criticism. Burnett recommended a series of full-page ads, to be placed in influential magazines such as *Time* and *Life*, explaining how P&G's wide range of innovative, affordable products benefited consumers.

In terms of working methods, P&G and Burnett were strictly opposed. P&G wouldn't budge without research, while Leo Burnett had founded his agency on the principle of unhampered creativity. Client and agency disagreed over the very first campaign – P&G wanted to test the ads on smaller markets before running with big titles such as *Time* and *Life*, while Leo would have preferred to trust his own judgement. In the end, the campaign tested badly and was cancelled. A TV campaign based on the same idea was somewhat more successful – and P&G was impressed enough to hand the agency its Lava soap brand in 1953. Over the years, Procter & Gamble turned the Leo Burnett Company into a more mature marketing organization, encouraging it to back up its creativity with solid research. The relationship survives to this day.

Also in 1949, Leo was called in for a meeting with WK Kellogg, the 89-year-old founder of a company supposedly dedicated to improving the diets of Americans through nutritious breakfast foods. In fact, Will Keith Kellogg had spotted the marketing potential of cornflakes when he first came across them at a health spa run by his brother, John, at the turn of the century. (The brothers were Seventh Day Adventists, which required a strict diet and a total ban on alcohol and tobacco.) After an abortive attempt to go into business with John – who was opposed to adding sugar to health food products – WK decided to go it alone. He founded The Kellogg Company in 1909, promoting breakfast cereal as a healthy alternative to bacon and eggs.

After meeting Leo (who was impressed by the elderly Kellogg's undimmed commitment to providing 'better nutrition for the human race'), Kellogg handed the agency the Corn Pops and Corn Soya brands. Burnett proposed television-oriented campaigns; the agency's advice on the matter was so convincing that Kellogg handed over the Rice Krispies account as well.

It was while redesigning the packaging for Rice Krispies that the agency came up with the idea of using the box itself as an advertising device.

Until then, cereal packets had been dominated by block letters identifying the product. The agency created a series of dummy designs that reduced the lettering and used the remaining space for colourful graphics. This was a packaging revolution – and it won Leo Burnett the Corn Flakes account. Soon afterwards, in 1952, Kellogg's handed the agency all of its advertising across the United States and Canada.

It was, of course, for Kellogg's Frosted Flakes that the Leo Burnett Company created one of its most enduring brand icons, Tony the Tiger. As we've established, the agency specialized in giving life to such characters, from the Jolly Green Giant (with his booming 'ho, ho, ho') to the Pillsbury Doughboy. 'None of us can underestimate the glacier-like power of friendly familiarity,' Burnett told executives in 1955.

Yet the agency's most successful invention was a tough, ornery, brooding figure.

The Marlboro Man rode into view to confront a straightforward marketing problem. In 1954, a delegation from Philip Morris met with Leo Burnett to explain that the company wanted to change the image of its filter-tipped Marlboro cigarette, which was regarded as a women's brand. The company was also excited about the new crush-proof flip-top box it had invented. In the end, Leo both changed the packaging and repositioned the brand.

He was certainly the right man for the job. Years earlier, conscious of the fact that his family had always lived in rented accommodation, Leo had purchased a 71-acre farm. Although toiling on his land was one of the few things that could distract him from advertising, work life inevitably overflowed into home, and weekend brainstorming sessions at the farm had become an established tradition. It was here that a handful of colleagues found him one Saturday morning, brandishing a magazine with a cowboy on its cover. 'Do you know anything more masculine than a cowboy?' he asked rhetorically.

Not content with providing a rugged new image for the brand, Leo also gave the Marlboro lettering on the packs a capital 'M' and switched the colour from red-and-white stripes to solid red. He wrote to Philip Morris executives: 'The cowboy is an almost universal symbol of admired masculinity... This almost sounds as though Dr Freud were on our Plans Board. He isn't. We've been guided by research and old-fashioned horse sense.'

No fancy psychological motivation techniques for Leo. According to Joan Kufrin in *Star Reacher*: 'The black and white cowboy ad titled

"The Sheriff" broke in local newspapers in New York, Florida, California, Texas, Washington DC and Philadelphia in January of 1955, closely followed by the rollout of the new Marlboro cigarette in 25 major cities over several months.' She goes on to quote Joseph F Cullman, who was executive vice-president, marketing for Philip Morris at the time: 'Marlboro became the number one brand in greater New York 30 days after the introduction, based solely on this one print ad.'

Subsequent executions featured other rugged, tattooed types who were not cowboys, but were not male models, either. But the agency later went back to the cowboy imagery and stuck with it. In this way, it turned Marlboro into the world's best-selling cigarette.

It would be ingenuous to avoid discussing the moral implications of cigarette advertising here. Over the years, the standard response from agencies has been that they are hired to persuade people to switch brands, not to start smoking. They are within their rights, they say, to market legal products. This has become something of a moot point since the mid-1990s, when public anger at the tobacco marketers reached such a height that tough advertising restrictions were introduced in the United States and Europe. Cigarette sales are still rising in Asia, but opposition to tobacco marketing is growing there, too.

Leo's own views are a matter of record. As far back as 1965, the *New Yorker* magazine wrote to him announcing that it would no longer carry cigarette advertising. Leo penned this response: 'As a long-time *New Yorker* reader, I have always considered myself capable of making my own judgements of products exposed to me in the advertising pages of your magazine and never looked to it either for preachments, protection or coddling.' After putting down his thesaurus, he added, 'I guess it's about time for another Marlboro.'

Of course, sensitivity about cigarette marketing rose to a far higher level in subsequent decades. But Burnett staffers are not forced to work on Philip Morris business. And Philip Morris has changed its marketing tactics. As long ago as 2003, an article in *Adweek* commented: 'The Marlboro Man, once a ubiquitous figure riding through the pages of US consumer publications, has disappeared from print altogether. Marlboro owner Philip Morris... began taking dollars out of magazines in 1999 and is virtually out of print now' ('The Party's Over', 5 May 2003). On its website, the company states: 'We have placed no consumer advertising for our cigarette brands in any newspapers or magazines since 2005' (**www.philipmorrisusa.com**). And yet a 2012 survey from research company Millward Brown still ranked Marlboro at number 7 in a list of the world's most valuable brands, with an estimated value of over US$73.6 million.

In the end, however you feel about tobacco marketing, there is no denying the Marlboro Man's status as an advertising icon – and a superlative example of simple, effective brand imagery.

## The international era

In 1956, the Leo Burnett Company moved into new headquarters in the Prudential Building, taking up 100,000 square feet of space. 'As I look down our seemingly endless corridors, I sometimes have to rub my eyes,' Leo wrote in his end-of-year summary to staff. Two years later, the agency passed the US$100 million billings mark. Burnett was 67 years old – and still reluctant to retire.

The sixties were as rosy for the Leo Burnett Company as they were for other agencies. United Airlines, Parker Pen, Kentucky Fried Chicken, Vick Chemical and Nestlé were some of the accounts that arrived during that bustling decade. By 1969 the agency's billings had soared again, to US$269 million.

In the meantime, Leo had finally started to let go, accepting that day-to-day operations were safe in the hands of his second-in-command, Phil Schaff. In June 1967, Schaff had become chairman and CEO, with Leo adopting the new title of founder chairman. A tougher moment came when he was asked to stop attending the Creative Review Committee (CRC) – the body that had the final say on much of the creative work that emerged from the agency. Now in his seventies, Leo conceded that it was time for him to step aside. But Schaff summarized the reality of the situation in an interview with Joan Kufrin: 'No matter what Leo's title was, whether he was chairman of the CRC or not chairman of the CRC, chairman of the board or founder chairman, his name was Leo Burnett and he was a legend, and people were going to pay attention to him, and not to whoever was in charge of the creative meeting.'

On 1 December 1967, at the agency's annual breakfast gathering, Burnett made a speech that would be considered his curtain call. It's known to insiders as the 'When to take my name off the door' speech, and it is something of a legend within the agency. It began: 'Somewhere along the line, after I'm finally off the premises, you – or your successors

– might want to take my *name* off the premises, too... But let me tell you when I might *demand* that you take my name off the door.'

The speech was a stirring evocation of the Burnett philosophy. Leo told staff he wanted his name removed 'when you spend more time trying to make money and less time making advertising – our type of advertising... When you lose your passion for thoroughness, your hatred of loose ends... When your main interest becomes a matter of size just to be big – rather than good, hard, wonderful work... When you start giving lip service to being a "creative agency" – and stop really being one...' Leo added that if these and other such horrors should come to pass, his staff could 'throw every goddamned apple down the elevator shafts'. By the time he had finished, several onlookers were tearful.

But Leo hadn't left the building yet – and he had a last chapter to oversee. In typically languid Burnett style, the agency had taken longer than many of its rivals to go global. Indeed, Leo rather disdained the expansionist policies of groups such as Interpublic, which he referred to as 'Interplanetary'. By the late 1960s, however, many rival agencies were reaping a large percentage of their billings from outside the United States – as much as 46 per cent in the case of McCann Erickson. Acknowledging that its clients required global reach, in May 1969 the Leo Burnett Company merged with the London Press Exchange – an agency of 23 offices around the globe. Burnett had at first been hesitant, but in the end he gave the merger his blessing at a decisive board meeting. Almost overnight, Leo Burnett became the world's fifth largest advertising agency, with billings of US $373 million. In a brochure sent out with his year-end letter, Leo remarked: 'I see in efforts like ours a modest advance towards the "single-family world" we so direly need.' Elderly he may have been, but Burnett could still envisage the future.

In 1971, at the age of 79, Leo was still going into the office four days a week. On 7 June, he dictated a letter to Jack O'Kieffe, saying that he planned to cut this down to three days.

He died of a heart attack that evening, at home on the farm.

## Life after Leo

A character like Leo Burnett was always going to be a hard act to follow – and in some ways the agency hasn't tried. Having spent his life creating brand icons for others, Leo has become a brand himself: a logo, a philosophy, an identity. To this day his picture is on the agency's walls, his black pencils lie on desks; on the website there is a grainy film clip of him telling staff when to take his name off the door.

And yet, life has undoubtedly changed at Leo Burnett. For a start, these days it is owned by the French. It's hard to imagine what the bluff, forthright Leo – who liked to imagine that Chicago copywriters 'spit on their hands' before taking up their pencils – would have thought of this development. In spring 2002, the *Chicago Daily Herald* announced with barely disguised alarm: 'The holding company for one of Chicago's most famous home-grown enterprises, Leo Burnett Worldwide Inc, is being sold to Paris-based Publicis Groupe SA for US$3 billion' ('Merger reshapes ad world', 8 March 2002).

By the time the Publicis deal went ahead, the agency that Leo Burnett had planned on his ping-pong table had grown into a conglomerate with billings of US$1.8 billion. Allowing itself a moment of nostalgic pride, the *Chicago Daily Herald* pointed out that when the adman had set out a bowl of apples on his reception desk, 'critics scoffed at his ambitions, predicting that he'd soon have to resort to selling apples in the street'.

Burnett saw off the scoffers long ago. And his name is still on the door.

# The Brit pack

## 06

*'Fags, booze and fashion'*

It was only a matter of time before the creative revolution made it across the Atlantic. 'There's no doubt that what happened in New York led to what is now regarded as the golden age of British advertising,' confirms experienced adman Alfredo Marcantonio, who has served time at some of the best-known agencies in the UK. In a scenario that could easily have been drawn from the period we're discussing, our meeting takes place in an Italian restaurant in London's Soho. Outside, a dreary winter drizzle is falling – but in here, there's a warm glow of nostalgia.

'Agencies like Doyle Dane Bernbach showed us how to use our own language,' Marcantonio says. 'Of course, in those days American advertising was not diffused as widely or as rapidly as it is today. Keen young creatives would rush to the newsagents as soon as magazines like the *New Yorker* and *Esquire* came out, because that was where you could see the sharpest ads.'

Marcantonio was actually working at the British arm of Volkswagen when DDB began producing its groundbreaking ads for the Beetle. The ads struck such a powerful chord that he quit his job in the VW marketing department to go and work at an agency. 'What happened next was admirable: instead of slavishly copying the American creative revolution, the Brits started one of their own, which was entirely different but just as much of a break with the past.'

It was also a product of its time. The early sixties struggled to emerge from the shadow of the previous decade, with its post-war burden of austerity and introspection. But when US agencies like Doyle Dane Bernbach and Papert Koenig Lois opened offices in London, their new take on advertising dovetailed with the experimentation that was occurring in the fields of music, fashion, photography and graphic design. Of course, they were not the first US agencies to arrive on British shores: J Walter Thompson and McCann Erickson had made their first forays into the market in the 1920s. Much later, Ted Bates, BBDO, Grey and Leo Burnett all acquired London outposts. Ogilvy & Mather eventually bought the venerable SH Benson, which had provided some of its seed money. But these were the shadowy reflections of the Madison Avenue monoliths, while DDB and PKL were trying to inject their trademark caustic wit into the somnolent British advertising scene.

Many names and agencies were associated with the British creative revolution, but one agency in particular quickly comes to the fore in any conversation about that era: Collett Dickenson Pearce.

## The British hot shop

The number of famous print ads, TV commercials and slogans created by CDP in the late sixties and throughout the 1970s is quite astonishing. Even now, for those of us who grew up in the period, a mention of them provokes a tingle of recognition. Stunning visual metaphors for Benson & Hedges cigarettes; 'Happiness is a cigar called Hamlet'; 'Heineken. Refreshes the parts other beers cannot reach'; Fiat cars 'Hand built by robots'... Not content with creating print ads for Pretty Polly hosiery that were disturbing enough to a growing lad, CDP even managed to make Clark's shoes look sexy. Agency co-founder John Pearce once summarized its main areas of expertise as 'fags, booze and fashion'.

With a knack for impact that augured well for its future clients, Collett Dickenson Pearce opened its doors on April Fool's Day 1960. The agency was not started by a band of young hotheads: its founding fathers were well into middle age when they went into business together. John Pearce and Ronnie Dickenson had met at Hulton Publishing, where Pearce was general manager and Dickenson worked on *Picture Post*, one of the most influential news magazines of its day. Dickenson went on to become programme controller at pioneering television company ATV, while Pearce was made managing director of the advertising agency Colman Prentis & Varley – probably the closest England had seen to a hot shop before CDP came along.

According to the book *Inside Collett Dickenson Pearce* (2000), compiled by two former staffers – deputy chairman John Ritchie and creative director John Salmon – the motivational spark for the launch came from Dickenson. He 'dropped in for a drink' at Pearce's flat in Devonshire Place one evening and said casually: 'Why don't we start an advertising agency?' Rather than start from scratch, the duo acquired John Collett's existing agency, Pictorial Publicity, which was 'going through a very rough patch' and had only one major client, a rather downmarket mail order company flogging an assortment of outdoor equipment, from binoculars to Wellington boots.

While starting the agency was Dickenson's idea, Pearce knew that there was a gap in the market. As Salmon and Ritchie put it, 'John Pearce felt there was a crying need for an agency that could produce unusually effective results for clients who did not have a fortune to spend. He reckoned that the bulk of advertising, while based on sound strategy, was terminally dull... [He] thought there was an opportunity for advertising that was inspirational, enterprising and most of all noticeable.'

Pearce's masterstroke was to bring with him from Colman Prentis & Varley a laconic Yorkshireman named Colin Millward, who became the creative director and imaginative force behind CDP. A number of famous names passed through CDP – and all of them pay homage to Millward. They include the film director Sir Alan Parker, who says, 'He was without a doubt the single most important person in the agency. It was his energy, vision and taste that made CDP what it was. He also had the good sense to employ all of us lot in his creative department.'

Various sources describe Millward as 'no-nonsense', 'eccentric', 'thoughtful', 'unruly', 'wise' and 'brilliant'. When asked why so many talented art directors came from Yorkshire, he replied that pollution covered every horizontal surface with a film of grime, so you could draw anywhere.

In *Inside CDP*, another famous alumnus, David Puttnam, recalls a typical meeting with Millward. 'I'd take an ad into his office for approval and he'd sit and bite his nails for a while and then, in his funny voice, he'd say "It's not very good is it?" and I'd say "Isn't it?" and he'd say "No, not very good at all." And I'd ask "What don't you like?" "You work it out. Take it away. Do it again. See you tomorrow."' Puttnam learned from Millward that 'competence is a point of departure, not a point of arrival'.

As if to emphasize its kinship with Doyle Dane Bernbach, CDP was one of the first British agencies to sit art directors with copywriters – elsewhere, they were still working in separate departments. Indeed, DDB tried to buy the agency two years after its creation, but Dickenson and Pearce were disinclined to sell despite the fact that, at that stage, CDP was still debt-laden and struggling.

Two factors that lifted the agency out of the danger zone were John Pearce's insistence on the importance of media placement, and the launch of the *Sunday Times Colour Supplement*, the first colour magazine to be offered free with a British newspaper. With his background in publishing, Pearce realized that the right choice of media and the quality, rather than the quantity, of the audience were critical to the success of a campaign. The *Times* supplement thus became a showcase for CDP's lavish, witty print ads for clients such as Benson & Hedges, Harveys Bristol Cream and Whitbread Pale Ale. Encouraged by the promise of additional advertising income, other newspapers soon launched their own colour supplements. In an echo of J Walter Thompson in the 1920s, Pearce considered that glossy magazines were ideal vehicles for advertisers because they often hung around on coffee tables – and in dentist's waiting rooms – waiting to be flicked through by an idle reader.

## Blockbusters in the basement

Alan Parker thought of CDP as a small agency that made great magazine ads when he arrived in 1968. He had started out at the age of 18 at Maxwell Clark, an agency so obscure that many employees felt it should change its name to 'Maxwell Who?', because that was what they were asked whenever they said they worked there. At first, Parker's responsibilities were limited to 'copy forwarding', which meant dragging proofs around various different departments and getting the stamp of approval. But on his travels around the agency he saw that the creative department was 'by far the most enjoyable place to work', so he set his sights on getting a job there.

'There was an art director called Gray Jolliffe, who later became a famous cartoonist and a great friend of mine. At the time I was just this young kid, but he encouraged me by giving me ads to do and marking them: "six out of ten, must try harder", that sort of thing. Eventually they got pretty good, these ads, so I was made a junior copywriter. That was when Doyle Dane Bernbach and Papert Koenig Lois opened, and everyone wanted to work for them. I went for an interview at DDB and didn't get in – but Peter Mayle [later the author of *A Year in Provence*], who was copy chief at PKL, hired me to work there.'

Cultural differences between the UK agency and its American parent soon made PKL an uncomfortable place to work, so Parker decided to move on. Mayle encouraged him to go for an interview at CDP, which Parker joined almost the same week as a certain Charles Saatchi. 'The agency attracted a lot of good people because it had a reputation for paying well,' says Parker. 'For instance, it got people from DDB, which was a great agency but paid crap money. CDP realized that to get talented creative people you had to pay them a decent wage, and it cracked open the industry's pay structures. We had notoriously crummy offices in Howland Street – they looked like the canteen of a secondary modern school – but John Pearce always said he preferred to pay for people rather than furnishings. That's how you ended up with Ross Cramer, Charlie Saatchi, Tony Brignull... this all-star creative department.'

Parker concedes, however, that the creative rebels would never have got their often startling work past the clients were it not for the 'fantastic, eccentric, maverick' leadership of John Pearce. 'The philosophy of the agency was that the account people had to sell whatever we did. They had no involvement in the creative process whatsoever; there was no research. They were simply great salesmen. It was a creative paradise – and no doubt a unique period in British advertising history.'

Demanding at the best of times, Millward put additional pressure on his creatives by dividing them into three groups and, as Parker puts it, 'setting us against one another'. 'Halfway down the narrow corridor of our crummy office, I hung a string with a sign saying "The creative department starts here". The trouble was that Ross Cramer had written the same thing on the other side.'

Parker's most important contribution was to turn CDP from an agency that made great print ads into one that was equally skilled at TV work. Unlike the London branch of DDB, which for a long time remained focused on the written word, CDP managed to reconfigure its creativity for the small screen. And Parker was the catalyst.

'At that stage commercial television in Britain was relatively new and the commercials were very pedestrian: they were silly cartoons or some-one holding a packet of washing powder. We had no history of making TV commercials, but I wanted to have a go at it. So I asked Colin Millward if we could have a budget to buy a 16 millimetre camera and a tape recorder and start experimenting in the basement. For some reason the basement at Howland Street was just a huge empty space, half-filled with junk and cardboard boxes. So I used the other half to shoot commercials.'

His initial approach was instinctive, to say the least. 'My art director Paul Windsor was good at lighting, and we had another guy operating the camera. In other words, I was the only one who didn't know how to do anything. But as I'd written the things, it was obviously going to be me who shouted, "Cut!" Pretty soon I was organizing everyone: "You do this, you do that... Okay, let's try again." They'd look at me with raised eyebrows as if to say, "Ooh, get him!" But at that moment, I became a director. It's strange, because my only ambition at the time was to become the creative director of the agency.'

Dragooning agency staff as actors, Parker grew increasingly embroiled in his experiments. He was inspired by Howard Zieff, who'd shot commercials for Doyle Dane Bernbach and Wells Rich Greene in the States. But union rules meant that Parker's ads had to be remade by a professional production company. 'This was frustrating because I thought our raw little pieces were better than the remakes. It all changed when John Pearce was showing a client around the agency one day. They got to the media department and there was no one around – the place was deserted. He asked, "Where is everybody?" and someone said, "They're all downstairs making a commercial with Alan." I was doing a commercial for Benson & Hedges Pipe Tobacco, set in a Russian embassy before the revolution, and I had the media department dressed up as ambassadors, with all the ladies from accounts in long dresses and tiaras... it was ridiculously elaborate.'

The next day, Parker found himself in an office with John Pearce, Colin Millward and Ronnie Dickenson. 'They said, "Alan, we want you to leave." I thought, "My God, I've never been fired in my life." Then they said, "We want you to start a television production company. We'll give you an interest-free loan to get you going and we'll give you some work." I was probably less excited than they'd anticipated, because all I wanted at that point was Colin Millward's job. As far as I was concerned, they were giving me the boot in the most elegant way imaginable.'

The Alan Parker Film Company went on to shoot award-winning ads for the likes of Birds Eye Beefburgers and Heinz Spaghetti. 'Almost everything was 30 seconds in those days – you were lucky to get 45 seconds or even a minute. It's a real art form to be able to tell a story, make a point, make someone laugh and sell something in such a short period of time. It can also be frustrating – which is why my ads increasingly began to look like miniature films.'

In the book *Rewind* (Jeremy Myerson and Graham Vickers, 2002), Parker is praised for introducing a 'new, more "realistic" style of TV commercials: engaging mini-dramas that brought a touch of wit and credibility to even the most contrived scenarios'. With his hit musical *Bugsy Malone* (1976), Parker became one of the first British commercials directors to cross over into feature films. But others were hot on his heels.

## Lowe and beyond

CDP not only attracted talented copywriters, photographers and film-makers, but also the people who nurtured them. Take account man David Puttnam for instance. As Parker recalls, 'He believed so strongly in the photographers he commissioned to shoot his ads that he finally decided to devote his time exclusively to promoting them. People tend to forget this, but he was the first truly professional photographers' agent in London.'

Puttnam later went on to produce *Bugsy Malone*, as well as Parker's antithetically gritty second feature film, *Midnight Express* (1978). Puttnam also produced *The Duellists*, the big-screen debut of another commercials director, Ridley Scott. For CDP, Scott made a series of nostalgia-bathed commercials for Hovis bread, set in the cobbled streets of an archetypal English village.

'Ridley went into films just after me, but he continued to make commercials, which I didn't,' says Parker. 'I was stung by an early review that said something like, "Alan Parker comes from advertising, which gives us a useful stick to hit him with". Directors who came out of advertising were considered crass – we were not real filmmakers. Ridley said the critics were just jealous because we made more money than them.'

The pair had occasionally talked about going into business together. 'Ridley made the pretty films and I made the ones with dialogue, so between us we reckoned we had it sewn up. But we kept arguing over whether it should be called Scott Parker or Parker Scott, so it never happened.'

Instead, in 1968, Scott formed the production company RSA Films with his brother Tony. It remains one of the world's leading commercial production companies, with offices in London, New York and Los Angeles.

As a commercials director, Scott's work had been championed by another account man at CDP – Frank Lowe. While account executives were under orders not to interfere with the creative department, the 'suits' were in fact the agency's secret weapons, as they had been charged with selling even the oddest, most challenging work to clients. According to Parker, Lowe not only defended but *demanded* outrageous creative work.

'When he joined the agency I was told I wouldn't like him, because he had opinions,' chuckles Parker. 'I said, "He won't get away with that here." On the day I met him he was dressed entirely in black, because it was the anniversary of the plane crash that had killed the Manchester United team [on 6 February 1958]. Of course we hit it off straight away, and he's been one of my closest friends ever since. He was a passionate advocate of great creative work.'

By the early 1970s, CDP was no longer a small agency. Outgrowing its cramped Howland Street offices, it had moved to larger premises on Euston Road. It had also developed global reach, thanks to a partnership with Paris agency FCA and subsequent similar deals with shops in Brussels, Amsterdam, Milan and Tokyo. Colin Millward's creative role had broadened, with John Salmon taking over the creative direction of the London office. Fortunately, Salmon's standards were every bit as high as those of his colleague.

John Pearce suffered a heart attack in 1971 – and although he returned to the agency when he recovered, it was in a more consultative role. Eventually, Frank Lowe was installed at the helm. 'To most creative people at the agency, Frank was simply the best account man they'd ever met,' recount Salmon and Ritchie in *Inside CDP*. 'He cared passionately about the work and would only present the agency's clients with advertising that he believed to be outstanding.'

In his own contribution to the book, Lowe reaffirms the inspiration provided by the uncompromising Colin Millward and the galaxy of talents that swirled around the agency. But Lowe also takes time to praise CDP's clients. He writes pointedly: '[They] seemed to value the opinion of their agency and, on balance, would go along with it. They didn't argue about money all day long trying to get things cheaper, they just wanted the best because they knew it would work for them. They always found a little extra time if the agency didn't feel they had cracked the problem. This, in turn, always seemed to pay off.'

After a golden decade, the 1980s began gloomily for CDP. Frank Lowe left the agency to set up his own operation with planner Geoff Howard-Spink and several members of the creative department (including Alfredo Marcantonio). Among many other achievements, Lowe's agency went on to create a popular and enduring campaign for that 'reassuringly expensive' lager brand, Stella Artois.

On 10 September 1981, at the age of 68, John Pearce had a second heart attack – this time fatal. The story was not over, but an era had ended.

As with every other hot shop in advertising history, CDP could not maintain its creative dominance forever. Though it continued to produce some excellent work throughout the 1980s, the spotlight moved slowly away from the agency to illuminate other areas of the London advertising scene.

## The master planner

Although it was no slouch on the creative front, the other British hot shop of the 1970s made its mark on adland history with the development of a rather more esoteric craft. Stanley Pollitt, of the agency Boase Massimi Pollitt, is generally considered the father of planning.

In fact, to be fair, he shares that honour with Stephen King of JWT. To complicate matters, the term 'account planning' was conceived by a third man, Tony Stead, at a JWT brainstorming session in 1968. This led to the merger of the agency's marketing, media planning and research departments into a single unit under the heading of account planning. For the purposes of concision, however, we'll concentrate on Pollitt – an appealingly colourful character – and the remarkable agency he co-founded with Martin Boase and Gabe Massimi.

Physically, Stanley Pollitt resembled a cross between the British comic Eric Morecambe and the American journalist AJ Liebling (he even shared Liebling's passion for boxing). Donnish, balding, overweight, scruffy and bespectacled, he was rarely seen without a cigarette and enjoyed a glass of wine with lunch. His wayward dress sense and lack of presentation skills (he is described as 'inarticulate and boffin-like') could not disguise his acute intelligence, however. A colleague summed him up as 'an orderly mind in a chaotic body'. He had a rather raffish background:

the son of an artist, he was born in Paris in 1930. He attended St Paul's College and then Cambridge, intending to become a barrister. Instead, through a family contact, he ended up working at the London advertising agency Pritchard Wood & Partners. It was here that he developed the concept of account planning.

Fortunately for us, account planning is more interesting than it sounds. It concerns bringing the voice and the desires of the consumer into the advertising process. In the sixties, this meant taking researchers out of the 'back rooms' of agencies and putting them next to the account teams as campaigns were being developed. In the book *Pollitt on Planning*, edited by Paul Feldwick in 2000, it is described as 'the greatest innovation in agency working practice since Bill Bernbach put art directors and copywriters together in the 1950s'.

To précis Pollitt's own description, the planner is a research expert who relies on first-hand interviews as well as data to develop an in-depth understanding of consumers. The planner forms a 'threesome' with the account manager and the creative and is expected to express a clear point of view on the direction of the campaign, rather than merely supplying useful statistics. An insight from a planner can inspire a creative team. The planner also analyses the effectiveness of campaigns.

In the 1950s, advertising agencies had their own research departments or worked with closely held research subsidiaries. This changed in the 1960s, when consumer goods companies began developing their own, in-house research departments, or paying for detailed studies of target consumers. To reflect this shift, agencies began to reduce their research staff. Rather in the way that their media departments would become separate entities later on (see Chapter 10, Media spins off), some agencies saw their research departments break away to form independent companies competing for business in the open market. At the same time, research methods and the means of analysing data were becoming more sophisticated. This created a paradox. Pollitt wrote: '[As] more data relevant to sharper advertising planning were coming in, more and more people qualified to handle it were leaving the agencies.'

Working on accounts at Pritchard Wood, Pollitt felt there was a danger that agencies would begin to pick and choose data, bending it to suit the direction of their thinking rather than the other way around. 'I decided therefore that a trained researcher should be put alongside the account man on every account. He should be there as of right, with equal status as a working partner.' Pollitt referred to this new type of researcher as 'the account man's conscience'.

When he set up the agency BMP with two colleagues in 1968, it was structured from the very start on an account manager/account planner team basis. 'From the outset at BMP we added an important new dimension to the planner's role, which has almost come to be the dominant one... we started to involve [them] more closely in the development of creative ideas.'

## A smashing agency

Boase Massimi Pollitt started in true late-sixties style. In order to advertise the new agency, a fleet of chocolate-brown Mini Coopers emblazoned with the initials BMP was driven around London. Account man Martin Boase, creative Gabe Massimi and, of course, planner Stanley Pollitt left Pritchard Wood & Partners with seven other members of staff. All 10 were shareholders in the new operation.

Martin Boase says, 'We were determined to produce not only original creative work, but also soundly-based advertising, which had provoked the whole account planning idea. In those days there was an awful lot of formulaic, soundly-based advertising and a great deal of original yet highly indulgent work. Pollitt realized that by introducing the planner into the creative process you could be original yet strategic. Most start-ups are about people wanting to run things themselves or simply make money. We were actually rather more crusading: we wanted to create an entirely new type of agency.'

Gabe Massimi left the agency about two years into its existence. He was replaced as creative director by John Webster, who had also come over from Pritchard Wood. Webster, it transpired, was an advertising genius – particularly in the field of TV commercials – and he became one of the industry's most revered creatives. (Sadly, he died shortly before I began researching this book.)

As with the work of CDP, anybody who was a kid in Britain in the 1970s is likely to have Webster's TV spots engraved on their memories. He created an animated, sunglasses-wearing polar bear for the soft drink Cresta, a large yet benign orange-haired Yeti called The Honey Monster for Sugar Puffs breakfast cereal and – best of all – the Smash Martians.

These animated tin men would roll around laughing as they watched films of earthlings washing, peeling and boiling potatoes. The Martians, of course, used Cadbury's instant Smash mashed potato – just pour on boiling water and give it a stir.

The irony and self-deprecation of Webster's TV spots – laced with a subtle dose of surrealism – combined the key ingredients of classic British advertising. In Webster's heyday people really did claim that the adverts were the best thing on the telly. Many British commercials still put entertainment first – and often succeed in looking as if there's nothing being sold at all.

In the late 1970s, BMP set up an outpost in Paris. It was unsuccessful, but the Paris link persisted and in 1977 French communications conglomerate Havas bought 50 per cent of BMP. Two years later, Stanley Pollitt died of a heart attack at the age of 49. This shock forced the agency's remaining founders to rethink its future direction. Boase says, 'We wanted to spread the shareholding to the generation who had come into the agency after us.' BMP bought itself out of Havas for £1.2 million and went public. After two years, it had a stock market capitalization of £50 million.

In the 1980s, BMP became embroiled in a tempestuous round of negotiations with another French agency, BDDP (see Chapter 8, The French connection), which had been busily buying up its shares. Boase fought off the hostile takeover by selling to the company that had once been Doyle Dane Bernbach. It is now the London outpost of DDB Worldwide. It remains one of the most awarded London agencies.

## The Saatchi saga begins

The agency with the intriguing double surname came later: in the beginning it was Cramer Saatchi. Charles Saatchi and Ross Cramer met at the London outpost of the US agency Benton & Bowles, which Saatchi joined in 1965. Charles was the copywriter of the duo. Having left school at 17 and hot-footed it to the States, Charles, like all the advertising stars of his generation, was electrified by the work being done there by the likes of Bill Bernbach. When he got back, he was ready to give the London scene a similar shot in the arm. Saatchi was 22 when he arrived at Benton & Bowles – one year older than another future star, John Hegarty, who was already working at the agency. Hegarty at first assumed Saatchi was an Italian name. ('I expected some bloke who couldn't spell and still lived with his mother,' he chuckles today.) In reality, Charles and Maurice Saatchi and their older brother David were born in Baghdad to an Iraqi Jewish couple, Nathan and Daisy. Forced out of an increasingly anti-Semitic Iraq after the Second World War, the family moved to the UK, where Nathan had started a textile business. Thus the brothers grew up in leafy Hampstead, a perfectly English childhood.

After a brief period working with Hegarty at Benton & Bowles, Charles was teamed with senior art director Ross Cramer. Before long, they found the atmosphere at Benton & Bowles too stultifying for their radical ideas and moved to where the action was: Collett Dickenson Pearce. Here the pair produced a string of remarkable ads, including racy ads for Ford – comparing various models to rival cars, an American technique quite unheard of in the UK at the time – and witty ones for department stores Selfridges and Lewis's. The D&AD awards flew in. Eighteen months after their arrival at CDP (following a brief but unsatisfactory stint at a smaller agency) Cramer and Saatchi went into business with their own 'creative consultancy'.

Cramer Saatchi was based above a fast-food joint in Goodge Street – in the same building where David Puttnam had set up his photography agency and BMP also occupied floor space. The pair recruited John Hegarty and another young adman called Jeremy Sinclair. The latter was to have a major impact on the Saatchi saga by devising one of Britain's most famous print ads.

The background to the ad that fuelled the Saatchi legend could not have been more mundane. While waiting for one of his children at the school gates, Ross Cramer had fallen into conversation with another parent, a woman who worked at the Health Education Council. When she discovered what Cramer did for a living, she mentioned that her boss was looking for an advertising agency. Soon, Cramer Saatchi was applying its forceful words and images to public health advertising. One print ad was a picture of some noisome brown sludge being poured onto a saucer, accompanied by the words: 'The tar and discharge that collects in the lungs of an average smoker.' The antismoking campaign attracted considerable press coverage – but not as much as the agency's best ad for the HEC.

It's a strikingly simple image of a young bloke in a V-necked sweater. His palm rests tenderly on his enormous pregnancy bump as he gazes at the camera with a doleful, resigned expression. The text reads: 'Would you be more careful if it was you that got pregnant?' Capturing at once the downside of permissiveness and the nascent women's liberation movement, the ad presaged the more thoughtful 1970s after the extended party of the sixties. Years later, the BBC voted the image one of the top 10 British ads of the century. At the number one position was another Saatchi ad, 'Labour isn't working'. But by then, the agency had evolved.

When Ross Cramer left the agency in 1970 to embark on a career as a commercials director, there was one obvious candidate to replace him. Maurice Saatchi had followed a different yet convergent career path to that of his brother. Less flamboyant and more strategic, he had graduated from the London School of Economics and joined a small trade press company called Haymarket Publishing. He was tasked with relaunching a dusty periodical called *World Press News*, aimed at journalists and advertising people. It was transformed into *Campaign*, the advertising trade magazine. Provocative and punchy, equal parts gossip and news, *Campaign* was the mirror of the business it portrayed. It quickly became the bible of British adland (which it remains). Maurice was a success.

And yet he was clearly confident enough in his brother's abilities to leave Haymarket and become the co-founder of Saatchi & Saatchi – a name 'so bizarre no one will forget it in a hurry', as Charles pointed out.

On 11 September 1970, *Campaign* carried the front-page headline, 'Saatchi starts agency with £1 million.' The brothers also took a one-page advertisement in *The Times*. It was possibly the only time they had to pay for column inches. The Saatchis were news, and would remain so for years to come.

## Mrs Thatcher's ad agency

Along with people like John Hegarty and Jeremy Sinclair – who stayed on from the Cramer Saatchi period – the new agency attracted an impressive line-up of talented young players. One of them was ebullient Australia-born account man Bill Muirhead, who recalls, 'Everyone was about my age and they had a certain attitude. I'd been at Ogilvy, where they had all this rule-book stuff. But we took the rules and threw them out of the window. We were always getting into punch-ups with regulatory bodies.'

Another recruit was a personable media director named Tim Bell. Highly charismatic, Bell later went on to become one of Britain's foremost public relations practitioners. In advertising history, however, Bell's name is most often associated with that of Margaret Thatcher – and with the 1979 Conservative Party election campaign. Although Charles Saatchi led the creative effort, Bell presented the work to the Conservative Party leader. As far as Margaret Thatcher was concerned, Tim Bell was the face of the agency.

Saatchi & Saatchi was appointed by the Conservatives at the prompting of Gordon Reece, the party's head of communications and the man who is often credited with honing Mrs Thatcher's steely image. As a sizeable British-owned agency that had developed a reputation for creativity, Saatchi & Saatchi met all the party's requirements. Bell made his first presentation to Thatcher in June of that year.

Much of the Saatchis' work for the Conservatives was exemplary, but the poster that the BBC chose as the advertising image of the 20th century was the idea of deputy creative director Andrew Rutherford. He came up with the line 'Labour isn't working', above a photograph of an unfeasibly long and winding queue outside an unemployment office. (The Labour party publicly attacked the photo as fake, which was beside the point: like all the best advertising, the poster crystallized a perceived truth.) In reality the poster only ran at a handful of sites, but the media furore it provoked made it one of the most cost-effective ads in history. The Saatchi & Saatchi campaign didn't exactly win the election for the Conservatives – the strikes and unrest during 'the winter of discontent' did that – but it was certainly a factor. When Mrs Thatcher came to power on 4 May 1979, the Saatchis could take at least part of the credit.

A few years earlier, in 1975, Saatchi & Saatchi had merged with a stock-market-listed agency called Compton, part of the larger Compton Advertising of New York. The deal gave the New York operation 26 per cent of the merged entity – and Saatchi & Saatchi access to a juicy list of clients, including Procter & Gamble and Rowntree Mackintosh. It also meant that Saatchi & Saatchi had gone public.

Around this time, the company gained a sharp young financial director in the form of Martin Sorrell, educated at Cambridge and Harvard. Sorrell's business acumen would help the Saatchis realize their increasingly ambitious expansion plans. As if to confirm that an era of growth and prosperity was about to begin, the agency moved out of its Regent Street base and into Compton's larger offices in Charlotte Street.

In 1982 Saatchi & Saatchi won the British Airways account – which was to become one of its signature pieces of business. The first TV commercial was genuinely spectacular. It began with an ominous shadow passing over the streets of Britain as if a giant spaceship was about to touch down. People emerged from their houses to peer anxiously up at the sky. Finally, the entire island of Manhattan came in to land at Heathrow Airport. 'Every year,' the endline explained, 'British Airways flies more people across the Atlantic than the entire population of Manhattan.'

The grandiose TV spot was in proportion to the magnitude of Saatchi & Saatchi's global ambitions. The eighties had begun.

# Eighties extravagance

## 07

## 'A question of prestige'

The 1980s are often regarded as the golden age of TV advertising. Cable television was in its infancy, expensive global campaigns were newly fashionable and agencies could afford the best directors, many of whom were honing their craft, creating shimmering images for music videos. Advertising and MTV – which launched in 1981 – pushed the products and the lifestyle that seduced a new breed of young, upwardly mobile consumers. This, then, was the time of the yuppie.

In the United States it was as if the world had been turned on its head – London's burgeoning creativity was inspiring Madison Avenue. 'For a long while TV ads were little more than moving print ads,' said Phil Dusenberry, who was the creative powerhouse behind BBDO through this period and beyond. 'I remember sitting in a darkened room in the 1970s looking at a bunch of ads from Britain and saying to myself: "This is the kind of stuff we should be doing!" It was so much more entertaining than most of the advertising that was coming out of the States at the time. TV advertising didn't really get into its stride until the 1980s. By 1984 it was really going places.'

But London ad agencies were indulging in more than just a frenzy of creativity. The entire restaurant and bar scene of Soho seemed to be catering solely to media and advertising people – and to those who wanted to bathe in their champagne-tinted glory. Smart young agencies like Saatchi & Saatchi and Bartle Bogle Hegarty had chosen Soho as a base over the advertising industry's previous centres of gravity, Mayfair and Covent Garden. This was mainly because all the cutting rooms and photography studios were in Soho – the area's traditional status as a red-light district, still tawdry around the edges, meant that minimal rents were charged for maximal spaces. Soho, effectively, became London's Madison Avenue.

Neil French, a well-known copywriter who worked at the London agency Holmes Knight Ritchie in the late seventies and early eighties, says nostalgically, 'I guess what made the era special was that so many erudite and talented blokes happened to be in the right place at the right time, when the art of communication was limited to press, posters, and TV – with radio if you knew a famous comedian to deliver the script. Life was so much simpler, and the only distractions were the pubs, the Zanzibar, and hordes of ra-ra skirts.'

Writing for *The Independent*, Stephen Bayley referred to the 'Porsche-driving, champagne-drinking, coke-snorting image of 1980s advertising' ('Goodbye to all that', 22 December 1996). Recalling the era, Bayley pointed out: 'As UK advertising agencies battled to win the increasingly large number of multinational, billion-dollar accounts that decided to centralize their business in London during the 1980s, entertaining clients became a high priority. So, in due course, did entertaining staff. An agency's capacity to party came to symbolise its capacity to do everything else: win business, attract the best staff, make advertisements... It was all a question of prestige.'

An article in *Campaign* a few years later featured anonymous accounts of unwise behaviour. 'My creative director at the time used to drink gin as if it were tap water,' said one art director. 'After all, how can you come up with a great campaign or a unique idea unless you're under the influence of some form of mind-altering drug?' A young personal assistant stated that when she entered the advertising industry, in around 1982, 'cocaine was considered a relatively harmless drug' ('The plague of addiction', 2 October 1992).

For the majority of people in the business, however, the 1980s were more about cash than coke. In the decade from 1978, total spend on advertising in the UK grew by 315 per cent. It was a time of mega-mergers, going public and achieving global reach. And at the centre of it all was Saatchi & Saatchi. As Stephen Bayley wrote, 'Everything the agency did in those days was larger, brasher and more confident than anyone else.'

## The Saatchi saga continues

In the spring of 1986 a salivating article in *Time* magazine commented: 'In this era of the entrepreneur, nearly everyone and his brother are thinking big. But Charles and Maurice Saatchi, London's most successful admen, are thinking gargantuan' ('The British admen are coming!', 28 April). It confirmed that the brothers were on track to turn Saatchi & Saatchi into the biggest advertising agency in the world.

The main subject of the article was the Saatchis' 'estimated US $100 million acquisition' of the US agency Backer & Spielvogel, best known for its Miller Lite ads. The deal put Saatchi & Saatchi at the number three position in the listing of the world's biggest agencies, behind Japan's Dentsu and the Madison Avenue monolith Young & Rubicam. The same piece defined the media image of the brothers. 'The reclusive Charles drives to his office every day accompanied only by his pet Schnauzer and often spends his lunch break playing chess,' it claimed. 'The more outgoing Maurice has excelled in courting outside financing for the company's rapid growth.'

Whether the image was accurate or not, it was the one that became fixed in the minds of journalists: Charles busy creating behind the scenes, while the more extrovert Maurice, with his trademark heavy-framed spectacles, fronted the company. They were the most famous admen in Britain, running an organization that was no longer a mere agency, but a global advertising empire. Their motto was 'Nothing is impossible'; and it seemed to be the case.

As well as Backer & Spielvogel, the group snapped up another US agency, Dancer Fitzgerald, and the giant Ted Bates Advertising – a deal that cost it US $450 million. It also bought management consultants, researchers and direct marketing operations. Its standard policy was to pay half the asking price up front and the rest in instalments, ensuring the loyalty of existing management for a fixed period.

By the end of 1986 Saatchi & Saatchi PLC had spent US $1 billion acquiring 37 companies. It had 18,000 employees in 500 offices across 65 countries. But the Americans had grown wary of the group, which had waded into the stable, cloistered environment of Madison Avenue and begun dismantling and reconstructing agencies. As a result of these reshuffles, clients occasionally found themselves in bed with their competitors. Some of them leapt right out again.

In 1987 – in a move that in hindsight seems to typify the excesses of the decade – Saatchi & Saatchi decided to buy a bank. It approached Midland, the fourth largest bank in Britain. The overture was summarily rejected, to derisive asides from the City. This setback prefigured a turning of the tide for Saatchi & Saatchi. In September 1987, the stock market crashed.

For a while it looked as though Saatchi & Saatchi would weather the storm – then all hell broke loose. Alison Fendley writes: 'In 1988 Saatchi & Saatchi was... the biggest advertising group in the world. Three years later, its shares had lost 98 per cent of their value and the company was no longer number one.' The advertising business was experiencing its worst slump since the war and the Saatchi organization was being dragged down with it. In 1989, after 18 years of consecutive growth, the company issued its first profits warning.

Although, like Charles, Maurice had sold some of his shares in the company, he was still chairman and CEO. Instead of walking away from the wreckage – as both of them could easily have done – the brothers sought outside help. They brought in Robert Louis-Dreyfus and Charles Scott, from a Pennsylvania-based research company called IMS, as respectively chief executive and finance director. The two newcomers accepted the challenge of bringing the group back from the brink – and Scott remained to take on the role of chief executive in 1993 when Louis-Dreyfus was lured away to help the ailing German sportswear firm Adidas.

According to Alison Fendley, the relationship between Maurice Saatchi and Charles Scott became strained, as Saatchi worried that Scott was not doing enough to put the company back on the right track. In the end, though, it was not this uneasy partnership that forced Maurice to leave the agency he had co-founded – but American shareholder activism. A group of rebel stockholders represented by David Herro decided that in order for the company to start over again, Maurice Saatchi had to go. His impressive salary, his flamboyant lifestyle and his tense relationship with Charles Scott were all produced as evidence against him. Acting in his favour was the support of important clients – including British Airways and Mars – and many members of staff, who saw him as the figurehead and brand identity of the company.

It was not enough to convince the shareholders. In January 1995, the news emerged that Maurice had been ousted in a boardroom coup. The media lapped up the story – after all, Maurice Saatchi had always been their favourite adman – and even the satirical *Private Eye* magazine paid him a backhanded compliment with the sardonic headline, 'Man with glasses leaves job'.

Maurice Saatchi did not let matters lie. Shortly after his ousting, *Time* magazine reminded its readers of the first line of the novel *Damage*, written by his wife, the bestselling novelist Josephine Hart: 'Damaged people are dangerous, they know they can survive' ('Damage and Destruction', 23 January 1995). And so he did. Saatchi still had loyal friends, in the form of Jeremy Sinclair – who had been with the agency since the Cramer Saatchi era – Bill Muirhead, and David Kershaw, an account executive who had risen through the ranks to become head of the London agency. They quickly began drawing up plans for Saatchi's return as a partner in a new agency. Charles, now more embroiled in the world of art than in that of advertising, lent his support to the business. After operating for a brief spell under the name The New Saatchi Agency, M&C Saatchi sprang to its feet in 1995 as an international agency, with offices in London and New York. One of the first things it did was to win back the Saatchis' most iconic account, British Airways.

Today, in the typically self-contradictory fashion of the advertising industry, two Saatchi-branded entities exist: Saatchi & Saatchi and M&C Saatchi. Those who know the background to the story can tell them apart – anybody else has a right to feel confused. For identification purposes, M&C Saatchi bills itself as a younger and more dynamic agency, specializing in 'brutally simple' ideas. In 2004, it floated 39 per cent of the agency on AIM in order to fund its expansion into mainland Europe. At the time of writing, it has 26 offices in 18 countries: 'As few offices as necessary rather than as many as possible,' its website comments, as if to distance itself from its estranged cousin.

But one thing neither of the Saatchi entities have is the British Airways account, which M&C Saatchi lost in 2002 – to an agency called Bartle Bogle Hegarty.

## Jeans genius from BBH

Saatchi & Saatchi was not the only advertising agency attracting attention from the media in the 1980s. Another, much smaller operation was grabbing eyeballs with a series of remarkable TV commercials for Levi's 501 jeans. The ads created a retro fantasyland – a 1950s that never existed – full of pouting girls in tight mohair sweaters and sharp-cheekboned boys with pomaded hair. The glossy images were accompanied by luscious soul hits that, having been discovered by a new generation, zoomed to the top of the charts. The most celebrated ad in the series was called 'Launderette'. To the sound of Marvin Gaye singing 'I Heard It Through the Grapevine', a young man clad in jeans and a black T-shirt sauntered into a launderette. Without further ado, he stripped down to his pristine white boxer shorts and put his clothing in one of the machines. Then he settled down to read a magazine, to the delight of female onlookers.

For something that lasted only a minute, the ad had a disproportionate effect on British popular culture. It brought back not only Levi's, but fifties fashion and soul music. As an unexpected bonus, it got men out of Y-fronts and into boxer shorts. Young women everywhere heaved sighs of gratitude. 'To this day,' admits John Hegarty, 'I'm not sure what we sold more of: jeans or boxer shorts. Ironically, we were originally going to put him in Y-fronts, but the advertising standards people thought it might be too risqué. Boxer shorts were less revealing – and they added to the authenticity of the ad.'

When *Campaign* was debating who to choose as its 'man of the decade' at the end of the eighties, it veered towards John Hegarty. 'Of the many advertising rules set in stone,' the magazine wrote, 'this is the most deeply-etched: "Thou shalt not set trends: thou shalt only follow them." In the 1980s, that stone tablet was split in two... BBH told us what jeans to wear; sent records to the top of the charts; and produced commercials whose launches became media events for a national press suddenly obsessed with advertising and admen' ('Who is the man of the decade?', 6 January 1990).

Hegarty complains that photos make him look a little too craggy these days ('I see them and think: "Who is that person?"'), but with what one could still describe as a mop of unruly hair, a broad smile that sets up pleasant creases beside his eyes and a voice calibrated for persuasion, he's very much the charismatic creative. As we know, Hegarty began his career at Benton & Bowles. He'd originally wanted to be a painter. 'I went to art school at Hornsey, but when I got there I was disappointed to discover that I was unlikely to become the next Picasso,' he says. 'One of my teachers, a wonderful man called Peter Green, told me I had lots of good ideas and that I should become a graphic designer. So I went to the design department of the LCP [the London College of Printing; now the London College of Communication], where I was rather perplexed to find that they all wanted to be artists.'

Fortunately, Hegarty found another mentor in John Gillard, who took a group of promising students under his wing: 'He introduced me to the work of Doyle Dane Bernbach, which for me was a seminal moment. It brought together all the things I'd been thinking and I suddenly realized, "This is what I want to do." It was as if a switch had been thrown and a light had come on. It showed that advertising could be witty and smart – but also inclusive.'

One wonders what the UK advertising industry would have become without the influence of Bernbach. In Hegarty's view, 'What [Bernbach's work] did was create an entire generation who actually wanted to work in advertising. Before us, advertising people still secretly yearned to be artists and novelists. But we wanted to be part of that whole sixties revolution in music, fashion and design – and we felt we could do that through advertising.'

Initially, however, the advertising revolution lagged behind the others. 'At that time advertising was still controlled by the big corporations. You couldn't just open a boutique in Carnaby Street, the way the fashion people had. You'd have to go along to an agency and say, "I've got these earth-shattering ideas for ads," and they'd say, "What are you talking about? – you're only a kid!"'

Fortunately, he found a job as a junior art director at Benton & Bowles, under creative director Jack Stanley. But he managed to get himself fired after 18 months. 'Obviously I was a pain in the arse, because I kept telling them where they were going wrong. Turned out I was right, but they didn't want to hear it from a 22-year-old art director. I would argue with the client, which in those days simply wasn't done. I wanted to convince them that their work could be creatively distinctive. The problem was that Doyle Dane Bernbach had created modern advertising in New York in the early sixties, but the concept hadn't quite arrived in England. The idea that you should entice, engage and entertain audiences was a million miles from the prevailing thinking. They just wanted to hit people over the heads with the same message hundreds of times.'

Hegarty then spent a short period at a small Soho agency working on the El Al airlines account – a client for which Doyle Dane Bernbach had done some groundbreaking work in the United States. Hegarty was pleased with the work he did there, but he upped sticks again when he was invited to join Charles Saatchi and Ross Cramer at their new agency, in 1967. 'We moved into this fantastic building in Goodge Street that was also home to David Puttnam's photographic agency, a new agency called BMP and the designers Lou Klein [who designed the D&AD's yellow pencil trophy] and Michael Peters. It was like the Chelsea Hotel in New York – a creative hub. Everyone was involved in everything, from ads to design to coming up with concepts for films. It was way ahead of its time, because in those days advertising people were supposed to stay in their box.'

And so Hegarty became one of the founding members of Saatchi & Saatchi. He stayed there until 1973, when he was recruited to set up the London branch of an organization that billed itself as the first European multinational agency, TBWA (see Chapter 8, The French connection). It was here that he met his future partners John Bartle, a planner, and Nigel Bogle, an account man. 'To be honest, although we were part of a European network, we were really operating as an English agency – we did wonderful work for brands like Ovaltine, Lego and Johnson & Johnson. In 1980, we became *Campaign*'s first ever agency of the year.'

But the trio became increasingly frustrated with TBWA's structure, which involved placing a certain percentage of each agency's profits into a central pot. 'The situation changed later, but at the time we felt that the best-performing agencies in the network, like our own, were propping up those who weren't up to scratch. So we decided to go our own way.'

Bartle Bogle Hegarty opened its first offices in Wardour Street in 1983. It pitched for its most famous client, however, before it had even moved in. The agency was barely a month old and working out of rented space when it received a letter from Levi's. 'It said they were compiling a list of agencies they might like to pitch for their European account and they wanted to meet us. At first we thought it was a joke. We rang Levi's and said, "We've got this letter, but we've only just started up so there must have been a mistake."' Not at all, said Levi's. 'Apparently we'd been recommended by a researcher who'd worked with us on Ovaltine at TBWA and had since moved to Levi's.'

The news threw the trio into a panic. The initial meeting was to be held in 'the worst conference room imaginable, decorated with hunting prints and ghastly wallpaper'. It was hardly the image of a hip young agency. So Bartle, Bogle and Hegarty plastered the walls with the work they'd done at TBWA, almost entirely obscuring the offending flock. The meeting went well. When the Levi's representatives had left, the BBH team took down the posters – and the wallpaper came off with them. 'We actually had to pay to have that bloody wallpaper put up again,' laughs Hegarty.

Still barely entertaining any thoughts of winning the business, BBH was surprised to hear that it had made it to the shortlist. The agency's policy was not to indulge in any speculative creative work. It was committed to the principle of devising the right strategy before it started making ads – so at pitch stage the trick was to convince the client that it had a thorough understanding of the brand and its future direction, rather than arriving with a stack of artwork. 'But we got nervous because we heard rumours that BMP had shot a commercial, and that McCann, the incumbent agency, also had a load of stuff prepared. We very nearly backed out – but that seemed ridiculously defeatist, so we decided to push on to the bitter end.'

Levi's desperately needed a new approach at that stage. Thanks to the post-punk phenomenon, jeans had become unfashionable: one only has to look at an early Spandau Ballet video to see just how irrelevant denim had become. Now installed in its new offices, BBH prepared to pitch. 'This time we had our own conference room, but the place was half-finished. The only things that made it look good were these incredibly cool designer chairs from Italy.' The pitch was simple: no poster designs, no pilot commercials – pure strategy. 'We told them that they should stop denying their roots. They were all about America and they needed a new way of expressing that.'

Hegarty suspected that the pitch had gone well, but he was a little disconcerted by the presence of Lee Smith, then president of Levi Strauss Europe. 'He was one of these good-looking American guys with a firm handshake. I thought he'd consider us a bunch of amateurs. At the end of the meeting, I nervously asked him if he had any comments. He suddenly broke into a giant grin and said, "Gentlemen, this is the finest chair I've ever sat in." The seat won the pitch.'

The story is characteristic of the self-deprecating Hegarty, who is justly known as one of the more human people in advertising. He even admits that, at a very early stage, the agency was forced to re-pitch for the Levi's business. 'We'd done some print work using rivets and stitching to establish an aura of authenticity around the brand. We'd also made a TV ad where a guy smuggles some jeans into Russia. Then suddenly there was an internal reorganization and we were back at pitch stage.'

Levi's sales were still in the doldrums, but the company agreed to give BBH more time, while also focusing attention on its classic 501 product. 'Launderette' was part of the agency's second wave of work for the brand. More than 20 years later, BBH was still working for Levi's, after a string of award-winning ads – accompanied by numerous hit pop songs.

But BBH, of course, is about far more than jeans. This is the agency that came up with the line 'Vorsprung Durch Technik' for Audi. Consider the audacity of selling cars to British consumers with a German phrase that most of them barely understood – but which *felt* right. Another key client is Johnnie Walker, for whom BBH devised the slogan 'Keep Walking'. More recently, the agency has defied political correctness with a series of deadpan ads for Unilever's Axe fragrance (the brand is known as Lynx in the UK). The ads insist with knowing implausibility that no woman can resist what is, in reality, a rather banal product. 'The Axe Effect' turns everyday guys into babe magnets.

During the rush to the stock market in the eighties, BBH stood on the sidelines and watched, considering that independence equalled creative freedom. Its logo, after all, is a black sheep. In 1997, however, it sold a minority stake to Leo Burnett. This enabled it to fund its 'micro network' model. Although it would open international offices, they would be regional hubs, inextricably linked with one another and able to collaborate on projects as well as operating independently. For the time being these are London, New York, Los Angeles, Singapore, São Paulo, Shanghai and Mumbai.

A great sea change in BBH's history came in July 2012, when Leo Burnett's parent, Publicis, took full control by acquiring the 51 per cent stake that still belonged to its founders. But BBH chief executive Nigel Bogle assured *The Guardian* newspaper that the agency would not lose control of its destiny. 'We were looking for an opportunity that would ensure that our agency maintained a high degree of autonomy and could continue to abide by the values characterized by the black sheep' ('Publicis takes full control of BBH', 5 July 2012).

Perhaps because of its relatively compact size, BBH still feels fresher and more relevant than many of its contemporaries. Like the original yuppies, BBH simply refuses to grow old.

## The gentleman copywriter

I was disappointed that I didn't get to meet David Abbott, co-founder of one of the most respected British agencies of the eighties – and indeed of all time. But Abbott has shied away from giving interviews for a while now. When the magazine *Marketing Week* requested an audience on his retirement, in 1998, he sent a polite fax saying, 'Sorry, but I don't want to be profiled. Even I'm bored with me. Thanks for asking.' It had all the hallmarks of this revered copywriter's style: concise, elegant and witty.

Abbott Mead Vickers, the agency that Abbott formed with his friends Peter Mead and Adrian Vickers, is now the most powerful in Britain, having evolved into AMV BBDO. At the time of writing, it was the most successful agency brand in the UK for the 10th consecutive year. When Abbott retired, *Marketing Week* worried that the 'cultural guts of the agency' would be 'ripped out'. But his legacy clearly lives on.

British readers of a certain age will be familiar with Abbott's work: his mouth-watering descriptions of food for Sainsbury's, his British Telecom advertising ('It's good to talk'), and of course the campaign he devised for *The Economist*, which we'll turn to in a moment. A much-loved TV spot from the 1980s promoted the *Yellow Pages* telephone directory. An elderly man was shown visiting second-hand bookshops in search of a rare volume. 'Do you have *Fly Fishing*, by JR Hartley?' he enquired. Each time the answer was no – until he became fatigued and despondent. In the next shot we saw him with a telephone directory on his knee, much revived as he hunted for the book from the comfort of an armchair. Finally, he got through to a shop that had the book in stock. He asked them to set it aside for him. 'My name?' he repeated. 'Yes, it's J... R... Hartley.'

The ad was polished, understated and humane – classic AMV stuff.

Abbott was born in Hammersmith in 1938 but brought up in the London suburbs, away from the Blitz. His father was a retailer who owned three stores. (It's no coincidence that many of adland's leading figures, from Bill Bernbach to Martin Sorrell, had entrepreneurial fathers.) Abbott shone at school and won a scholarship to read history at Oxford. It was here that he met Adrian Vickers, who was studying law. Some reports describe them chatting animatedly in Oxford coffeehouses, which is a nice image, so let's stick with it. But Abbott never completed his degree: he was summoned home to run the family business for his ailing father, who eventually died of lung cancer. Later, when he ran an advertising agency, Abbott refused to take on any tobacco accounts.

Unable to save the family firm, Abbott found himself out of work. In the meantime, he'd been inspired by a book about advertising. It was *Madison Avenue, USA*, by Martin Mayer – the same book I toted up and down that street last spring, unaware of the connection at the time. Abbott liked the sound of the colourful world contained within its covers. 'At the time [1961] I was a backward 22-year-old,' he once told *The Financial Times*. 'It never occurred to me that someone spent their time writing words in ads' ('A deceptively spare style', 25 October 1984).

He managed to get a job in Kodak's advertising department, where he edited an internal publication and wrote ads for industrial x-ray film. But his goal was a big advertising agency, so he applied to Mather & Crowther. They gave him a copy test – which he failed. He begged them to let him sit it again. They acquiesced – and this time he passed. In those days the agency was still run in time-honoured fashion, with the copywriters working in a separate pool, away from the creative department. The most junior copywriter sat by the door; the most senior got a desk near the window. Once you'd written your copy, you placed it in the out tray, from which it was collected by a young Alan Parker type. That was the last you saw of it until the finished ad appeared in the press ('Man of letters', *Design Week*, 18 April 2002).

After two years of this, Abbott spotted an ad for Remington electric razors made by the newly opened London branch of Doyle Dane Bernbach. He became another Bernbach disciple and – after spending a few months honing a DDB style – successfully applied for a job there. Working with art directors for the first time, he began producing bolder and more confident work – and getting noticed. In 1966 he was sent for a spell at the New York office – the ultimate consecration. On his return, he was made copy chief. Not long after that, he became creative director. According to *Design Week*, Abbott had no fewer than 26 pieces in the 1969 D&AD annual.

The magazine also unearthed this charming description of Abbott's craft, from an essay he wrote in 1968: 'Let's start at the beginning: abcdefghijklmnopqrstuvwxyz – you are looking at the copywriter's toolbox. With these 26 little marks on paper we have to persuade people to buy our client's products, ideas or services. If we jumble them one way, we can sell with a laugh. Mix them up another way and we're provocative. Another, and we're sympathetic. It beats Scrabble. And we get paid for it.'

Abbott's first stab at his own agency came with the creation of French Gold Abbott. But this doesn't seem to have worked out, and soon he was being wooed by his old friend Adrian Vickers, who had worked at SH Benson, and his former colleague Peter Mead, whom he had met at Mather & Crowther. Finally, in 1977, Abbott Mead Vickers was born.

Abbott created a wealth of fine advertising during his 20 years at the agency, but *The Economist* case study is worth going into in more detail. The relationship began in 1984. Ironically, Abbott almost didn't work on the campaign at all. Something about the way his pitch had been received persuaded him that *The Economist* had been unimpressed, so he let the publication know that he had changed his mind about working on the account. Abbott was justly confident in his own abilities and, with plenty of clients beating down his door, he had little to lose. The magazine had other ideas, and found itself in the unusual position of having to persuade Abbott to take the job.

Initially, the campaign followed the rules of almost every promotional drive for a media product, which was to focus on the content. But Abbott realized that a more effective approach, which would also dispense with the need for time-consuming meetings with *The Economist*'s editorial team, would be to focus on the publication's brand identity. At that stage, the ads were still black-and-white; but as Abbott stared down at the magazine on his desk, he realized that if he blew up its distinctive red-and-white masthead, it would be more or less the size of a 48-sheet poster. So why not use the masthead as the basis for a campaign? The red and white would be highly distinctive and inextricably linked with the product. And as a copywriter, Abbott instinctively felt that the ads should be about words, rather than images.

Among the first ideas that Abbott produced for the new campaign was the one that has remained a firm favourite: '"I never read The Economist". Management trainee. Aged 42.' It set the tone for the witty, sophisticated and ever-so-slightly smug posters that have followed, each May and October, until the present day.

As a poster campaign, it was a risky idea in the first place – using a mass medium to promote a niche product. But while the posters clearly position *The Economist* as an exclusive club, they also suggest that it is easy to enter. Whether you are rich or poor, a banker or a garbage collector, you require only one attribute – intelligence. At the same time, although outdoor campaigns traditionally run the risk of 'wastage' – being seen by many people for whom they are not relevant – the *Economist* posters generate a feeling of warmth about the brand; and they attract advertisers to the publication.

Shortly after winning the *Economist* business, in 1985, AMV followed the trend of the times and went public. Abbott, Mead and Vickers brought in an outsider, Michael Baulk – then managing director of Ogilvy & Mather in London – as agency chief executive and managing director, 'to manage their brand,' as he puts it. Baulk remembers the eighties fondly: 'Collett Dickenson Pearce creatively and the Saatchis commercially were examples to everyone else. A whole wave of new agencies got started and the City encouraged them to go public. A lot of personal money was made and a lot of public interest was created. Advertising suddenly became news. It was really the time when a new generation took on the establishment and won.'

In 1991, AMV sold out to BBDO and merged with the London arm of the US agency network, creating a £130 million entity. 'The nineties were very generous to us,' says Baulk. 'Once the advertising industry had recovered from the recession of the early 1990s, it began to grow at double digit rates, so everyone was doing well. That was the catalyst for our growth. But you get to a certain point where you need an international network of some kind if you're going to grow any further. Of course, we chose our partner very carefully. We considered BBDO to be the most creative network, which also had a great respect for local sovereignty. And it gave us access to clients like Pepsi and Gillette.'

AMV whizzed past Saatchi & Saatchi as the UK's biggest shop in 1997. The following year, with this achieved, David Abbott retired. In 2001, however, he was inaugurated into the New York Art Directors Club Hall of Fame – the second English writer to be accorded this honour after David Ogilvy. But by then, Abbott's place in advertising history was assured.

## The buccaneers of Venice Beach

Although it might be unfair to suggest that, in the eighties, the real action was taking place away from Madison Avenue, let's go ahead and do that anyway. In 1990 the US trade bible *Advertising Age* chose as its Agency of the Decade an operation based in Venice Beach, California. Its boss was a renegade perfectionist who believed 'good enough is not enough', its resident creative genius considered shorts and flip-flops acceptable working attire, and its unofficial symbol was a pirate flag. For connoisseurs of colourful characters, Chiat/Day was a mouth-watering story.

Although he is closely associated with a peculiarly West Coast brand of creativity, the late Jay Chiat was born in New York – in The Bronx, to be exact, the son of a laundry deliveryman. He graduated from Rutgers University in 1953 and tried out a handful of unsatisfactory jobs – including a stint as a tour guide at the studios of NBC – before being called up for military service. Describing his job as 'broadcasting', he was assigned the post of information officer at an airbase in California. After being discharged, he worked briefly on recruitment advertising for an aerospace company. Then he landed a job at a small Southern Californian advertising agency called the Leland Oliver Company. He's said to have written five advertisements on his first day.

Inspired and ambitious, Chiat realized that not only was there money to be made in advertising, but that California might be the place to do it. In her book about Chiat/Day, *Inventing Desire* (1993), Karen Stabiner writes, 'At that time, Southern California was the wild frontier; all the famous, established agencies were based in New York or Chicago. There was little competition, there were great expense account lunches... and he enjoyed the work.'

He launched Jay Chiat & Associates in Los Angeles in 1962. After a conversation with Guy Day, the owner of another agency, over hotdogs at a baseball game, the pair decided to merge their companies and create Chiat/Day, in 1968. The relationship was a turbulent one and Day eventually left. He later told *Advertising Age* that the only thing the pair 'agreed on 98 per cent was the advertising' ('Jay Chiat, ad pioneer', 29 April 2002). The agency swooped and dipped through the seventies, winning and then losing Honda – a brand that it had dragged from obscurity.

Blows like that did not rattle Chiat for very long, however. Stabiner characterizes him as a powerhouse, driven by a quest for what he called 'ads that jolt'. 'He was propelled by an odd disdain for any objective he managed to obtain,' she writes, 'as though his ability to accomplish it diminished the inherent value of the achievement.'

Chiat saw his agency as a crew of wild buccaneers harrying the stately galleons of Madison Avenue. 'We're the pirates, not the navy,' he would say. And yet there was some cold, cerebral science behind the showmanship. In 1982 Chiat became the first to introduce the British practice of account planning to the US industry, supporting creativity with strategic thinking. The agency's ads were spectacular, but they weren't founded on vapour.

Nor did the agency's successes come without sweat. Chiat drove his people as hard as he drove himself, which prompted one wag to nickname the agency 'Chiat/Day and night', as a commentary on the number of hours staff were expected to put in. 'If you don't show up for work on Saturday, don't bother coming in on Sunday,' was another quote attributed to Chiat. But he was also known for organizing sybaritic parties and ensuring that there was more than enough food on hand to fuel his employees' creativity. 'In the Chiat/Day vernacular, food meant love,' writes Stabiner. 'The Venice office spent US$1,000 a month on pizza alone.'

The results of this tough love were advertising landmarks. The agency created the overactive Energizer Bunny, for example. Perhaps more impressively, it hijacked the 1984 Los Angeles Olympics for Nike by covering the city with oversized posters, giving citizens the impression that the brand was the event's main sponsor, when in reality Converse had paid US$4 million for just that privilege. At the same moment, Chiat/Day created the vogue for spectacular posters that had a jaw-socking visual impact and only a mute logo by way of explanation.

But the Chiat/Day ad that everyone adores was for Apple Computer.

## '1984' and the Super Bowl factor

When Phil Dusenberry said that TV advertising got into its stride in 1984, he could hardly have picked a more appropriate year. '1984' was the name of a TV spot that aired only a handful of times, yet achieved instant and lasting acclaim.

Apart from the ad's director, Ridley Scott, the name most often linked to '1984' is that of Lee Clow. The creative force behind Chiat/Day, Clow was (and is) the long-haired, bearded, sartorially relaxed surfer I mentioned earlier. Committed to California, Clow once told *Adweek* that he grew up on the beach and 'only moved about ten miles in my life' ('Clow riding high on Chiat/Day creative wave', 6 August 1984).

Although he attended art school, he effectively taught himself advertising, comparing his own work to the ads he found in *Communication Arts* magazine and the New York Art Directors Show annuals. After starting out at a graphic arts firm, he spent four years as an art director at the agency NW Ayer/West. At the beginning of the 1970s he decided that he wanted to work for Chiat/Day. According to *Adweek*, he targeted the agency with a year-long self-promotion campaign called 'Hire the Hairy', of which the most amusing element was a jack-in-the-box that popped open to reveal a bearded Clow simulacrum.

Clow was by no means the only creative thinker drawn to the Chiat/Day dream factory. Steve Jobs, the boss of Apple, felt that the agency's iconoclastic attitude meshed with his own. Apple paid US $1 billion for the 60-second commercial that was to launch the Macintosh.

Written by Steve Hayden and directed by Scott in the dystopian style of *Blade Runner*, '1984' took its cue, obviously, from George Orwell's novel. The spot featured an army of ashen-faced drones marching into a darkened hall, where a bullying dictator harangued them from a giant video screen. An athletic blonde in sports gear charged down the aisle, pursued by black-clad riot police. Pausing, she whirled a sledgehammer above her head and hurled it into the screen, smashing the dictator's image into a billion fragments. With the arrival of the nonconformist new Macintosh, promised the ad, 'you'll see why 1984 won't be like *1984*'. The ad has often been taken as an allusion to the then-dominant IBM, something Apple denied at the time.

Another oft-recounted story, almost certainly true, is that the Apple board was uneasy about the spot, and that Jobs saved it from oblivion by insisting that it ran. To pile on yet another myth, most accounts state that the ad aired only once, during the Super Bowl broadcast. However, reports published closer to the time indicate that it ran for at least a week, in the form of a teaser campaign in smaller markets and a 30-second version in selected cinemas. One of these sources, *Adweek*, adds that the spot even 'enjoy[ed] an appearance on the CBS Evening News' ('Adweek's '84 All-American Creative Team', 4 February 1985). Only a year after its January 1984 screening, the magazine described the ad as 'making advertising history'. It helped to push initial sales of the Mac to more than 40 per cent above projections, with 70,000 computers flying out of stores in the first 100 days. It set a trend for 'event advertising', in which commercials were expressly designed to be so eye-popping that they generated a halo of media attention.

'1984' also established the National Football League's Super Bowl game not only as an essential sporting fixture, but as the annual show-case for the best TV advertising. Every year, on the first Sunday in February, agencies and their clients roll out their most sensational work for more than 100 million American TV viewers. And because it's a premium live event, it stubbornly resists ad-skipping technology. On the contrary: great commercials have become part of the reason for tuning in. If you're looking to build brand awareness among American adults aged 35 and under, the Super Bowl is one of the quickest ways of doing it – if not exactly the cheapest. In recent years the cost of a 30-second advertising slot during the Super Bowl has soared to as much as US $4 million, from US $42,000 when broadcasting of the event began in 1967. Even the internet has turned out to be an ally of Super Bowl advertising – agencies now regularly trailer their work on YouTube as the big day approaches.

Ironically, two years after the success of '1984', Apple pulled its advertising out of Chiat/Day, adding to the impression that Chiat was almost as good at losing big accounts as he was at winning them. (Of course, Steve Jobs had gone by then too – and turbulent times lay ahead for Apple.)

Although it's probably a fallacy, there is a widespread belief in the advertising community that when an agency gets bigger, its creative output becomes less daring. Big, in other words, equals bad. Jay Chiat spent much of his career wondering how big his operation could get before it became bad. At its peak, in 1992, it had billings of US $1.3 billion and 1,200 employees, as well as a Frank Gehry-designed headquarters shaped like a pair of binoculars. (Chiat once described himself as a 'frustrated architect' – and it is partly to his theories about creativity and the working environment that we owe the cliché of loft-like advertising agencies stuffed with punch-bags, pool tables and other toys. He robbed executives of offices and then everyone else of personal desk space, inventing 'hot desking' in the process.)

Chiat had also attempted to grow the agency through acquisition, acquiring an Australian outfit called Mojo MDA in 1989. But the deal unravelled. Global expansion plans sputtered to a halt and the recession suddenly began to take its toll. Laden with debt and struggling to reduce overheads, in 1995 Chiat finally agreed to sell the business to the Omnicom Group, where it became part of TBWA Worldwide. Against his better judgement, Chiat had finally joined the navy.

He left the agency soon after the deal was completed. His last job was as chief executive of Screaming Media, an internet content provider, which he joined in 1999 but had been observing since its founding in 1993 – always ahead of his time. He died of cancer, aged 70, in 2002.

Commenting in *The New York Times* after Chiat's death, Clow said that his boss had combined 'the aggressiveness of a New Yorker with the freedom of California' ('Jay Chiat, advertising man on a mission, is dead at 70', 24 April 2002). On a more poignant note, he added that Chiat 'pushed us to the edge – and when we got there, he challenged us to find a way to fly'.

# The French connection

## 08

*'Vive la publicité'*

**M**aurice Lévy had just stepped out of a restaurant on the Champs-Elysées when he noticed a sickly amber glow in the sky. Lévy, a technology wizard, was in charge of computer systems at the advertising agency Publicis, based a little further up the celebrated avenue. He turned to his dining companions and said without a soupçon of humour, 'I think the agency is on fire.'

His friends assured him that this was unlikely and advised him to go home. Unconvinced, Lévy marched up the street and discovered to his horror that his premonition had been correct: fire trucks were clustered around the blazing building at number 133 Avenue des Champs-Elysées. It was the night of 27 September 1972 – one that would have a major impact on the history of the agency, and on Lévy's career.

Lévy knew that the future of Publicis depended on the data stored on disks and magnetic tapes in the computer room. Sickeningly, he realized in the same instant that his information technology team's night shift was still on duty. 'I became so determined to get into the building that I got into a fight with the firemen,' he recalls. 'They had to physically pin me to the ground. Finally I calmed down and they let me hang around outside. I stayed there until about two in the morning, but it was clear that I wasn't going to be able to get into the agency. So I went home and tried to sleep for a couple of hours.'

At 5am, however, Lévy returned. 'The main blaze had been put out, but the building was still smouldering in places. I met several members of the IT team's morning shift, who were looking on. There was a fire brigade command car parked nearby with a leather jacket and a helmet sitting on the bonnet. Without really thinking, I grabbed the jacket and the helmet and put them on. There was one guard on the door. He nodded at me distractedly and I walked straight into the building – the first member of staff to gain access.'

The building was little more than a blackened husk – anything that hadn't been destroyed by fire had been ruined by water. The computer room on the ground floor was a twisted mass of charred steel and melted plastic. Still, Lévy reckoned some material could be saved. He broke a window and began passing wreckage out to the lingering members of his team. 'What was left of the disks, the tapes, half-burned papers, programmes... in a few hours we removed anything that might be useful. And it turned out that we did the right thing, because a few hours later the building was sealed for good.'

Lévy and the team took the material to IBM, where they began working to retrieve data from the damaged tapes. 'By now it was Thursday morning. We worked without a break and by Monday, miraculously, we were able to provide every member of staff with details of their clients, their suppliers, work in progress, ongoing campaigns... And we were able to invoice clients for work we'd recently completed, which you can be sure they weren't expecting. As a result, the agency was back up and running relatively quickly.'

The Publicis fire was an accident. *Le Monde Diplomatique* once tried to suggest that it was an arson attack by the Palestinian terrorist group Black September ('*Publicis, un pouvoir*', June 2004), but this was strenuously denied by the agency. What is certain is that Maurice Lévy's quick thinking and subsequent hard work earned him the undying gratitude of the agency's founder, Marcel Bleustein-Blanchet. A French ad industry legend, Bleustein-Blanchet had become a mentor and something of a father figure to Lévy. Recalling the events surrounding the fire, Lévy admits, 'Certainly, the fact that I showed a bit of initiative did not go unrecognized.'

Today, Maurice Lévy is president of the Publicis Groupe, one of the world's most powerful communications empires, which owns, among others, Saatchi & Saatchi and Leo Burnett. French industry mythology has it that Lévy's close relationship with Bleustein-Blanchet and his subsequent rise to the top of the agency were the direct results of his actions during and after the fire. The truth, as usual, is a little more complex.

# The father of French advertising

Marcel Bleustein started Publicis in 1927 in two rooms above a butcher's shop at 17 rue du Faubourg Montmartre. He was 20 years old. The son of a Jewish furniture salesman, he had been born in the Paris suburb of Enghien-les-Bains, but was raised in Montmartre. Although unquestionably bright, he left school early, at around the age of 14, to work with his father. He discovered not only that selling came naturally to him, but also that he enjoyed the process of the sale more than its conclusion. He soon became intrigued by what the French called '*réclame*'. Adapted from the verb '*réclamer*', meaning 'to call for', 'to claim' or even 'to beg', it was at the time the accepted term for the act of advertising. (It has since been replaced by the more genteel '*publicité*'.)

Explaining his motivation, Bleustein once said, 'I chose the vocation of advertising because I felt irresistibly drawn to it; and because it would provide me with the thing I'd desired above all else since childhood: independence' (*Musée de la Publicité* website: **www.lesartsdecoratifs.fr/ francais/publicite**). His father was reportedly unimpressed, commenting, 'So you're going to sell air.'

The name of the agency was a simple contraction of '*publicité*' and the French pronunciation of the number six – because 1926 was the year in which Bleustein had conceived the project. He adopted a lion's head as the logo of the nascent operation. Some 50 years ahead of his time, he decided to base his kind of advertising not on 'begging' for trade, but on building long-term relationships between brands and consumers. Early clients included Brunswick fur coats and furniture maker Lévitan. Slogans like the one Bleustein wrote for Brunswick, '*Le fourreur qui fait fureur*' ('Wildly fashionable furs'), appear quaint today, but at the time they were innovative – singsong forerunners of the radio jingle, which Bleustein also introduced to French advertising.

Three years later, Publicis was named the exclusive advertising representative for state-owned radio. When the government decided that public radio was to become an ad-free medium, in 1935, Bleustein resolved the problem by buying a small radio station and turning it into a successful private broadcaster. A few years later, he launched a company that made and distributed advertising films for the cinema, called Cinema et Publicité (which evolved into today's Mediavision). By the end of the

1930s, Bleustein was also handling advertising sales for many of the country's leading newspapers.

Central to the Bleustein legend is his valorous conduct during the war. During the Occupation, he joined the Resistance and changed his name to Blanchet, melting into the shadows as the company he had created was dismantled by the Nazis. Wanted by both the Gestapo and the Vichy government, he escaped first to Spain and then to England, where he became a fighter pilot for the Free French Forces. When the war ended, he was awarded numerous medals for bravery – but he had been ruined financially.

Fortunately, his pre-war contacts and clients stood by him. With radio now fully nationalized and resolutely non-commercial, the entrepreneur known henceforth as Bleustein-Blanchet concentrated on rebuilding his newspaper advertising sales house, and on creating ads for the cinema. He also moved into the transport advertising business, selling space on bus-sides and in the metro. Towards the end of the 1940s he travelled to the United States. He returned convinced of the importance of motivational research – and dreaming of opening his first branch agency in New York.

That ambition was achieved in the 1950s, a boom period for Publicis. Its advertising sales unit now represented newspapers with a total circulation of more than a million copies a day. Its mainstream advertising department won clients such as Shell, Singer and Nestlé. The New York office, the Publicis Corporation, opened in 1958. That same year, the agency moved into its new headquarters at 133 Avenue des Champs-Elysées, the site of the former Hotel Astoria. On the ground floor, in imitation of the cafés/grocery-stores he had seen in New York, Bleustein-Blanchet opened the Publicis Drugstore. This innovation – which remains unique – was more than a way of inviting consumers into the agency; it also ensured that the Publicis brand name became almost as well known as those of its clients.

By the sixties, the 'kid from Montmartre', as he occasionally referred to himself, barely recognized the agency he'd started in two unprepossessing rooms 40 years earlier. Publicis pioneered TV advertising in France, creating campaigns that are still fondly remembered today for the likes of Renault, L'Oréal, (hosiery brand) Dim and Boursin cheese (*'Du pain, du vin, du Boursin'*).

In 1970, Publicis went public.

# The man who said *'Non'*

Maurice Lévy remembers the first time he met Marcel Bleustein-Blanchet, on the afternoon of 2 March 1971. It was Lévy's first day at Publicis. Having built up a considerable reputation in the IT field, he had been headhunted from a smaller agency that had, coincidentally, just offered to make him managing director. Although Lévy had embraced management and account-handling responsibilities alongside his IT duties, he didn't feel ready for the top slot. He thought to himself, 'If they think I'm the best person to run this agency, I'm at the wrong agency.' A few days later, he got a call from Publicis, which had fallen behind in the information technology race and needed him to upgrade its systems. Lévy would end up working from dawn to the depths of night for almost a year on that project – consequently saving the agency from ruin.

In the meantime, on the afternoon of his first day, Lévy had been ushered in to meet Marcel Bleustein-Blanchet. 'It was a meeting I can only describe as "enlightening",' he says. 'I was immediately charmed by this formidable gentleman. You have to remember that he was extremely famous at that stage, the equivalent of a personality like Richard Branson today. Right then I instinctively adopted him not only as my boss, but as my mentor. The meeting was supposed to last 10 minutes, but it went on for an hour. He told me about his life, shared his vision of the future, and encouraged me to express my own ideas. At the end of the meeting, he shook me by the hand, looked me in the eye and said, "One day, young man, you will be running this agency." When I proudly told my wife, she said, "He probably says that to all the youngsters."'

Lévy had never thought in terms of career plans, but from that moment on he had a mission: to earn the respect of Bleustein-Blanchet. 'He seemed to sense that I would rise to any challenge he gave me. It was like being in the army. If he told me to charge a machine-gun emplacement or blow up a bridge, I would do it. He made sure that each challenge was more difficult than the last, to see how far he could push me. And I was determined to prove that no matter how hard he pushed me, I would never fail him.'

Following the fire, with the agency staff dispersed around Paris, Lévy was part of the core team that helped Publicis get back on its feet. Exactly a year after the blaze, Bleustein-Blanchet – who was a great fan of symbols – decided that a management reshuffle was in order. 'He came to me and said, "Listen, Maurice, I've thought hard about this, and I've come to the conclusion that you should become CEO of the agency." I told him I was very flattered, but that it would be a mistake. Publicis was the most respected agency in France, it thrived on creativity, and I hadn't earned my spurs as an advertising man. I saw myself as an administrator – running an agency was not my metier.'

Lévy's rivals still take delight in pointing out that he does not come from a classic advertising background; that he trained as a computer programmer. These days, of course, he can afford to shrug off such barbs, but at the time he felt something of an outsider. Nevertheless, he agreed to take on the role of secretary general, which meant that he was responsible for preparing the agency for its return to 133 Avenue des Champs-Elysées, where an avant-garde new building in glass and steel was under construction. 'After the fire we lost time, money and clients. My job was to return Publicis to the level of health it had attained before the agency burned down.' He was also handed responsibility for the agency's two largest clients: Renault and Colgate-Palmolive. At the same time Publicis began pitching for, and winning, new accounts.

In 1975, 27 months after the conflagration, the agency moved into its revamped headquarters. Bleustein-Blanchet now reiterated his offer. And this time he waved Lévy's protests away: 'Don't bother arguing – the decision has been made.'

Lévy took over the running of the agency first at a local, then gradually at an international level. By the early eighties it was clear that Marcel Bleustein-Blanchet considered Lévy his natural successor. 'From 1987, almost right up until his death in 1996, we worked extremely closely together,' recalls Lévy. 'He pushed me hard, but it became a sort of game. He wanted to find out how far I could take the company. He would say to me, "Let's see what your limitations are." And I replied, "I assure you, you'll never find out." I wanted to demonstrate that I was worthy of his trust.'

Towards the end, when Bleustein-Blanchet had withdrawn to the role of non-executive chairman, one of Lévy's jobs was to relate the inner workings of the agency to him, down to the smallest detail. 'If I ever presented him with merely the conclusion of a story, he'd become irritable. "You're spoiling it! I want to feel as through I was there! Tell me everything!" When the mood took him, he'd burst into my office and demand to be brought up to date, even if I was already in a meeting.'

The elderly Bleustein-Blanchet could be cantankerous, Lévy admits. 'We yelled at each other on more than one occasion. But all the way through our relationship – even before we became close friends – I was often the only person who dared to say, "No, I don't agree with you." Like all great leaders, he hated "yes" men. He didn't want courtiers – he wanted characters.'

To an extent, Lévy says today, he has never stopped working for Marcel Bleustein-Blanchet. 'For all those years, my foremost ambition was that this man, this truly great man, would look upon me with the same amount of respect that I afforded him. Even now, I like to think that he would be proud of our achievements as a group.'

Under Lévy's watch, Publicis has grown to a scale that the kid from Montmartre could never have imagined. But we'll return to that story later (in Chapter 11, Consolidation incorporated).

## Provocation and impact

Apart from Marcel Bleustein-Blanchet – and indeed Maurice Lévy – there have been other notable French admen. One of them was the late, lamented creative Philippe Michel, co-founder of the agency that evolved into today's CLM/BBDO. A sympathizer of the Situationists – the group of artist-agitators who inspired punk – Michel wanted to devise a more intellectual form of advertising, one that deconstructed clichés and winked at, rather than patronized, the consumer. Philosophical and provocative, with a trenchant wit, he could only have been born in France.

Michel 'stumbled' into advertising after initially studying medicine, ending up in 1966 at Dupuy-Compton, where he quickly rose to creative director. In 1973 he founded CLM with Alain Chevalier and Jean-Loup Le Forestier. The agency went on to work for brands such as Total, Volvic, Vittel, Apple and Monoprix. For the fashion brand Kookaï, it created an entire attitude: feminine yet independent, bitchy yet seductive. Michel's philosophy was summarized by the title of a 2005 book devoted to his thoughts on advertising: *C'est Quoi, L'Idée?* ('What's the Idea?'). When Michel asked you that question about a proposed ad, according to former colleagues, he expected you to come back with a quick answer.

Perhaps not his best, but certainly his best-known campaign outside France (and one that was appreciated by David Ogilvy) was for the billboard contractor Avenir in 1981. The first of three posters showed a sexy French waif named Myriam, standing on the beach in her bikini. 'On the 2nd of September,' the ad promised, 'I'll take off the top.' Sure enough, on the appointed date, Myriam appeared with her breasts bared. But now she made an even saucier pledge: 'On the 4th of September, I'll take off the bottom.' When the date arrived, the poster showed Myriam from behind, with her pert bottom on display. 'Avenir,' read the tagline, 'the poster company that keeps its promises.' Taking the advertising concept of a 'teaser campaign' to its logical conclusion, it underlines Michel's taste for provocation.

Eminently quotable, Michel once observed that, as far as ideas were concerned, 'complex doesn't necessarily mean complicated'. Referring to Chiat/Day's '1984' spot, he noted: 'The job of advertising is not to sell, but to create a cultural link between the desires of the entrepreneur and those of the public.' He died of a heart attack in 1993, but his ideas live on.

Another of France's classiest copywriters was Pierre Lemonnier, founder in 1959 of the agency Impact, who passed away in 2002. Having started out as a salesman for Philips, Lemonnier saw himself – and came to be regarded as – the French equivalent of David Ogilvy. A consummate wordsmith, he once said that he wanted to ban slogans and taglines from print campaigns. 'To catch a reader's eye, all you have to do is write S**T across a double page,' he observed dryly. Instead, the body copy should be so good that it hooked the reader from the first sentence. 'A piece of advertising copy is no good unless it's infinitely superior in technique, in facts, in emotion and in rhythm to something a good journalist could have written on the same subject,' he claimed ('L'homme qui voulait bannir les slogans', *Stratégies*, 19 July 2002). He was as good as his word, writing taut, compelling copy for clients as diverse as Tefal and Ferrari. His copy for Ferrari was based on his personal experience as a driver. 'Nobody can put themselves in the place of the owner of a Ferrari 308,' he wrote, defying the reader to do just that.

Although Lemonnier and Michel were admired by their peers, arguably only one French adman has achieved celebrity status among the wider public. The 'S' of the agency Euro RSCG, his name is Jacques Séguéla.

# The house that Jacques built

When I arrived in France to work at the advertising magazine *Stratégies*, the name 'Séguéla' was one of the first I heard. Eyebrows were raised when I admitted that it meant little to me. Officially the co-founder of Euro RSCG and the chief creative officer of Havas, to a large section of the French public Jacques Séguéla *is* the advertising industry. He master-minded two successful election campaigns for François Mitterrand in 1981 and 1988, engraving the slogan *'La Force Tranquille'* on the collec-tive French memory. Yet he has never positioned himself as a suave spin doctor. In 1979 he wrote a bestselling book called *Ne Dites Pas à Ma Mère Que Je Suis Dans la Publicité... Elle Me Croit Pianiste Dans Un Bordel* ('Don't Tell My Mother I Work In Advertising – She Thinks I'm a Piano Player In A Brothel'). Today, at an age when most men would have long retired, he takes the same infectious delight in his craft. 'There's no point in asking me to give up advertising,' he says. 'When I stop working, I'll die.'

Séguéla is proud to be part of yet another French exception. Outside the United Kingdom, France has the strongest advertising sector in Europe. For a start, the country boasts two giant communications groups: Publicis and Havas. Some claim that during the post-war period the pair formed an unofficial entente, agreeing to divide the biggest French clients between them, so they could freeze out the invading American networks. In fact, it's more likely that they had a vicelike two-pronged grip on the market before the overseas networks arrived. The French are nothing if not nationalistic.

But this doesn't explain a second intriguing fact, which is that French agencies perform exceptionally well in international creative competitions, compared to their rivals in Italy, Germany and Spain. Séguéla believes this has something to do with the French mentality. 'I always say there are three kinds of advertising. The English make advertising that comes from the head but touches the heart: it's always rather intellectual. The French make advertising that comes from the heart and touches the head: it often relies on imagery that is romantic, emotional and sensual. The Americans make advertising that comes from the head and touches the wallet. It's possible that the French approach, at least outside the Anglo-Saxon markets, has a more universal appeal.'

It's exactly this kind of quotable material that makes Séguéla such a media favourite. He's always known how to seduce the press. Born in Paris and raised in Perpignan, he studied for a doctorate in pharmacy before setting off to travel the world in a Citroen 2CV – ostensibly to research his thesis on medicinal plants. His adventures resulted in a book that, in his words, 'landed on the desk of the editor of *Paris Match*'. Abandoning the white lab coat of the pharmacist, Séguéla accepted an invitation to become a journalist.

After *Paris Match* he moved to *France Soir*, where he rose to the post of editor before realizing that he was in the wrong department. 'In my new role I had to liaise with both the editorial and the advertising departments,' he explains, 'and I became increasingly curious about advertising. It occurred to me that there had been many great journalists in history, and that I had only a limited chance of joining them. But something told me there were still interesting things to be done in advertising. At that stage, in the 1960s, it wasn't considered a particularly reputable profession. It attracted a lot of people who simply didn't know what else to do, which showed in their work. But with my training as a journalist, I felt that I could genuinely create better advertising.'

In other words, he knew how to research clients, write copy and devise media-friendly events. With these attributes in his favour, he approached the advertising department at Citroën, a company that had brought him luck in the past. Before he knew it, he found himself working for the automaker's agency, Delpire – run by the talented art director Robert Delpire. Unfortunately for Séguéla, at that point Citroën was pouring practically its entire publicity budget into luxurious brochures, while he still dreamed of 'doing real advertising'. His next stop was a small agency called Axe Publicité, whose accounts included Lanvin, Olympic Airways, Volvo and Electrolux. Inspired by the revolutionary events of May 1968, when students and workers took to the streets, Séguéla and his colleague Bernard Roux approached their boss to demand equal shares in the agency. Instead, they were shown the door. Out of work, they decided their only option was to start their own business. With the creation of Roux Séguéla, they were halfway into the advertising history books.

Creating an independent agency in France in the early 1970s was practically an act of recklessness. As discussed above, the government-owned communications empire Havas and the long-established Publicis formed an almost impenetrable block against newcomers to the market.

In addition, the fledgling agency's means were somewhat more than limited.

'In those days there was no such thing as a golden parachute, so we started literally with nothing,' says Séguéla. 'For a couple of months we sublet an office from another advertising man who never arrived at work before lunch. So we'd use the place in the morning and he'd use it in the afternoon. We had a sign made saying "Roux Séguéla" and each morning we'd unscrew his and hang ours in its place. When we left, we'd replace his sign. In the afternoons, we'd work in the café below the office, where the barman found himself doubling as our receptionist. The only problem was that if we met prospective clients in the afternoon it had to be in the café, which was often frequented by prostitutes. We'd get them to chat up the clients while we dashed upstairs and begged to use the office for an extra 10 minutes.'

The agency's first campaign was for Mercury outboard motors. It placed an ad in the news magazine *L'Express*: an old paparazzi photo of then President Georges Pompidou steering a boat powered by a Mercury outboard. When he saw an advance copy of the magazine, Pompidou was enraged at this unauthorized use of his image. He called the publisher and demanded that the ad be pulled. According to Séguéla, 600,000 copies of the ad had to be ripped out by hand, over three days. The story made it on to the radio, which effectively launched the new agency. 'We owed our sudden fame to an ad that never saw the light of day,' he says.

Positioning itself as feisty and anti-establishment, Roux Séguéla built up a modest portfolio of clients, mainly in the property field, and moved to larger premises in the 8th arrondissement. The founders were joined by Alain Cayzac, who had spent some time at Procter & Gamble before working at a small agency called NCK. Cayzac helped the agency break into the field of fast-moving consumer goods.

Then, once more, Citroën appeared in Séguéla's life like a four-leaf clover. He says, 'By chance I found myself back in contact with Robert Delpire, who told me that he was on the point of selling his agency. Although I'd had several conversations with Citroën about working for them, I'd always said that I respected Delpire too much to steal one of his clients. Now, however, he was thinking of moving on. He asked me if I knew anybody who might want to buy his agency. I thought, "Why not us?" Eventually we made a deal, and almost overnight we were one of the biggest agencies in France, with one of the most prestigious accounts. I've been working for Citroën ever since.'

In 1978 Jean-Michel Goudard, another Procter & Gamble alumnus, became the final letter in RSCG. The agency's key role in François Mitterrand's 1981 election campaign, which swept the socialists to power for the first time in 40 years, sealed its reputation. The Mitterrand success was repeated in 1988. For a while it looked as though the agency could do no wrong – until, suddenly, it could. Now one of France's top three agencies, it went on an acquisition spree, snapping up several agencies in the United States. This expansion programme might have gone smoothly had it not coincided with a downturn in the advertising market. By 1990, RSCG had amassed debts of around US $220 million and was teetering on the brink of ruin.

'Building an international network had been incredibly costly,' admits Séguéla. 'We'd gone as far as we could, but now the well had dried up. The banks threatened to cut off our credit. I think we were about 15 days away from going under.'

Ironically, a life raft appeared in the form of the organization that the non-conformist RSCG had once considered its polar opposite: Havas. The group's advertising arm, Eurocom, stepped in and acquired RSCG in a deal that cost it US $300 million. The merged entity would be headed by Eurocom chief Alain de Pouzilhac. Together, the agencies formed Euro RSCG, a giant agency network with a global reach. It was a dramatic comeback, although at the time a rumour circulated that President Mitterrand himself had gently encouraged Eurocom to save his former advisers.

Euro RSCG Worldwide worked hard to stabilize its international offering throughout the 1990s, when its network was criticized as inconsistent and lacking in central coordination. Confirmation of a successful turnaround came at the end of 2006, when it was named the world's biggest agency (in terms of number of accounts handled) by *Advertising Age*. In 2012, however, under the guise of simplification, the network was rebranded with the name of its parent company: Havas Worldwide. Perhaps the word 'euro' had taken on unpleasant connotations of economic shakiness. Like so many agency brands before it, Euro RSCG was consigned to adland history.

One of the jewels in the network's crown was BETC, the Paris agency formed in 1994 by bringing together French talents Rémi Babinet, Mercedes Erra and Eric Tong Cuong. By that stage Euro RSCG had become bloated and firmly establishment – the new young agency was designed to revive its creative image. On the evidence of the awards that have flooded in ever since, the gamble paid off. And BETC's Paris office is still possibly the coolest headquarters in town: an airy retro-futuristic space in the shell of a former 19th-century department store, where vintage chairs from the city's flea markets cosy up to Jean Nouvel desks. Needless to say, it bears little resemblance to the agency that Jacques Séguéla started above a café in 1970.

## TBWA: absolutely European

In late 1970 an intriguing pamphlet fell onto the desks of several French business leaders. Its headline looked as if it was written in code: Tragos, Bonnange, Wiesendanger, Ajroldi.

The first page revealed that these were the names of four advertising men who had set out to solve a major problem facing European advertisers. The situation, the pamphlet explained, was this: after the war, despite the opening up of borders for international trade, European advertising agencies had largely failed to expand overseas. Not only were their accounts generally too small to fund the opening of offices abroad, but they felt linguistically and culturally tied to their domestic markets.

The big American agencies, on the other hand, had not been so apprehensive. The need to service multinationals such as Ford, Coca-Cola and Procter & Gamble had furnished them with ample reason to traverse the Atlantic. Once they'd set up branch offices in the major European capitals, they deigned to handle a few local accounts – provided there wasn't a client conflict. Their resources and experience were highly sought after; but their hearts lay in New York and Chicago. 'For the American agencies,' the pamphlet claimed, pointedly, 'European clients will always be a second priority.'

Bill Tragos (American of Greek descent), Claude Bonnange (French), Uli Wiesendanger (Swiss) and Paulo Ajroldi (Italian) had worked together at Young & Rubicam France. Now they intended to create the first European agency network: TBWA. It would set up shop in Paris and quickly open branches around Europe. Its vocation was not to be a creative boutique, but a major network capable of working with even the biggest clients. It would be 'the first agency born international,' as Tragos put it.

Claude Bonnange, a strategic planning pioneer, had joined Young & Rubicam's Paris agency in 1964. 'The agency was doing fine, but not much better than that,' he recalls over lunch in his Paris apartment. 'So they brought in Bill Tragos, who'd turned around Y&R's Benelux operation in just 18 months. Bill called his old friend Paulo, whom he knew from Y&R in New York. And the quartet was completed by this young Swiss copywriter, Uli. Not only did we become friends, but we had totally complementary skills. Bill was management, I handled planning and research, Uli was the creative and Paulo was the account manager. In three years, we took the agency from 15th place to 3rd. And more than half its billings came from non-American clients.'

With success came temptation: all four received calls from other agencies (Bonnange recalls a conversation with Pierre Lemonnier of Impact, for example). This naturally pushed them down an alternative line of thinking: what if they set up their own agency? They had discussed the dominance of the American agency brands. They passionately believed that there was a need for a coordinated European network, rather than one cobbled together from agencies acquired here and there. 'Built not bought,' was how Tragos would later describe the TBWA structure. 'We sat down in Paulo's apartment and wrote the document that became the agency's mission statement,' says Bonnange. 'Then we told Y&R that we were going to leave – and that they had a year to find replacements for us.' He chuckles. 'That just shows you how much times have changed.'

Another event that would be unlikely to occur today came when the quartet finally quit Y&R. 'We had such a good relationship with the media owners – the billboard companies and so on – that when they heard about our project, they offered us nine million francs [about US$1.7 million] worth of advertising space free of charge. So in August 1970 we were able to run posters, print ads and radio spots announcing the launch of TBWA, the first European advertising network.'

The quartet quickly received calls from advertisers intrigued by their proposition. Despite the fact that they had signed a non-competition agreement with their old agency – meaning that they couldn't take any accounts with them – by the end of their first year, they were making enough to open a Milan office. 'We wanted to move fast because we knew that if we didn't expand out of Paris quickly enough, our pledge to become the first European network would start to lose its credibility,' says Bonnange. A year later came Frankfurt – and then London, where TBWA engaged a young creative called John Hegarty.

Hegarty underlines the fact that TBWA was considerably ahead of its time. He observes that the very concept of 'Europe' was still fuzzy back in the mid-1970s. 'In those days if you talked about Europe to a British client, their eyes would glaze over,' he says. '"What's all this about? I'm not even interested in what's going on in Newcastle, so don't talk to me about Milan. That's somewhere you go on holiday."'

But Europe was not enough: TBWA realized that to compete with the biggest players it needed a presence in the United States. In a diversion from its usual strategy, it acquired New York agency Baron, Costello & Fine. This merged outfit snagged what became TBWA's most famous account: Absolut.

The obscure vodka made by Sweden's Vin & Sprit was imported to the United States by a company called Carillon, headed by a dynamic French salesman named Michel Roux (not to be confused with the London chef of the same name). Roux had arrived in the United States in 1964 with a degree in hotel management and worked his way to the top slot at Carillon. 'A classic liquor salesman, he… used to make a nightly tour of eight or ten Manhattan nightspots, staying out into the wee hours night after night while always managing to put in a full day at the office' ('Absolut Michel Roux', *Business Week*, 4 December 2001). This was how Roux became a regular at Andy Warhol's legendarily bacchanalian Manhattan parties, an entrée that was to play a part in Absolut's success.

When Carillon hired TBWA in 1981, Bonnange and his team did some research to find out how consumers were likely to respond to Absolut. 'We were given three pieces of advice,' says Bonnange. 'First change the name, because Absolut sounds arrogant. Second change the bottle, because it looks like it's designed for urine samples. And third change the logo, because the blue lettering is printed directly onto the glass, which means you can't see it on the shelf. We took these results to Roux, who told us to ignore them. He said, "At least it doesn't look like anything else on the market. The bottle stays as it is."'

TBWA's strategy – driven by the affable Roux – was to turn Absolut into a fashion accessory. The bizarrely shaped bottle was placed in every cutting-edge bar and nightclub in town. And to make sure opinion leaders knew exactly what it contained, the print advertising transformed the

bottle itself into a logo. The first ad, devised by TBWA's New York creative director Geoff Hayes, featured a bottle with a halo, and was entitled
'Absolut perfection'. This visual pun set the template for every ad that
followed. The number of executions now runs into the thousands –
feverishly cut out, collected and traded by fans of the cult campaign.
(The full rundown can be seen at a website called Absolut Ad, run not
by the brand, but by a collector: **http//absolutad.com**.)

A crucial moment came in the mid-1980s, when TBWA and Roux
managed to enlist Andy Warhol to design an ad for the brand. (Although
the artist didn't drink the stuff, he occasionally liked to dab it on as
cologne.) After Warhol's contribution came designs from Jean-Michel
Basquiat and Keith Haring. Anointed by Manhattan's counter-culture,
Absolut vodka became, in Bonnange's words, 'the snobbiest drink in the
United States'. In the decade up to 1989, shipments of Absolut rose from
under 100,000 litres to almost 30 million, and it sped past Russian
brands to grab the biggest slice of the imported vodka market. At the
same time, the campaign confirmed TBWA's reputation as one of the
world's most creative advertising organizations.

## The seeds of disruption

TBWA's success brought it to the attention of the US communications
conglomerate Omnicom, now owner of the DDB and BBDO networks.
Omnicom realized that TBWA was about to hit a wall: if it wanted to
move into Asia and Latin America, as well as strengthening its presence
in the United States, it was going to need additional funding. Omnicom
made TBWA an offer it would have been foolish to refuse. In 1990, not
without irony, the first European advertising network became the third
pillar of an American conglomerate. And in 1995, Omnicom chose
TBWA as the perfect home for its newly acquired West Coast agency,
Chiat/Day.

The merger provoked high drama in London, where Chiat/Day's UK
office decided that it had no intention of becoming part of TBWA. Andy
Law, who headed the office, was convinced that a merger with TBWA
would mean 'spiritual death' for the agency. 'I knew we'd all end up in
the basement of TBWA,' he said at the time ('The ad agency to end all ad
agencies', *Fast Company*, December 1996).

Returning from a tense meeting with Omnicom, Law drew a line across the floor of his office. 'I'm leaving,' he told his staff, tacitly suggesting that those who wanted to follow him should cross the line. One by one, they did so. Omnicom was left with little choice but to sell the London office of Chiat/Day to Law and his associates. The breakaway was named St Luke's – after the patron saint of artists or, pushing it a bit, 'creative people'. It became one of the most high-profile hot shops of the 1990s, generating reams of press coverage with its desk-free offices and its cooperative structure – in which every member of staff was given an equal stake in the agency. It seemed almost too trendy for its own good. Law has since left St Luke's, which lost some of its initial verve. But as one of a group of feral agencies that gnawed at the wainscoting of an increasingly monolithic nineties advertising business, it was undoubtedly influential. (See Chapter 13, The Alternatives.)

Meanwhile, TBWA had another merger to digest. One of the star French agencies of the 1980s was BDDP, founded in 1984 by Jean-Claude Boulet, Jean-Marie Dru, Marie-Catherine Dupuy and Jean-Pierre Petit. (For fans of the minutiae of advertising history, Marie-Catherine Dupuy's grandfather, Roger-Louis Dupuy, founded one of the first agencies in France in 1926. Later, Jean-Pierre Dupuy, Marie-Catherine's father, ran the agency, which in time became Dupuy-Compton.)

The last time we met BDDP on our tour of adland, it had failed to snap up London's BMP (which was bought instead by DDB), but successfully acquired New York's Wells Rich Greene for the colossal sum of US$160 million. Initially this didn't hurt BDDP, as its billings were close to US$930 million. But when the dank fog of recession closed in, the agency began to lose its way. Arguably, as often happens in the advertising business, Wells Rich Greene's oldest clients felt destabilized by the departure of agency figurehead Mary Wells. In her book, Wells writes that she was 'too familiar with the fates of former chairmen and I assumed [BDDP] had their own ideas about how to run the agency'. She suggests that the agency 'was not the reign of Mary, it was a history of groundbreaking television advertising created by pioneering thinkers with tremendous talent'.

Nevertheless, clients began to leave. Some of these losses were provoked by the recession: Continental Airlines filed for Chapter 11, and the newly-named Wells BDDP was forced to cover the unpaid media bills. IBM subtracted a chunk of business when it consolidated its global account with Ogilvy. Slowly, the billings began to trickle away. In a surprising move, the British agency GGT acquired a weakened Wells BDDP for US$174 million in 1997. But the apparent culture clash between these three different elements – Wells, BDDP and GGT – further destabilized the agency. Now Procter & Gamble pulled out its US$125 million account. BDDP was a shadow of its former self.

Once again, Omnicom saw its chance and swooped. It paid US$230 million for GGT BDDP in 1998. The acquisition was fused with the TBWA network. Gradually, even in its French homeland, the name BDDP vanished into the annals of history. But a reminder of its glory days lives on in the form of BDDP & Fils, a creative spin-off, founded in 1998, that continues to be highly respected in the French market.

The worldwide chairman of TBWA is Jean-Marie Dru, one of the original founders of BDDP. Tall, broad-shouldered and silver-haired, Dru has the look of an energetic professor who may be a bit handy on the rugby field. He is the architect of the network's USP of 'disruption'. This is a marketing technique designed to force a brand out of its comfort zone. It's about challenging – or even overturning – the status quo. Quite simply, it's about breaking the rules. 'Brands that don't innovate begin to deteriorate,' Dru explains. 'Our job is to help them change.'

Dru says that the roots of Disruption date back to the earliest days of BDDP. 'As a new, challenger agency, we realized that we had to offer something more than the mere promise of "creativity" to differentiate ourselves. For a start we decided to take on "problem brands". Our approach was, "give us your brand if it's in trouble, and we'll turn it around"… We arrived at the idea of reinvention as a "rupture" with the past – a word that works much better in French than in English. As our international network grew, the idea evolved into "disruption", which can still sound negative in the wrong context, but is slightly less shocking in English.'

As BDDP grew larger and Dru became more preoccupied, he had less time to spread the gospel about Disruption. For a while, the idea went into hibernation. After the fusion with TBWA, Dru assumed that Disruption was dead, 'because it's very difficult to impose the culture of one agency on another; especially when you're the one who's just been bought'. But the theory resurfaced when Dru teamed up with John Hunt, of TBWA's highly creative South African office (see Chapter 16,

International outposts), to create one of the first Disruption Days. These are brainstorming sessions during which clients are challenged to dissect their brand values and identify those that signify outmoded or conventional thinking; and which could be successfully 'disrupted'. 'The great advantage of these sessions is that, even when they don't generate a great new idea, they make the client more receptive to innovation. In the future they'll be more open to genuinely creative ideas – ideas that, for them, represent real change.'

Further Disruption Days were held around the world, and gradually the philosophy entered the bloodstream of the agency. Dru accepts that Disruption is a simple idea, based on the truism that change can ensure relevance – but the skill lies in its execution. 'When you've identified the elements of a brand that could be subject to change, which one do you choose? Change takes time, and when you embark on a long-term strategy you need to be fixed on a goal. Is the key value of our new positioning going to be "health", or is it going to be "taste"? Clearly, it's vital to make the right choice at the outset.'

Apple is a classic example of the Disruption process at work. In 1997, the company was in trouble. Following the departure of its co-founder, Steve Jobs, in 1985, it had changed chief executives more times than it had changed advertising agencies. It was haemorrhaging cash, losing up to US $1 billion a year. In addition, the brand had lost its sense of identity. With Chiat/Day's '1984' commercial, the computer maker had positioned itself as a tool that liberated man from machine. It was the unconventional yet human face of computing. But home PCs were now commonplace: computers were no longer the focus of wariness or anxiety on the part of consumers.

When Steve Jobs returned to Apple and resumed contact with his old agency – now in the form of TBWA – a new approach was required. Apple ransacked one of its old brand values and repositioned itself as the tool of predilection for creative thinkers. The resulting campaign was entitled 'Think Different'. It paved the way for the launch of the iMac, Apple's turnaround product. And the 'disruptive' insight that Apple was about creative utility rather than computer screens led ultimately to the development of the iPod.

Disruption is still a central pillar of TBWA's offering, supported by what it calls 'Media Arts'. The business of achieving visibility in media was once largely a matter of spend – with some strategic planning bolted on – but in today's multi-platform media world, breaking through the cacophony requires more finesse. Media Arts sums up this idea. It essentially urges advertising people to go beyond selling – and even beyond the basic idea of providing entertainment. The goal is to create an event; a highly memorable experience.

One classic example is TBWA's work for energy drink Gatorade in 2009. The agency reunited two rival US college football teams 15 years after a frustrating (and famous) 7–7 tie. The original players, the original coaches, even the original cheerleaders returned for a re-match that was breathlessly followed by traditional and online media. The match itself was played on 26 April before 15,000 spectators (the Phillipsburg Stateliners beat the Easton Red Rovers 27-12).

Not only was this crowd-pleasing event cooked up by an ad agency, it also provoked massive (and free) media coverage, as well as a spin-off TV series. Disruption and Media Arts, flexing their muscles. Traditional advertising forms were beginning to look distinctly creaky.

# European icons

## 09

*'The product is the same – the difference is the communications'*

Every Christmas, without fail, a parcel the size and shape of a hatbox appears on my doorstep. Inside, entirely made of chocolate, are the intertwined letters A and T. It's the logo of Armando Testa, Italy's leading creative agency, in candy form. The parcel is a souvenir of the first visit I made to the agency no fewer than seven years ago. I've been back a few times since – but if I had never darkened Testa's door again, I doubt it would have made much difference. All cynicism aside, this seems a little warmer than the average PR gesture. I wrote a positive article once, so I've been adopted.

Maybe the fact that we're in Italy encourages metaphors concerning the family. And Testa is all about family. Armando Testa, a Turin-based graphic designer, founded the agency in 1946. He died in 1992, but by then the agency had been taken to even greater heights by his son, Marco, who took over as managing director in 1985. The agency remains stubbornly independent, refusing to be snapped up by an American leviathan.

Contributing to the familial atmosphere is the fact that, to a certain extent, Testa is the Italian Leo Burnett. The agency handles household names like Pirelli, Lavazza, San Pellegrino and Fiat-Lancia. And it has created much-loved characters like Pippo, a friendly blue hippopotamus, for a brand of diapers, and the immortal Caballero and Carmencita, two cone-shaped cartoon characters brought to life for Café Paulista in the 1960s and still going strong.

But there is another, hipper side to Armando Testa. It has a strong graphic design heritage and its print work, particularly, has an undeniable punch. Consider the groovy posters it creates every year for Lavazza coffee: ultra-glam confections shot by photographers such as David LaChapelle, Jean-Baptiste Mondino and Ellen Von Unwerth. Outdoor advertising is often dismissed as visual pollution – but these babies actually brighten up a cityscape. The spin-off calendars wrench a vivid hole in your wall. Armando Testa would have approved, as his greatest goal in life was to make an impact.

## The graphic world of Armando Testa

Armando Testa has something in common with the French *affichistes* Cassandre and Raymond Savignac. Unlike those masters of poster art, however, Testa managed to translate his talent into a full-service advertising agency that remains a force in Italy to this day.

He was born in Turin in 1917 and – like most of his generation who came from a humble background – he attended the school of life. By the age of 14 he had already been apprenticed to a locksmith, a sheet metal worker and a typesetter. The latter seems to have awoken his artistic impulses, because he began attending night classes at the Vigliardi Paravia School of Graphic Arts. Here he met Ezio d'Errico, a teacher at the school and one of the best-known abstract artists of the day, who became his mentor. Under d'Errico's influence, Testa began winning competitions to design letterheads and leaflets.

But Testa was a perfectionist: he worked slowly and had, at that stage, an over-inflated opinion of himself, which combined to make him a difficult employee. Each printing company he joined fired him a few weeks later – until at the age of 18 he had been let go by 28 different employers.

In 1937 he won a competition to design a poster for ICI (Industria Colori Inchiostri SA), a Milanese company that made coloured inks for the printing industry. The brutally simple design – which resembles the letters ICI in origami form on a black background – indicated Testa's future direction. In a catalogue of his work produced for an exhibition at the Parsons School of Design, New York, in 1987, he commented: 'My love of synthesis – conveying a message by means of a single gesture, a simple image – and my use of white backgrounds, primary colours and the most basic symbols of visual communication (circle, cross, diagonal, angle) have unfortunately endowed me over the years with a distinctive style, and many people recognize my work on sight.'

After the war – which he spent as an aerial photographer – Testa opened a graphic design studio in Turin. He attracted commissions from the likes of Pirelli and (hat maker) Borsalino. Throughout his early career, he wrestled with the conflict between his desire to create abstract art and his interest in producing commercial imagery. Fortunately, he was able to work with clients who, like him, felt that art and commerce were not mutually exclusive.

Maurizio Sala, president of the Italian Art Directors' Club and vice president of Armando Testa Group, still becomes animated when he talks about Armando: 'Advertising today just refers to other advertising. But Armando made advertising that referred to art, to books, to cinema. He had a very wide frame of reference.'

As for the man himself, Sala remains knocked out by him. 'When he entered a room it was like being hit by an ocean wave – he was extraordinarily energetic. And because of this charisma he could always get what he wanted. He was very good at seducing clients. He would sit down, draw his chair up close to them and ask, "So how much money have you got?"'

Testa needed his charm because his creative work was often provocative. Sala says, 'He felt that great advertising should make the viewer a little uncomfortable. If it was designed to please everyone, it wouldn't get noticed; it would just sink into the sea of banality that surrounded it.'

In 1956, Testa created a full-service advertising agency with his first wife Lidia and her brother Francesco de Barberis, a marketing expert. A year later, commercial television began in Italy. Sala says, 'Many advertising companies went out of business because they didn't know how to do television ads, while clients were shifting large chunks of their budgets to the new medium. Instead of being defeated, Armando set up his own production company to experiment with stop motion animation techniques. He was very inspired by Eastern European animation. The characters he created mirrored his poster work – very simple and graphic, like the blue hippo or the Paulista coffee characters, which are simple cones with eyes, mouths and hats.'

The success of Testa's TV work was initially due to a quirk of Italian legislation that resulted in *Carosello*, a 10-minute daily ad break screened every evening at around 8.50 from February 1957 to the end of 1976. The slot forced agencies to create advertising that resembled TV content: series of cartoons and comedy sketches, which had to be entertaining and/or educational. The sell was so soft it was positively downy. At its peak it was the most popular TV show in Italy, boasting an audience of 20 million (half of them children). Sala explains: 'This was a period when well-known directors and actors were making advertising.

Audiences adored *Carosello*. Parents would say to their kids, "You can watch *Carosello* and then it's time for bed." That's why Armando was able to develop such memorable characters for brands.'

Although the legacy of *Carosello* is occasionally blamed for Italian TV advertising's comparative lack of bite today, it had the kind of following that agencies can now only dream about, and it transformed brands into popular culture icons. Meanwhile, Armando Testa had achieved considerable celebrity, dating back to 1959 when he was commissioned to design the official logo for the Rome Olympics. By the 1970s the agency had swelled in size and opened regional offices in Milan and Rome.

Testa's son, Marco, came on board in the early 1980s. At first Marco had been reluctant to join the family firm, and his desire for independence was sometimes a source of strain. When he returned to Italy from Benton & Bowles in New York – where he had gone to develop a more international approach to advertising – he set up his own agency called, pointedly, L'Altra ('The Other'). 'We lost our biggest client in the first six months, and spent the next six months trying to get the money back from 20 small clients,' he recalls, with a grim smile. Eventually, however, he was reconciled with his father. 'He asked me, "Do you want to start where I am now, or do you want to spend your whole life getting here?" I realized he had a point.'

But Marco Testa retains his independent streak, which is perhaps why he hasn't sold out to a conglomerate. He puts it in more strategic terms: 'If the industry is divided between giant groups and small creative hot shops, where are the big clients who are not global mammoths supposed to go?'

Under Marco, Testa's ads abandoned the saccharine of the *Carosello* era and became faster, wittier, and more transatlantic in inspiration. Yet one of the challenges facing the Italian industry is its relatively lack-lustre performance on the international awards circuit, leading to the impression that the country is no longer a source of groundbreaking creative work. The Brits and the Americans have led the field for years; but the Thais and the Brazilians also attract far more plaudits. The Italian jeans brand Diesel may have produced a string of innovative, award-winning advertising campaigns – but none of them were made by Italian agencies. It's a subject that preoccupies Armando Testa creative director Maurizio Sala – and a situation he is determined to change. He believes the answer lies not in aping the work of US or British agencies, but in redefining Italian advertising.

'Recently I sat down to consider the elements of Italian culture that could be reflected in our advertising. The most obvious one is humour. Italians are very relationship oriented. They like to talk, they like to gesture... and they like to laugh. In general, their humour is quite innocent – it's warm and southern. British humour tends to be crueller, darker and more cynical than ours. For some reason we don't seem able to express our own style of humour in advertising.'

His second big Italian plus-point is 'style'. 'We have a strong heritage when it comes to fashion, film, design and graphics. I think we should look back at some our triumphs in these areas and try to identify our own visual style, which we can then apply to our advertising.'

While Armando Testa is greatly admired at home, international accounts are still proving elusive. Despite the fact that it has offices in London, Paris, Frankfurt, Madrid and Brussels – and longstanding partnerships with agencies in more than 100 countries around the world – these generally service Italian clients. But is it necessary to become a moderately successful global network when you are already a phenomenally successful domestic one, with clients that have trusted you, in some cases, for more than 40 years? The family-owned Armando Testa remains Italy's most powerful agency brand. It is, as its website states, 'the world's largest Italian agency'.

## Copywriting, Italian style

If Armando Testa is the father of Italian advertising, then the late Emanuele Pirella was at the very least the father of Italian copywriting; Italy's answer to David Ogilvy in the United States, David Abbott in the UK and Pierre Lemonnier in France. He gave his name to the agency Lowe Pirella. He died in 2010, but lives on in an interview conducted for the first edition of this book.

Pirella knew he had been born to write. After a degree in modern literature he took up his pen, never to put it down again. Determined to spill ink for a living, he wrote day and night. He wrote short stories for children, cinema reviews for a daily newspaper, copy for comics and cartoons – even a history of Italy from Ancient Rome to the post-war years, dashed out with three other journalists. 'I knew I was a good writer,' he recalled, 'quick, funny, accurate, and able to put a paradoxical spin on a sentence. And I sold that attitude.'

In short, Pirella was a natural for advertising – but until he stumbled into a copywriting job by accident, he knew almost nothing about the industry. 'At that time, advertising in Italy was still a mysterious world. Few people had heard of these entities called "advertising agencies". They thought that inside companies there must be a secret room where a guy sat doing a job that was a mixture of advertising and public relations.'

When he moved from his home town of Parma to Milan in the early 1960s, he looked for a job at a newspaper or a printing company. Then one of his friends told him about a job as junior copywriter at an American advertising agency, Young & Rubicam. With armloads of written work to his credit, Pirella glided into the job. Most of the agency's employees were English or American, but Pirella found his creative 'other half' at Y&R in German art director Michael Göttsche. Together, the pair went on to devise slick, funny advertising in the vein of (naturally) the ads being created in the States by Doyle Dane Bernbach.

'I wasn't getting paid much at first, so I'd be making ads during the day and doing freelance work at night,' said Pirella. 'I was lucky with my first couple of campaigns and in my second year at the agency – this was 1965 – I was named Copywriter of the Year. That meant I could demand a salary increase and give up some of my out-of-hours activities.'

Nevertheless, he didn't entirely abandon freelance work. A lengthy collaboration with the news magazine *L'Espresso*, for whom he wrote a TV review column, ended only recently. And he still creates satirical cartoons with a friend, the artist Tullio Pericoli.

But with more recognition and a decent wage under his belt, Pirella was now firmly hooked on advertising. 'It seemed to me that we were the best agency in Italy – the one that was using the most expensive photographers and directors, with an American copy chief, an English creative director, German and English art directors... All around us the other agencies were making dull and phoney advertising; typical home-grown Italian stuff, featuring poorly conceived illustrations with the product always in use.'

Pirella stayed at Young & Rubicam for five years, followed by a two-year stint at Ogilvy & Mather. Then, with Michael Göttsche and another colleague, Gianni Muccini, he went into business, launching Agenzia Italia in 1971. 'For 10 years, we were the most creative agency in the business. We worked like hell, night and day and all weekend, just because it was fun to find new ways to say the usual things – to challenge one another.'

The ad that really got Pirella noticed was for a brand called Jesus Jeans, launched in 1974 by MCT (Maglificio Calzificio Torinese), the company that makes Kappa sportswear today. According to Pirella, the brand was vaguely inspired by the previous year's hit musical *Jesus Christ Superstar*. Clearly something provocative was needed, so a young photographer named Oliviero Toscani was hired to shoot a young woman wearing the jeans, the zipper open in a manner that indicated she was not wearing any underwear, while casting a coy shadow over the evidence. Pirella's copy read: 'Thou shalt not have any jeans but me.' Mixing fashion, sex and religion – in a Catholic country? No wonder Pirella got himself in the papers. The second execution was the line, 'Whoever loves me, follows me', printed over a pert bottom in denim hot-pants. (The bottom, by the way, was that of Toscani's girlfriend at the time.) The Jesus Jeans brand clearly hasn't stood the test of time, but the furore surrounding the campaign did much for Pirella's career.

After five years, Agenzia Italia did a deal with BBDO that allowed the US agency entry into Italy. But in the end the new relationship didn't suit Pirella, and he and Göttsche pulled out in 1981 to start another independent shop called Pirella Göttsche.

'The first clients that called us are the type I prefer working with. Not the market leaders or the big brands that stick to the rules and try to maintain the status quo. I like the challengers, the number three in the market, the brand that is forced to take risks and break the rules. And we got a lot of those. In a few years we went from four guys to seventy, then eighty.'

In the early 1990s Pirella succumbed to the advances of another international group: this time Interpublic, which made Pirella Göttsche part of the Lowe group – the network that had grown out of Frank Lowe's original London agency. The marriage seemed to work, although Pirella hadn't finished innovating. In 2000 he launched the Scuola di Emanuele Pirella ('The Emanuele Pirella School'), a training centre for budding creatives that was also a real live agency – a modern version of apprenticeship.

The rebel who sold Jesus Jeans had gone respectable: he had become the sage of Italian advertising. Even in those days, Pirella was part of a vanishing generation. But while their artisanal approach may seem out of step with the digital world, writing is still a craft that needs to be honed.

In the meantime, Oliviero Toscani had taken an altogether different approach to his career.

## Blood, sweaters and tears

'I am not an advertising man,' Oliviero Toscani points out, 'I am a photographer.'

Of course – but Toscani's disquieting images for Benetton enlivened the advertising scene of the nineties, and may have been responsible for the vogue in so-called 'shock advertising'. It was certainly hard not to gawp at photos of a priest kissing a nun, a newborn baby with the umbilical cord still attached, or a dying AIDS patient surrounded by waxen-faced relatives – hardly the images you expected to see from the window of your commuter train. With the blessing of his client, Toscani created a giant public photography exhibition that was also an ambiguous running commentary on society. It made audiences think – and it made Benetton notorious.

The son of a photojournalist for *Corriere Della Sera*, Oliviero Toscani was born in Milan in 1942. He studied photography and graphic design at the Kunstgewerbeschule in Zürich from 1961 to 1965. He became a sought-after fashion photographer, working for *Elle*, *Vogue*, *GQ*, *Stern* and other leading titles. (After a while he found the job unfulfilling, once comparing a well-known supermodel to 'a washing machine'.) In addition, his lens provided imagery for brands such as Fiorucci, Esprit and Chanel. But in adland his name is most closely associated with that of Benetton.

Luciano Benetton started the family firm in 1965 with his brothers Gilberto and Carlo and his sister Giuliana. In fact, it was Giuliana who knitted the first ever Benetton sweater for Luciano, an item that prompted many admiring remarks and sparked the idea for a business. In 1982, when Benetton hired Toscani, the company had never advertised. But export sales were rising and communications had taken on a new importance.

Benetton was introduced to Toscani through their mutual friend, the fashion magnate Elio Fiorucci. Recalling their first meeting in an interview with *The Independent* newspaper, Benetton said, 'I didn't have any particular suggestions or restrictions to guide [Toscani], except that the campaign had to be different – very different – and that it had to be international. I had figured that the traditional system of advertising with a different campaign in each country wasn't the way ahead. I... wanted to make people aware of the spirit of the company' ('How we met', 22 August 1999).

For his part, Toscani felt that Benetton was 'essentially a teenager... in the sense that he doesn't have the cynicism that comes as we grow up: he is rash, he has the courage to try new things and see whether they work. I thought, "Here I can learn something, do something new."'

In the same article, Benetton recalled Toscani's first campaign: 'It was for a line of children's clothes, and instead of using kids he used teddy bears. I realized early on that he had extraordinary vision.'

But the teddy bears gave laughably little indication of how far Toscani would push his Benetton campaigns. His earliest images appropriated the theme of multiculturalism ('United Colors of Benetton'), and although they remained within the boundaries of acceptable taste, they were already ahead of their time. Towards the end of the decade, though, Toscani's work became more provocative, with an image of a black woman breastfeeding a white baby. This was followed a short time later by a picture of two little girls, one white and one black. The black girl's hair had been sculpted into the shape of two devilish horns. Was the ad racist – or was it a comment on racism? It was impossible to tell, which was exactly what Toscani had intended. This was no longer advertising: it was fuel for debate.

The provocations continued throughout the 1990s: a nun kissing a priest, mating horses, a bloodstained Bosnian soldier's uniform, black and white wrists manacled together, the aforementioned AIDS victim... The willingness of the press to deplore images that it would not have hesitated to exploit for its own ends guaranteed swathes of media coverage for Benetton and Toscani. In the meantime, the pair launched a stylish photography magazine, *Colors*, and a pioneering art school, Fabrica – 'an electronic Bauhaus'.

Some articles sneeringly referred to the fact that Toscani had once compared his relationship with Benetton to that of Michelangelo and the Pope; but the jibes missed the point. What he meant was that he saw his work as art, and that he did not see any contradiction in the fact that it was funded by advertising. The original source is probably a quote in *The Guardian* newspaper: 'Historically, a lot of art was publicity. It was selling an ideology or a product. In the Church, for example, Renaissance artists worked for the Pope. We all work for the Pope. There is always a Pope somewhere' ('Death is the last pornographic issue left', 2 February 1998).

Toscani could have quietly exhibited his imagery in a gallery in the depths of New York's SoHo, where it would have generated little more than a raised eyebrow. Instead, thanks to the patronage of Benetton, he was able to confront the wider public with discomfiting scenes torn from the world around them. To an extent the images were pointless: they weren't offering any solutions, and Benetton didn't appear to actively support any of the causes it latched on to. But Toscani was not in the business of providing easy answers, just raising difficult questions. And one thing was for sure: he certainly didn't set out to sell sweaters. Instead, he considered that Benetton was funding research into alternative approaches to communication. 'A sweater has two sleeves, wool is wool,' he told *The Guardian*. 'The product is more or less the same. The difference is the communications.'

Other advertisers of the 1990s seemed keen to emulate Benetton. Confrontation was the order of the day. Coyness was abandoned, taboos were attacked; sex and swearing came streaking out of the closet. The British 'master of shockvertising', as *The Express* newspaper dubbed him (8 June 2001), was TBWA's Trevor Beattie. In truth, Beattie's much-talked-about ad for the Wonderbra was more sensual than shocking. The poster featured the supermodel Eva Herzigova showing off a décolletage that could literally stop traffic, accompanied by the words, 'Hello Boys'. A little nearer the knuckle was Beattie's campaign for French Connection UK, which made use of the fashion brand's initials in the form FCUK. 'FCUK Fashion!' yelled a poster, to growls of media disapproval.

Not long afterwards, fashion designer Tom Ford commissioned an image of the voluptuous Sophie Dahl lying invitingly naked apart from, presumably, a dab of advertiser Yves Saint Laurent's Opium perfume. Was the picture shocking, sexist – or just harmlessly titillating? Opinion was divided. The ad was the latest in a trend that the fashion community had branded 'porno chic'.

Commenting on the 'shockvertising' phenomenon, Trevor Beattie observed, 'These ads aren't shocking; what is shocking is the rank mediocrity of 90 per cent of British advertising, which means that anything remotely different stands out.'

The same article pointed out that, thanks to Toscani's advertising, Benetton had recently been judged the 10th most powerful brand in fashion ('Why shock tactics work like a dream', *Sunday Business*, 29 August 1999).

But if shock advertising was in vogue (not to mention in *Vogue*), Toscani was the doyen of the genre. His work was far darker and more serious than anything attempted by his contemporaries. His final campaign for Benetton was the most controversial of all. It featured pictures of men facing execution on death row. As might have been expected, it generated a storm of outrage in the United States, with calls for a boycott of Benetton products.

A little while later, in May 2000, Benetton and Toscani went their separate ways, ending an extraordinary 18-year partnership. In a press release at the time, Luciano Benetton thanked Toscani for his 'fundamental contribution' to the company. Toscani simply stated that it was time to move on.

The clothing company may have come to regret Toscani's departure, as its advertising slumped into cosy conformity. Certainly, nobody defaced its posters or was gnashing and wailing about it in the press. In fact, nobody spoke about it much at all.

Which may have been why Benetton returned to something approaching shock advertising with its 'Unhate' print campaign of 2011. The PhotoShopped images showed world leaders with conflicting views throwing aside their differences and themselves into one another's arms, locked in a passionate kiss. And so US President Barack Obama was pictured snogging Chinese leader Hu Jintao, then-French President Nicolas Sarkozy puckered up for Angela Merkel and Palestinian leader Mahmoud Abbas was shown kissing Israeli prime minister Benjamin Netanyahu.

A picture of Pope Benedict XVI passionately kissing Egyptian imam Ahmed Mohamed el-Tayeb was inevitably denounced by the Vatican, which threatened legal action. Benetton withdrew it, but not before it had generated reams of media coverage, tweets and blog posts. The campaign was the work of Fabrica, not Toscani himself – but it was firmly in his spirit. It also showed that, in a world where advertisers strive to create material that will generate a buzz across the social web, 'shockvertising' has a role to play.

## The German conundrum

On the face of it, the advertising cultures of Italy and Germany don't appear to have much in common. And yet they share certain problems. They are both seen as lacking in creativity – or at least, in the kind of accessible, border-busting creativity that reaps international awards. And they are both accused of insularity. Although Spain has traditionally had strong links with South America (see Chapter 15, Latin spirit), and both Britain and France are the hubs of multinational communications combines, German agencies have struggled to expand beyond their own borders. 'For [us], 80 million people is quite good enough,' one of the country's top agency bosses told *Campaign* magazine in 2004 ('Germany's agencies to watch', 10 September).

One explanation for Germany's lack of creative edge might be its strong manufacturing base. Britain, like Holland and Spain, has a trading history. Germany is a producer. Thus Britain makes terrific ads for cars – but Germany actually makes cars. The country has also lacked a central creative hub, a Soho or a Madison Avenue, to act as a Petri dish for talent. German creativity is shared between Frankfurt, Hamburg, Düsseldorf and, increasingly, Berlin. The relative fidelity of German clients may also contribute to a more complacent creative environment. Finally, the very late arrival of commercial television, in 1979, has also been blamed.

But early into the new millennium, Germany's stolid, housebound image began fraying at the edges. In 2003, when McDonald's challenged its agencies worldwide to come up with a new branding campaign, a German shop called Heyer & Partners won, creating the basis for the global 'I'm lovin' it' positioning. Nimble creative agencies emerged, particularly in the digital arena, to take the place of the established giants.

A clear if depressing sign that times were changing came in 2010 when iconic agency Springer & Jacoby filed for bankruptcy. It had been one of the most significant operations in the history of German advertising, along with Jung von Matt... and Scholz & Friends.

Juergen Scholz is another of those 'founding fathers' who play a role in every country's advertising history. A respected creative, in the sixties he was one of the founding members of Team, which later became Team/BBDO. In 1981 he broke away to set up Scholz & Friends in Hamburg. Just over 10 years later he retired, having created what local trade magazine *Horizont* described as 'the agency of the decade'. Following his departure, the Bates network moved in and acquired 80 per cent of the agency.

Scholz & Friends flourished by staying one step ahead of the game. When it lost a chunk of Mars' pet food business, it threw its energy behind another of its biggest clients, the tobacco brand Reemstma, aiding that company's expansion by setting up branch offices in several European capitals. Following the fall of the Berlin Wall, Scholz was the first agency into the former East Germany, opening an office first in Dresden, then in central Berlin. In 2000 it merged with the TV production company UVE, giving the agency the ability to create branded TV shows for clients. And in 2003 it bought itself out of its network owner – then the Cordiant Group – with the aid of a private equity company.

Scholz even managed to wrench opportunity from the jaws of the recession that decimated the German advertising industry. By 2005, following its management buyout from Cordiant, it was effectively the biggest independent network in Europe, with 900 staff and turnover in the region of 80 million euros. It had also won clients including Ideal Standard, Siemens, Masterfoods, Nike and AOL – not to mention the job of promoting the 2006 World Cup.

'We have the recession to thank for our success,' joint chief executive Sebastian Turner told *Campaign*. 'If we hadn't found ourselves in a situation two years ago where we didn't show a profit, we wouldn't have had the courage to drastically overhaul the company' ('German creativity blooms as recession persists', 22 April 2005).

The revamp knocked down the walls between marketing disciplines. Instead of treating, say, TV advertising and direct marketing as separate issues with compartmentalized budgets, integrated teams would apply their expertise to each campaign from the beginning. The idea was to create a fully integrated network, although the agency used the term 'orchestra of ideas'. It's the kind of thinking that is becoming increasingly common as agencies adapt to the digital environment (see Chapter 20, The agency of the future).

Nevertheless, one of Scholz's most famous campaigns is a long-running series of print ads for the newspaper *Frankfurter Allgemeine Zeitung* (FAZ). Well-known personalities are photographed in dramatic settings, their faces hidden behind the broadsheet newspaper, in which they are clearly engrossed. The tagline reads, 'There's always a clever mind behind it.'

While Scholz & Friends has managed to remain coolly aloof, two of Germany's best-known creative agencies, Springer & Jacoby and Jung von Matt, had a vaguely incestuous relationship.

But let's not get ahead of ourselves. The wild card in the history of German advertising is the Swiss-based agency network GGK (which later linked up with the Lowe Group). The original agency was founded in 1959 by the highly respected graphic designer Karl Gerstner, along with Paul Gredinger and Markus Kutter. GGK established several European branches – and in the 1970s its German office was considered the country's most creative agency. It was at GGK that Reinhard Springer and Konstantin Jacoby met.

Reinhard Springer left to open his own agency in 1979, at the dawn of the country's commercial television service, with copywriter Konstantin Jacoby joining him a little while later. Some say Springer & Jacoby invented modern German advertising. Together they mastered what was effectively a new medium, injecting a universal humour into their work while at the same time providing a disciplined, professional working environment.

Leading German creative Jean-Remy von Matt, who joined the agency in 1986, recalls, 'There were many strict rules. The agency's founders were the protagonists of a tough, rigorous approach.' Self-respect was encouraged. 'Reinhard Springer, for example, never waited longer than 10 minutes for a meeting – even if it was his first contact with a big prospective client.'

Although the agency operated on a modest scale for some years, it leapt into the big time in 1989 when Mercedes awarded its account to the agency. With this highly prestigious win under its belt, S&J gained more clients and secured the top slot in the country's creative league table.

The advertising industry, you will have noticed, resembles a slide of amoeba under a microscope, with elements constantly breaking off and reforming. The German advertising scene is no different. And so in 1991 Jean-Remy von Matt and his colleague Holger Jung left Springer & Jacoby to set up their own agency, Jung von Matt.

Jean-Remy von Matt entered the advertising business in 1975 as a copy-writer in Düsseldorf, 'which at the time was a boomtown of creativity'.

His first task was to create a print ad for a company that made shower screens: 'I wrote the headline and the copy – and because the male model for the photo was sick, I did that job too.'

He later went to Ogilvy & Mather in Frankfurt, and then to a hot shop in Munich. Finally, after another five years of hard work at Springer & Jacoby, he – like his business partner Holger Jung – was ready to take a risk. Acquiring a former corset factory as their headquarters, they installed a 14-foot-high Trojan horse in the foyer. The horse reminded staff and clients that 'good advertising... has an attractive exterior, resembles a gift and delights the heart. But inside, the hard-hitting core is consistently aimed at a specific target' ('Germany's creative hot shops', *Campaign*, 17 April 1998).

Jung von Matt grew quickly. 'We started with seven people,' says Jean-Remy, 'ten years later we had 500 – so our biggest challenge in the early years was to find enough talent to fulfil our ambitions, as well the expectations of the market. Today we have a staff of 650 in four countries – with hopefully more to come in Eastern Europe.'

One of the agency's flagship accounts was BMW. In a memorable TV spot, a good-looking guy gets into an open-top BMW Z3 sports car and roars off down a country road. He pops a cassette into the player and a song begins: 'Oh Lord, won't you buy me a Mercedes Benz...' In an obvious jibe at the auto maker's competitor (and its advertising agency?) the driver pops the tape out of the machine and chucks it over his shoulder.

This was a fine sentiment until the summer of 2006, when Mercedes announced that it was taking its account away from Springer & Jacoby and giving it to Jung von Matt. After much soul-searching, Jung von Matt had been forced to resign the BMW account. It started work as the lead agency for Mercedes in January 2007.

After being buffeted by the recession, Springer & Jacoby found itself back in the role of creative outsider, under pressure to prove itself again. The agency pledged to reconfigure itself for the new era of digital marketing. It remained, as one German executive stressed, 'a school and a reference for the German advertising community'. But past glories were evidently not enough to assure its future: in April 2010, shortly after its 30th birthday, the agency filed for bankruptcy, having failed to survive the departure of Mercedes.

However, as an article in *Advertising Age* pointed out, its spirit lived on; not only in Jung von Matt, but also in Kemper Trautmann – another respected independent agency co-founded by an S&J alumnus – and in Germany's growing number of creative hot shops ('Iconic German agency Springer & Jacoby closes', 15 April 2010).

Constantin Kaloff, a former creative director of S & J, summed up: 'Springer & Jacoby was the mother of all creative agencies in Germany, the architect of our creative landscape.'

# Media spins off

## 10

*'Let us spend your money'*

The 'full service' advertising agency ceased to exist some time ago. By 2000 there was barely an advertising agency left that still had its own media department. The business of selecting and buying media space had practically become a separate industry – comparable with research, direct marketing, or event management. And there lies the rub: in a world of converging media, it has become almost impossible to separate these disciplines. Clients are now demanding multimedia campaigns that combine the firepower of TV, digital, outdoor, sponsored events and a host of other points of contact with consumers, with one underpinning creative strategy. This requires highly skilled media planning. Crucially, it requires a tight partnership between the creative and media teams. It might help if they were in the same building.

This development has left the advertising agencies rather shamefaced. Having spun off their media departments into highly profitable self-contained units, they may now have to figure out a way of getting them back. Some say that the links between the 'creative' and 'media' agencies are strong enough to address clients' needs. Others are less convinced. At a forum organized by the British creative advertising journal *Shots* in March 2006, one executive said, 'Separating media from creative was the worst mistake the industry ever made.'

We'll return to this argument at the end of the chapter. But for now the key question is: how did we come to this pretty pass? For the answer, we must first return to Paris.

## The 24-carat idea of Gilbert Gross

Gilbert Gross was born on 3 April 1931, the son of shopkeepers. As a young man he worked for a tiny advertising agency at the top of rue Lafayette, the long straight avenue that runs between the Gare du Nord and the Opéra Garnier. For the time being, there was little to indicate that he would create a new branch of the advertising profession.

'It was tough, but not as tough as it had been just before my arrival,' says Gross – who now is an imposing, bronzed, silver-haired gentleman in his mid-seventies. 'As you know, we made our money by accepting a commission of 15 per cent from the media every time we placed a client's ad with them. At that time, the government had just overturned a rule that said if you took a client from another advertising agency, they continued to receive the commission for *two years*. This had completely blocked the market to new entrants.'

Despite the scrapping of this terrifying regulation in the mid-1950s, Gross was forced to go from door-to-door along the rue Lafayette, soliciting for business. 'I remember my first client was a shoe store called Aux de Lions, a minuscule small ads account. The next client was a tailor... basically, it was a struggle.'

Eventually, Gross won the creative account for a brand of coffee owned by Perrier. He was told that while he would be paid a fee for his creative work on a freelance basis, the media placement would be handled by Havas. 'There were a series of meetings at which I met a certain Monsieur Clément, who was responsible for the media placement. During our conversations, I realized that he was able to negotiate the media space for a much lower price than the client might have imagined. I also noticed that he drove a very nice car. It still took me a while to work out what was going on, though.'

Gross became friendly with Clément, who invited him along to a lunch with the advertising sales director of a large regional newspaper. 'It was like being in the bazaar at Marrakech,' he chuckles. 'I'd always accepted that the rates for advertising space were fixed... but no, not at all! It was, "If I buy two pages what kind of deal can you do for me?" and so on. All this while sipping wine and eating fine food in a very jovial atmosphere: I began to realize I was in the wrong job.'

Inspired by this experience, Gilbert approached the beer brand Champigneulles and offered to place its media at reduced rates. 'The boss, René Hinzelin, was a friend of mine. He didn't think my idea would work but he gave me a chance. After all, if I came to you and said "If I can get you a cheaper electricity bill, can I take my fee out of the difference?" you'd probably agree. You've got nothing to lose! And so

I went to a newspaper and began to use the same arguments as Clément: "If I buy two pages and guarantee a lot more in the future, can you do me a deal?" It worked like a charm.'

And so a new metier – the independent media buyer – was born. Shortly afterwards, the BSN group (now Danone) acquired Champigneulles along with another beer brand, Kronenbourg. 'I thought that was it; my short run as an independent media buyer was over. But they called me in for a meeting and said, "We've noticed you've been able to negotiate some very advantageous rates. How would you like to take care of media for the whole group?" Suddenly, I had the biggest media account in France.'

Shortly afterwards, Gross won the French media-buying account for Coca-Cola. Soon the combined media clout of his accounts enabled him to buy blocks of space a year in advance and resell them piecemeal to clients, guaranteeing a fixed income for his media contacts. It was this media buying operation that became Carat (*Centrale d'Achat, Radio, Affichage, Television*) in 1966. In order to offer an extended service to international clients, Gross began to set up offices in Europe and beyond.

All went well until the introduction in 1993 of the Loi Sapin ('The Sapin Law'), designed to create 'transparency' in the French marketplace. It effectively fixed media rates and cut the media agency out of the transaction between advertisers and media supports. Gross uses a neat metaphor: 'It meant that instead of going to the market and buying vegetables in bulk, then selling them to customers and pocketing some of the money we saved them, we were reduced to telling them whether carrots or cauliflowers were better for their health. We became consultants rather than traders.' (The law exists only in France – elsewhere, media independents are free to act as both traders *and* consultants.)

Although Gross admits that the Loi Sapin 'cost us a lot', Carat eventually flourished in its new consultancy role. The advantage it offered to clients became qualitative rather than quantitative: thanks to its media expertise, it could advise brands on exactly where and when they should be seen in order to achieve maximum impact for their campaigns. This expertise would be paid for on an entirely above-board fee basis.

Carat is part of the British communications group Aegis, which bought a stake in the company in 1990 and became a full owner in the years following the introduction of the Loi Sapin. Carat's headquarters were then shifted to London. Entirely free from agency ties, it is the world's largest independent media consultancy. A host of other media specialists were spun out of full-service advertising agencies. The motivation for creating them was partly practical, but largely financial.

## From barter to Zenith

Independent media buying in the United States essentially grew out of barter arrangements. You might provide some studio equipment to a small TV company. In return, rather than paying cash, they would give you TV advertising slots. Then you'd have to sell them on.

One barterer-turned-buyer was Norman King, founder of a company called US Media. In 1970, he prophetically told the Association of National Advertisers that their 'giant agencies' were not buying media efficiently. 'For years, now, your agency has been spending millions of dollars and nobody's been really watching them,' he said. 'My suggestion is, let us spend [the money] and let your agency watch us' ('The day the prices fell', *Inside Media*, 1 January 1992). Unfortunately, a year later, US Media went out of business.

At around the same time, Dennis Holt started Western International Media in Los Angeles. A far more solid concern, over the years this swelled into a media-buying behemoth with blue-chip clients such as Disney. In 1994 Holt sold it to the communications group Interpublic, which re-named it Initiative Media.

In London, in 1972, a young man named Chris Ingram was made responsible for merging the media departments of seven agencies belonging to the KMP group. He suddenly found himself running a standalone division of 50 or so people, which was cunningly christened The Media Department. 'This was the birth of the agency-owned media specialist,' he says. But during the 1973 recession, Ingram feared that the media function would be merged back into the main agency, so he left to start his own media planning and buying shop, CIA (Chris Ingram Associates).

Another important landmark came in 1985 when Ray Morgan, who headed Mercury Media at Benton & Bowles, left with most of his staff and clients to set up a standalone media operation, Ray Morgan & Partners. Three years later it was acquired by the Saatchis, who wanted it to handle media for their growing collection of agencies. The operation was re-branded Zenith. This opened the floodgates for the tide of re-named agency media operations that emerged throughout the 1990s: MediaCom, MindShare, Starcom... the list was long and bewildering.

The birth of the media independent was partly driven by industry consolidation (see next chapter) which meant that single agencies were subsumed by larger communications groups. A standalone operation could buy media on behalf of all the agencies in the group, giving it enormous negotiating clout with media owners. At the same time, it could pitch for clients whose creative work was not held by any of its associated creative agencies. It could also bolt on a whole range of consultancy services for which it could charge additional fees. The overall result: more income for the parent group.

## Turning back the clock

Although the creative agencies clearly feel uncomfortable talking about it, there is a lingering suspicion that letting go of the media planning function may have been an error. An early hint of this came in 2000 with the formation of Naked, a new breed of independent agency designed to help clients coordinate the scattered disciplines (see Chapter 20, The agency of the future). More recently, a number of agencies have launched initiatives designed to bring the media and creative functions closer together. BBH called this new discipline 'engagement planning'. TBWA preferred the term 'connections planning'.

But there is certainly no consensus that a return to full service is an attractive idea. Media specialists argue that in the full service era, clients were too often persuaded that the best way to raise their profile was via television advertising – which coincidentally meant bigger bucks and a greater chance of creative awards for the agency. The media planners' oft-touted philosophy of 'media neutrality' means that if a cheap but targeted blog is more appropriate to the client's needs, then that's what they should pay for.

Jack Klues, who created Leo Burnett's spin-off media operation, Starcom, insists that unbundling actually took place at the behest of the clients. 'Clients push for change. We try to keep pace with them, or even interpret what they want and get ahead of them, but at the end of the day the advertising landscape is moulded by them. I'd be disappointed if anyone thought that the media businesses were formed to serve the egos of people like Chris Ingram or myself. This turned out to be the best way of doing our job – but we're not trying to do it at anyone's expense. Some of my friends in the creative agencies say, "You guys are trying to take over the world!"' He laughs. 'Well, maybe that will happen – but it's not my agenda.'

Kevin Roberts, the straight-talking worldwide boss of Saatchi & Saatchi, dismisses the very notion of a return to the old days: 'It's the burning question that everybody's asking – but it's the wrong bloody question. Old notions of media are no longer relevant. In my view there is no such thing as media any more: all we've got are consumers and connections. What clients need is a group of consumer experts from all over our world, sitting around the same table, before the brief has even been set. In fact, briefs are useless because the clients usually don't even know what they want. So give me a group of people who can *feel* what the consumer needs. Do those people all need to come from the same company? Of course not.'

In any case, there's no going back. It's impossible, not to mention pointless, to compare the original single-celled advertising agencies with today's highly complex marketing giants.

# Consolidation incorporated

## 11

*'Almost everyone in advertising works for one of five different companies'*

## Omnicom: the Big Bang

Orchestrating a mega-merger is a stressful business. Some evenings, Keith Reinhard would stand at his office window, overlooking St Patrick's Cathedral on Madison Avenue, and wonder quietly, 'What the hell have I done?' Reinhard had just helped to coordinate the pairing of giant agencies DDB and BBDO under a new holding company called Omnicom. At the same time, he'd merged his own agency – Needham Harper – with DDB. What seemed like half of Madison Avenue, and a fair chunk of Chicago, was moving under one roof. No wonder Reinhard's office felt a little stuffy.

He could hardly believe that he was now running Doyle Dane Bernbach, an agency he'd revered since before he got his first job in advertising, when he was fresh out of high school in Berne, Indiana. 'My fascination with Bill Bernbach and his band of revolutionaries started very early,' he recalls, years later. 'I was absolutely certain that advertising was the career for me, even though I had no education, no experience and little evidence of any talent. Nonetheless I would look forward eagerly to the weekly issues of *Life* magazine, where the Volkswagen ads were appearing. I would tack them up on my wall.'

Reinhard initially wanted to be an art director, and he spent a long time 'hanging around art studios and bumping into agency big shots', while never quite snagging the agency job he coveted. Finally he got an interview with a Chicago outfit called Needham Louis & Brorby. 'They looked at my art book and said, "Would you consider being a copywriter?"' He laughs. 'I said, "Sure, that would be great." Turned out I'd written a couple of scripts that they liked. So at the age of 29, in 1964, I became the oldest new copywriter at the agency.'

Over the years the agency evolved into Needham Harper Worldwide (in 1965 it merged with a New York agency to create Needham, Harper & Steers – with the incoming agency's chief, Paul Harper, in the top slot). And Reinhard's career evolved too, as he climbed the creative ladder and eventually became president and CEO of the agency. Not bad for a guy who started out as a 'paste-up boy' in the Midwest. He'd also relocated from Chicago to run the agency from New York, where it was now headquartered.

Reinhard had never lost his admiration for Bernbach. And as it happened, there was a link between Needham Harper and the late DDB co-founder. Bernbach had had several meetings with Paul Harper, whom Reinhard had succeeded as president. 'Harper had a much lower profile in the industry than Bernbach, but they respected one another. He and Bill got together as early as 1978 to see if there might be a possibility of merging the two companies. Even then, people were beginning to see the emergence of a global advertising industry, and on paper, at least, the merger made sense: geographically we were stronger in different regions around the world, and of course Needham was strong in Chicago, where DDB had little presence.'

They also had similar values: both were committed to creativity as their raison d'être. Yet the two agency bosses couldn't come to terms – Reinhard suspects that there may have been a clash of egos over whose name would go on the door. In any event, the merger never happened and it remained a missed opportunity when Bill Bernbach died in 1982.

That same year, Reinhard took over as the boss of Needham Harper. 'I gathered everyone together and said, "Look, we have to do something. We're the number 16 agency in the world. It seems clear to me that the advertising industry is going to become a two-tier business. There will always be vitality in the bottom tier, the boutique agencies. And then there will be a top tier of maybe six or seven giants. There will be no middle. Unfortunately, we're in the middle. And we better find a way out."'

There was no way the agency could climb out of the gap on its own – it would have needed to grow another 40 per cent year on year. Other possibilities were considered, but Reinhard remained convinced that DDB was the solution. Bernbach's agency was past its glory days at that point, languishing in a similar position to that of Needham Harper, at about 13th in the market.

'I'd only met Bill in person a couple of times, and perhaps had a handful of telephone conversations with him, but I felt that the two agencies could be right together. It had been reported that Bill felt uncomfortable with international – he liked to have a hand in every-thing that came out of the agency. My idea was to take his insights about human nature and communications, and apply them to a world which bore almost no resemblance to the one in which he'd created his busi-ness. My passion was to take his principles of creativity and apply them to new media and to the global marketplace.'

Reinhard began wooing Bernbach's successors at the top of DDB – to no avail. The issue dragged on into the autumn of 1985, when Reinhard began a series of discreet discussions with Allen Rosenshine, then president and CEO of BBDO. The pair would meet at the Stanhope Hotel, 'because ad people never went there'. Initial conversations about the state of the industry deepened into talk of a merger. Reinhard says, 'I admitted to Allen that my real passion was for Doyle Dane Bernbach. And he said, "Wait a minute – we've also had some conversations with DDB." That's when things got serious. We thought, OK, a three-way merger was such a big idea that the lawyers and the nay-sayers would never be able to stand in our way.'

The pair began a series of secret meetings with Bernbach's son, John, and the president and CEO of DDB, Barry Loughrane. Using the code-name 'Stanhope', they'd change hotel suites with every meeting so finan-cial journalists didn't sniff out the merger. (Two of the three companies were publicly held at the time and the stock price would have been affected if the news had leaked out.) On Friday 25 April 1986, the deal was finally sealed. The announcement would be made the following Monday.

The process took on a vital urgency when, at the last minute, Saatchi & Saatchi arrived at the table with more money. But the DDB board was wary of the swashbuckling British brothers and after an agonizing meeting voted to move ahead with Needham Harper. On that Friday, the palpable air of tension was increased by the fact that *The Wall Street Journal* had heard a rumour about the merger, but couldn't stand it up enough to run a full story. 'Meanwhile, we had an army of young people poised to ring the clients and managers of three different agencies to tell them what was going on. And we had to do it before Monday morning.'

The following Monday, 28 April, *The New York Times* ran a story headlined: 'Three-way merger to create largest advertising agency.' Three of the world's top 20 agencies had merged in a deal that gave them combined billings of US$5 billion a year and a workforce of more than 10,000 people. Bearing in mind this was more than 20 years ago, the article was prophetic. It read, 'Advertising has gained enormous status... because [it is] responsible for adding perceived differences in products where actual differences, because of technological advances, often no longer exist... Another pressure is driving agencies into international expansion to accommodate their clients' multinational marketing goals. Some analysts of the advertising scene are convinced that the agency side will soon consist of just a few giant multinational organizations and a multitude of small local and regional makers of advertising.'

And the merger presaged a further trend – that of global communications groups as providers of vast arsenals of marketing services, far beyond mere advertising. To this end, the fused operation included an entity called Diversified Agency Services (DAS) to take care of 'below-the-line' activities; such as direct marketing, public relations and sales promotion that did not employ traditional advertising techniques.

No personal fortunes were created by the deal: this was about three creative agencies bonding to safeguard their identities in an increasingly rapacious market. The merger was accomplished through an exchange of stock. Each of the three companies got new shares in the holding company, based on a merger of equals and judged by what each was worth. The press nicknamed the deal 'The Big Bang'.

Owing to client conflicts, a merger of this size was bound to result in account losses. *Campaign* magazine reported that, altogether, the three agencies had lost clients worth US$250 million a year in billings, including the US$85 million Honda account – which departed due to a conflict with DDB's famous VW account and BBDO's work for Chrysler Dodge. Other losses included RJR Nabisco, IBM and Procter & Gamble ('What cost the mega-mergers?', 26 September 1986).

As the new chief of DDB Needham, Reinhard had another challenge on his hands: converging the cultures of two giant agencies. Although the DDB staff understood that he was a 'creative guy' and a Bernbach fan, they remained prickly about the new set-up. 'You can't imagine the "us versus them" attitude; the number of "we don't do things that way" remarks. It was bad enough in New York, but overseas – where we couldn't be present to smooth things over – virtual civil wars broke out. The managers of both merging agencies would tell the local press, "Yes, there has been a merger – and I'm in charge."'

As for the press, it was overwhelmingly critical. 'I think only *Ad Age* had anything positive to say about us. They commended us for our courage – because we'd done what we thought was right without asking any clients. But everyone else was overwhelmingly negative.'

Bearing in mind the previously lacklustre status of the three agencies involved, some journalists wondered whether the Omnicom merger really solved anything. One Madison Avenue commentator joked that the name stood for 'Operations May Not Improve Considering Our Merger'.

To add to the overheated atmosphere, Saatchi & Saatchi – having failed to win control of DDB – paid US$507 million for the Ted Bates agency, creating an operation worth US$7.5 billion and immediately cutting short Omnicom's reign as the world's biggest advertising group. 'The press felt that mega-mergers were not about serving clients – they were about greed,' says Reinhard.

And so he would stand at his window – in the office that had once belonged to Bill Bernbach – and gaze into the night while wondering if he'd ever be able to straighten things out. His passionate belief in the long-term rightness of the project weighed against any transitory misgivings, however. 'Allen [Rosenshine] and I were convinced that we could create a holding company dedicated to creativity... There's a perception that size is the natural enemy of creativity; but what's important is not size, it's the culture and philosophy of the network.'

A respected creative in his own right, Allen Rosenshine initially stepped up from his post at BBDO to run Omnicom. In 1999, however, he returned to running the agency – a job he preferred – and Bruce Crawford took over at the helm of Omnicom. A former chairman of BBDO, Crawford was running the New York Metropolitan Opera when Rosenshine invited him, half in jest, to take on the job. Rosenshine worried that BBDO was beginning to lose its identity. Besides, as he explained to *Adweek* shortly before his retirement in 2006, 'running Omnicom was not right for me. My experience didn't lie in managing and running a public company and dealing with analysts and promoting the stock and all the things you have to do.'

Rosenshine's self-awareness proved critical to the future of Omnicom, which flourished under Crawford. One of his first acts was to revamp

DAS into a streamlined collection of marketing operations. He was helped in that task by John Wren, who took over as chief executive in 1996. DAS is now the biggest earner for the Omnicom group.

At the time of writing, Omnicom serves more than 5,000 clients in 100 countries and has an operating income of US$1.6 billion a year (2011 annual report). As well as BBDO and DDB, its subsidiaries include TBWA and the media specialists OMG and PHD. Surprisingly, given its vast size, it has largely managed to maintain the 'creative' identity envisaged by Reinhard and Rosenshine. It is praised for its hands-off management policy, which allows outfits like AMV BBDO, TBWA, Goodby Silverstein & Partners and others to carry on doing their creative thing.

For many years Omnicom occupied the top slot in a shifting peloton of holding companies that included WPP, Interpublic, Publicis Groupe and Japan's Dentsu. But in 2011 WPP bustled its way to the top, having snapped up market research company TNS in 2008.

# WPP: wired to the world

'Forty is a dangerous age,' says Sir Martin Sorrell. 'When male executives turn 40 they should put a red flag on their computers. It's the male menopause, or andropause. There's always a chance they might do something unpredictable.'

Like start a company that grows into one of the biggest marketing communications groups in the world, for instance? After all, that's what Sorrell did. This feisty, energetic man – who is often described as 'aggressive' by the press, which suggests that journalists rub him up the wrong way – built an empire from a damp basement office. And the male menopause provided the spark. 'I thought it was my last chance to start a business,' he says. 'There's an optimum period in your mid-thirties. At 30 you still lack experience. At 40 you look back at what you've achieved and decide what you want to do next.'

Twenty-five years later, the company he started owns four historic advertising agencies – J Walter Thompson, Ogilvy & Mather, Young & Rubicam and Grey – as well as a host of other communications, research and branding operations; around 100 marketing services companies in total. Sorrell dislikes the description 'conglomerate' because it implies that these businesses are disconnected, while WPP aims to offer its clients access to any or all of its component parts. *Fortune* magazine once described it as a 'marketing machine'.

Sorrell's extraordinary story is a testament to the potential rewards that await entrepreneurs with the right formula of determination, talent and luck. Knighted in 2000 for services to the communications industry, Sir Martin grew up in an ordinary middle-class Jewish home. His grandparents were émigrés from Eastern Europe; his father Jack a successful businessman in the electrical retail trade. Sorrell's father died a few years ago, but he remains the WPP chief executive's ultimate hero. 'Above all he taught me the value of persistence. He also told me that the secret to success in life was to find one thing, one company, and focus on it. He thought the whole idea of portfolios was nonsense.'

But while his father had left school at the age of 13, Sorrell was armed with a first-class education. After Haberdashers' Aske's Boys' School, he attended Christ's College, Cambridge – where he studied economics – and then Harvard Business School. His career began with stints at Glendinning Associates, a marketing consultancy now half-owned by WPP, and Mark McCormack's sports marketing company. At his next job, working for investment and management advisor James Gulliver, Sorrell came into contact with Saatchi & Saatchi. Gulliver advised the brothers to take on a full-time finance director and Sorrell was offered the job.

Unlike many of those who worked in London in the 1970s, Sorrell is disinclined to look back upon the period as a 'golden age' of advertising. 'I think that's the attitude of nostalgic old men,' he says. 'If anything, the industry is more interesting today than it was then. But it was a time when creative brands were beginning to grapple with global opportunities.'

Having grappled on behalf of Saatchi & Saatchi since 1977, Sorrell reached that 'dangerous age' in 1985 and realized that if he wanted to do something for himself, it was now or never. He and stockbroker Preston Rabl raised a loan to acquire Wire & Plastic Products, an innocuous manufacturer of shopping baskets. Appropriately enough, this was to be the receptacle for a collection of below-the-line businesses. Sorrell felt that the non-advertising components of marketing were undervalued. After a dozen or so carefully judged acquisitions in that sphere, his attention was diverted, almost despite himself, by J Walter

Thompson. It was an opportunistic move, he admits. 'Somebody wrote at the time that the agency had problems in places where most companies didn't even have places.'

The takeover of the legendary American agency brand was plotted from an unlikely base in London. At that point, Sorrell and Rabl were still working in a basement office in Lincoln's Inn Fields. 'The place was quite modern, reasonably trendy; let's not exaggerate. But it was below road level and whenever it rained the water would pour in. In the middle of the JWT bid we had plasterers in repairing the wall to keep the damp at bay.'

Sorrell had taken a look at J Walter Thompson and seen its potential. There was still the great brand name. It would make WPP genuinely global, opening the door to Asia. Plus, it remained strong creatively in London and New York. But profit margins were shrinking and Burger King, a major client, had just put its account up for review. Initially, WPP built up a 5 per cent stake. This escalated into the advertising industry's first hostile takeover, which Sorrell finally pulled off in June 1987, after just 13 days, acquiring JWT for US $566 million.

But there was another, unexpected fillip to the deal. Half-buried on J Walter Thompson's balance sheet was a freehold property – a building that Sorrell had assumed to be the agency's Berkeley Square headquarters. It turned out to be a building in Tokyo, which Sorrell subsequently sold for US $200 million, walking away with US $100 million after tax.

With that deal under his belt, two years later Sorrell turned his attention to the next agency prize: Ogilvy & Mather. As mentioned earlier, David Ogilvy was far from overjoyed by the prospect, infamously describing Sorrell as 'an odious little shit' who had 'never written an advertisement in his life'. At the time, they had never met. Realizing that the prospect of letting O&M go would be emotionally wrenching for the adland veteran, Sorrell had been half-expecting such a response. He won Ogilvy over by reading and quoting from all his books and offering, in person, to make him non-executive chairman of the merged company. Ogilvy apologized for his comments and their relationship was one of equanimity from that moment on.

Not so the future of WPP, which lurched like a galleon overloaded with booty. Sorrell had paid US $860 million for Ogilvy & Mather, using debt and preferred stock rather than equity. In the wake of the takeover,

O&M lost some senior staff and key clients. And then, in 1991, the recession struck. Analysts issued warnings and WPP's share price plummeted. Sorrell's company came close, very close, to going under. He survived only thanks to his, as *Campaign* put it, 'forensic knowledge of how banks operate' ('WPP at Twenty', 29 April 2005).

When I ask Sorrell if he feels that this was a necessary part of the learning process, I can almost hear his knuckles whitening around the phone. 'No, absolutely not: I would never have wanted to put myself or anybody else in the company through that. I made a mistake, that's all. If I'd done the deal with half-debt, half-equity, it would never have reached that stage. Our shares were down to about 30p at one point. It was a dreadful period.'

But WPP clawed its way back to the surface – as did O&M, landing the consolidated IBM account in 1994. WPP grew steadily thereafter, with no dramatic acquisitions for a time. Instead, Sorrell concentrated on his founding principle of knitting together a cohesive range of marketing services operations. 'Clients want solutions to problems,' he says, unknowingly echoing Kevin Roberts over at Saatchi & Saatchi. 'And they want the benefit of access to as many varied solutions to their problems as possible. At the end of the day, I don't think they care too much about agency brands.'

This ability to provide solutions was demonstrated in 1997 when Sorrell brought the JWT and O&M media departments together to create MindShare, a unique operation at the time. By 2000, he was ready to net a big fish again, this time securing Young & Rubicam for US $4.7 billion. In short order, WPP acquired The Tempus Group (the former CIA) for £400 million. Admittedly it tried to pull out at the last minute as the markets went into convulsion following the 11 September 2001 attacks; but the negative was turned into a positive with the creation of yet another hefty merged media buying organization. More recently, in 2005, Sorrell bought the Grey Global Group for US $1.75 billion.

Is this size for the sake of size? You might think so; but over the years WPP has bagged some huge consolidated accounts – HSBC, Samsung and Vodafone, for instance – and its wide range of agencies means that it can work for conflicting accounts, such as Unilever and parts of Procter & Gamble. Additionally, WPP's diversified portfolio shelters it, somewhat, from the economic cycle. As Sorrell told *Business Today*, 'There's a wave phenomenon that happens in a recession... The thing that gets affected first is advertising and media management; then, public relations and public affairs, next, branding. The... functional spread gives us a little bit of insularity' ('Advertising is local, regional and global', 21 December 2003).

Today WPP is the world's largest marketing communications group, with billings of US $7.1 billion, revenues of US $16.1 billion and a staff of around 160,000, working out of 3,000 offices in 110 countries. Alongside the advertising entities mentioned above, its vast box of tricks includes research companies, PR networks, branding and corporate identity specialists, direct marketing outfits and healthcare communications; as well as every imaginable element of the marketing mix, from internet strategy to sponsorship.

Sir Martin Sorrell remains very much involved in WPP, even to the extent of occasionally being labelled a 'micro-manager'; something he does not regard as an insult. 'This is not business, it's personal,' he says. 'I didn't inherit anything – there was no Marcel Bleustein-Blanchet before me – I built this thing up from scratch. So yes, I'm heavily involved. When you're this close to something, you don't behave like a hired gun.'

No doubt Sorrell realizes that even the most enlightened clients need something to focus on when looking at a vast organization like WPP – and so he provides a figurehead; a brand identity. During a conversation about overseas markets, he mentions that coins featuring the likeness of Alexander the Great have been found in India; 'one of the earliest examples of branding'. Sorrell plays a similar unifying role within his own empire. The last time I saw him in person was at a Unilever management get-together. He knows that clients appreciate the personal touch. Indeed, although he laments the fact that many clients now regard advertising as 'an extension of show business', Sorrell is one of the industry's few genuinely statesmanlike figures, afforded the sort of respect commanded, in another era, by David Ogilvy.

It seems not to matter, then, that he is guilty of the great copywriter's accusation that he has never written an ad. 'There is creativity in all walks of life,' he observes. 'It shouldn't be assumed that creative directors have the monopoly on it. There's plenty of creativity in direct [marketing], for example. There are creative financial people. I occasionally get a vague urge to come up with a campaign, but to everyone's benefit I've always resisted. At the end of the day, I am a businessman.

Some creative people find the idea uncomfortable, but advertising is a business.'

During the Unilever event, Sorrell remained in constant touch with the outside world via smartphone. He is famously linked in. 'It doesn't matter what time it is,' Mel Karmazin, the former Viacom CEO, told *Fortune*, 'if Sir Martin didn't get back to me within 15 minutes, I'd call to see if he'd been injured' ('Bigger and bigger', 29 November 2004).

It is evident that Sorrell works not for riches, but because he adores it. He does not strike tycoon-like postures – outside work, his passions are family and cricket. WPP's London base is a discreet townhouse in Mayfair, not a skyscraper designed to send a message to those who stand awed at its base. Far from being the austere, driven figure one might imagine, he is surprisingly easygoing. He once observed that 'hard work isn't stressful as long as you're having fun'. But make no mistake: it is fun that Sorrell takes seriously. 'I feel the same way about WPP that [Liverpool Football Club manager] Bill Shankly felt about football: "It's not a matter of life and death – it's much more important than that."'

## Interpublic: the horizontal ladder

Marion Harper, the late boss of McCann Erickson, had a rather different approach to his job. In the midst of an acquisition rampage in the sixties, Harper had a private DC-10 aircraft kitted out like a flying French chateau, with a king-sized bed, a library and a sunken bath. According to Stephen Fox in *The Mirror Makers*, the plane was part of a small fleet nicknamed 'Harper's Air Force'.

Although his Napoleonic ambition eventually got the better of him, Harper laid the foundations for the very first marketing communications combine. His innovation may be the reason that, today, almost everyone in advertising ultimately works for five different companies. In 1954, he acquired a small agency called Marschalk & Pratt. Feeling that McCann Erickson was already organized along the most efficient lines possible, he was unwilling to embark on a messy, destabilizing merger. Instead, he allowed Marschalk & Pratt to flourish as an independent agency, with separate offices and staff.

Over the next few years, as Harper snapped up more agencies in varied marketing fields, he maintained the same policy. In 1960, he formed the holding group Interpublic. It was divided into four divisions: McCann-Erickson, to handle domestic accounts; McCann-Marschalk, a second-string agency capable of handling conflicting accounts; McCann-Erickson Corp International, taking care of more than 50 offices around the world; and Communications Affiliates, a collection of below-the-line operations. Harper said that he had taken the ladder structure of the business and 'turn[ed] it to a horizontal position'.

In 1961, with the acquisition of London agency Pritchard Wood, Interpublic overtook J Walter Thompson to become the world's largest advertising company. But Harper's horizontal ladder also required a delicate balancing act. As the acquisitions continued throughout the 1960s, the structure began to wobble dangerously. Not every client was convinced by the separate agency policy: Continental Airlines, for example, pulled out of McCann-Erickson citing a conflict with Braniff Airlines, which was handled by fellow Interpublic agency Jack Tinker & Partners.

McCann's creative successes – notably 'Put a tiger in your tank,' for Esso – were being undermined by the instability of its parent company. At that point, Interpublic had 24 divisions and billings of US $711 million – but Harper was unwilling to delegate and there was little coordination of these entities. Interpublic's debt rose from US $1 million in 1962 to US $9 million in 1967 (WARC profile in association with AdBrands, March 2006). Chase Manhattan Bank agreed to stave off disaster with a US $10 million loan – on the condition that Harper left the company. He was duly ousted by the Interpublic board. A few years later (after a brief, ironic attempt to set up a small creative agency) he left the advertising business altogether. He died in 1989 at the age of 73. But he presumably had time, as he sat on the sidelines, to observe other groups adopting and honing the structure that he had pioneered.

Interpublic recovered from the Harper era and in the 1980s it went shopping again, acquiring the Lowe Group and Lintas International. In the 1990s it fused Lintas with another purchase, the US independent agency Ammirati & Puris, to create Ammirati Puris Lintas.

Both entities had interesting histories. Established in 1929, Lintas had once been the in-house advertising department of packaged goods manufacturer Unilever (Lever International Advertising Services). It began to take on separate clients in the 1960s and was eventually spun off as a standalone agency, ending up in the Interpublic stable. Ammirati & Puris was a New York creative agency set up in 1974 by Martin Puris, Ralph Ammirati and Julian AvRutick. Its most famous client was BMW, for whom Puris conceived the slogan 'the ultimate driving machine'. Briefly owned by London's BMP in the eighties, the agency was once again independent by the time Interpublic got hold of it and merged it with Lintas.

Interpublic now possessed the three-agency structure that was becoming familiar throughout the industry; but neither Lowe nor Ammirati Puris Lintas was strong enough to offer a realistic alternative to the mighty McCann-Erickson. So Interpublic engineered another fusion, this time combining Lowe and APL to create Lowe Lintas. Then it went hunting again. It had set its sights on MacManus, the holding company of the DMB&B network – but that was snatched from under its nose by Leo Burnett. Finally, in March 2001, it acquired True North, parent to FCB Worldwide, for US$1.2 billion.

FCB was a direct link back to two of the most prestigious names in advertising history: Lord & Thomas and Albert Lasker (see Chapter 1, Pioneers of persuasion). In 1942, when Albert Lasker retired from advertising, he sold the Chicago-based Lord & Thomas agency to his three top managers: Emerson Foote in New York, Fairfax Cone in Chicago and Don Belding in Los Angeles. The following year, the agency was reborn as Foote, Cone & Belding. Over the next couple of decades it devised some of the most famous slogans in advertising: 'Does she or doesn't she? Only her hairdresser knows for sure,' for Clairol hair colour; 'You'll wonder where the yellow went when you brush your teeth with Pepsodent'; 'Up, up and away with TWA'... Although its founders had long passed away by the time Interpublic acquired True North – the name of FCB's holding company – the agency had retained its prestige.

Unfortunately for Interpublic, however, the acquisition could not have come at a worse time. In 2001 the dotcom bubble burst and the events of 11 September sent the advertising market into a downward spiral. This hampered the restructuring process that was needed to bring True North inside the already unwieldy Interpublic group. In addition, FCB had just lost the DaimlerChrysler account, worth US$116 million. And to pile on the agony, flagship McCann client Coca-Cola (for whom the agency had penned 'I'd like to teach the world to sing' in the 1970s) was beginning to pull out of the agency, placing work with smaller operations. It would be years before Interpublic was back on a fully even keel, especially as it was soon buffeted by claims of accounting imbalances. While 'neither admitting nor denying' the allegations, the group agreed to pay a civil penalty of US$12 million to the Securities and Exchange Commission ('Interpublic, SEC reach $12 mil settlement', *Adweek*, 1 May 2008). The following year, just as its recovery seemed imminent, IPG fell into another global economic trough.

In 2011 it was forced to concede its third place in the list of the world's largest advertising holding groups to Publicis. Yet it is and will remain an entity to be reckoned with: 42,000 employees in more than 130 countries and net income of over US$551 million.

## Publicis: readjusting the compass

One of Marcel Bleustein-Blanchet's challenges to Maurice Lévy had been to take the agency global. This proved an even more fraught expedition than he might have imagined. In 1988, Lévy discovered that Foote, Cone & Belding was looking for international partners in order to grow in Europe and Asia. Having been named Agency of the Year in 1986 by *Advertising Age*, largely on the strength of its Levi's and California Raisins campaigns, FCB looked like an attractive proposition to Lévy. But he recalls, 'The initial approach came from FCB. They said, "We're interested in buying you." I replied, "That's not a bad idea – but I'd prefer it if we bought you." So rather than trying to buy one another, we sat down and worked out an alliance.'

With complex cross-shareholding arrangements and a coordinating body, the partnership was far more than a gentlemen's agreement. And for a while it worked for both parties, with the combined agencies netting billings of US$6 billion at the height of the union. 'We spent several excellent and profitable years together,' says Lévy. 'And Publicis learned a lot during that period.'

But however formal the partnership might have been, it was still dependent on the will of those concerned. This became clear when the FCB CEO with whom Lévy had negotiated the deal, Norman Brown, retired and was replaced by Bruce Mason. It transpired that Mason was not favourable to the alliance, and the relationship between the two agencies grew strained. When Publicis acquired a small advertising agency in the United States, FCB charged that the French agency was competing on its turf and claimed a breach of the original agreement.

After a painful legal wrangle, the partnership was dissolved in 1996. FCB was free to continue along its path as part of the holding company True North, with the results described above.

Publicis had grown in 1993 with the acquisition of the French network FCA-BMZ, which gave it offices in Germany, the UK, the Netherlands, Belgium and Italy, as well as additional strength in France. But the end of its agreement with True North meant that it had lost its American presence, and could make no claims to being global. 'Like a woman can't be half pregnant, you're either global or you're not,' observes Lévy. 'If you want to work for clients that are present everywhere, you have to be present everywhere too.'

To make up for lost time, Lévy set off on what he admits was 'a crazy acquisitions trail'. 'At one point we were moving into a new country every week,' he says. One valuable prize was the San Francisco creative agency Hal Riney & Partners, which had already repelled advances from Omnicom, WPP and Interpublic. But Lévy won over founder Hal P Riney by showing his appreciation for the creative work and taking a personal, rather than a corporate, approach to the deal. 'From a more cynical point of view, I think it helped that we were a long way from San Francisco and less likely to interfere,' says Lévy. 'The deal earned us a great deal of respect within the creative community – and also from advertisers – because they saw that we were committed to creativity.'

The creative agency Fallon McElligott was acquired shortly afterwards. And then Saatchi & Saatchi sailed onto the horizon.

The wounded giant of the eighties was striving to build a new image under its chairman Bob Seelert (a former General Mills executive) and flamboyant CEO Kevin Roberts. The agency had needed a colourful character like Roberts in order to break with the past. Roberts had discovered the power of brands while working for fashion designer Mary Quant in London in the 1960s. He'd then taken his experience to posts at Gillette, Procter & Gamble, Pepsi and Lion Nathan Breweries in New Zealand – where he was chief operating officer before accepting the invitation to run Saatchi in 1997.

With an accent that tumbles from Northern England to New York to New Zealand and back again – often in the same phrase – Roberts is one of those informal, switched on, global citizens in which the advertising industry seems to specialize. He's good at providing inspiration and controversy in equal measure. While working for Pepsi, he machine-gunned a Coke vending machine on stage during a conference. More recently he created the concept of 'Lovemarks' – brands that inspire loyalty beyond reason.

Back in 2000, Roberts and Seelert found themselves running a debt-laden, discredited agency that was unlikely to grow much further without a large injection of cash. (By that stage, Saatchi & Saatchi had been de-merged from Cordiant, the holding company it had shared with Bates. Cordiant and Bates later ended up in the hands of WPP, where they were dissolved into other parts of the operation.) Saatchi enjoyed an unconsummated flirtation with the Japanese agency Dentsu and rejected a proposition from WPP, which was regarded as too controlling. The answer, then, perhaps lay with Publicis.

The dance started on another foot, when Publicis, Saatchi and Bates began discussing a merger of their media operations. Lévy was cool on that deal, but he instigated behind-the-scenes talks with Bob Seelert about the future of Saatchi & Saatchi – starting with a discreet breakfast meeting at London's Connaught Hotel. The informal discussions about a potential fusion were continuing when Lévy was approached by Young & Rubicam, which was trying to stave off a takeover by WPP and wondered if it could throw in its lot with Publicis. But Publicis was considered an unlikely white knight for Y&R – the latter handled the Ford account, which would have clashed bumpers with key Publicis client Renault. It seems that even Lévy took his negotiations with Saatchi more seriously. 'I knew that once news of my talks with [Y&R] became public, my conversation with Saatchi & Saatchi would turn into something more concrete – which proved to be the case.'

Lévy also won the support of Kevin Roberts, who after a crucial meeting decided that he trusted the Frenchman with the Saatchi brand and those who worked for the company. The US$1.9 billion deal was completed on 20 June 2000. Now there could be no question that the Publicis Groupe was a global player. 'There were three excellent reasons for acquiring Saatchi,' says Lévy. 'It was still an excellent brand with a reputation for creativity. I had a great deal of respect for Bob Seelert and Kevin Roberts. And finally, it gave us instant global status: the name Saatchi & Saatchi is known everywhere, all over the world.'

A year and a half later, Lévy found to his surprise that he was still hungry. For months he'd been reading in the press that there were now two tiers of global communications groups – and his was in the second tier. 'To me, the insinuation was "top class", "second class",' says Lévy.

'If we wanted to enter the top tier – to become "top class" – we needed to make another acquisition.'

Lévy had previously had some informal contact with Roger Haupt, CEO of Bcom3. As you'll remember, Bcom3 was the awkwardly named holding company of Leo Burnett and the MacManus Group, in which Dentsu had taken a 22 per cent stake. Many at Leo Burnett felt that the name sounded temporary – as if it was a step on the way to someplace else. That place turned out to be Publicis.

Soon after 11 September 2001, Lévy resumed contact with Haupt to discuss the potential for a merger. He recalls that they met in 'strange, unlikely places, like the Hilton at Heathrow Airport, with no lawyers or financiers present' to draw up the deal, which was then presented to Dentsu. The Japanese agency gave its accord and the US$3 billion deal was announced in March 2002. During several meetings with staff, Lévy mustered all his charm and tact to reassure Leo Burnett employees that their new owner would not attempt to interfere with the agency's unique heritage.

The acquisition turned Publicis into the fourth largest advertising group worldwide. At the time of writing it sits at number three, with an annual net income of US$791 million.

# Havas: child of the information age

The modern history of Havas ended with a boardroom battle. Its ancient history began with a secret mission.

Charles Louis Havas was born in Rouen on 5 July 1783 into a wealthy Jewish family of Hungarian descent. His father had a number of business interests, including a small local newspaper. As described by Jacques Séguéla in his book on the history of Havas, *Tous Ego* (2005), Charles became in his turn a notable merchant, banker, publisher and wheeler-dealer – but he seemed to lose fortunes as quickly as he made them.

In 1861, Charles departed on a mysterious journey. Nobody knows where he went or why – there has been some speculation that it was a spying or diplomatic mission (or a mixture of both) for the king, Louis-Philippe. 'I am going on a long and dangerous journey,' he wrote to his sister-in-law. 'Should I succeed, I will make everyone happy; if not, God knows what we will become.'

While the details of his voyage remain murky, the mission seems to have provided the capital for his nascent press agency. He may also have recruited several foreign correspondents along the way. On his return he began translating news items from the overseas press and gathering dispatches from the stock exchange. He forged contacts with businessmen and politicians. But Havas was more than a prototype freelance reporter. His rise coincided with the first information boom: Louis-Philippe was warily tolerant of a free press and by 1835 there were 600 newspapers and periodicals in France, all hungry for the kind of information Havas could provide. In addition, Havas's political connections led him to become the almost exclusive diffuser of government information, creating an awkwardly cosy relationship between press and state.

In 1835 the Havas agency was installed in a three-room, 80-square-metre space at what is today 51 rue Jean-Jacques Rousseau. The agency's news dispatches were crowned with the words VITE ET BIEN ('Fast and good'), indicating that Havas had a flair for self-promotion. In order to deliver on his promise he made use of every available form of information technology, from carrier pigeons to the brand new electric telegraph. By 1840, the agency was publishing a range of bulletins for politicians, bankers and industrialists, as well as providing publicity services for many of the same.

Havas died on 21 May 1858, succeeded at the head of the company by his two sons. Charles Auguste Havas rapidly assumed the leadership role. Shortly after his father's death, he bought a stake in the newspaper advertising sales house Société Générale des Annonces (SGA), which would come under the full control of the agency in 1914. The slow swing of Havas away from news and towards advertising had begun.

During the Franco-Prussian War (1870–71), however, news was still at the heart of the organization. With Paris under siege, Auguste Havas based himself in Tours in order to relay news of the capital to the rest of France, using carrier pigeons to communicate with the Paris office. In an attempt to cut off the supply, the Prussians released falcons to bring down the pigeons.

Towards the end of his reign, Auguste sold his share of the business to Emile d'Erlanger, an international financier. Other stakes were already in the hands of influential politicians, industrialists and businessmen. This contributed to the persistent impression that Havas was the intelligence service of the French industrial and political elite. Auguste died in 1889, the last Havas to head the agency. He was succeeded first by Edouard Lebey, and then by Léon Régnier.

The agency found a new figurehead in Régnier, who ran Havas from 1916 to 1944 – a period of immense growth. As well as diversifying into international advertising and investing in telegraph links with northern Europe and the United States, Régnier won the contract to provide advertising space for the Paris métro system and news kiosks. In 1920, he merged advertising sales house SGA with Havas (although it remained a separate division called Havas Publicité). The agency now handled ad sales for the five largest French newspapers.

After the Nazis marched into Paris on 14 June 1940, the offices of Havas were requisitioned by the Occupation government. Havas took on a strange new half-life. Its ownership was split three ways, with 32.4 per cent remaining with its existing owners, 47.6 per cent going to the Germans and 20 per cent to the French state. And so the news agency became a propaganda tool for the occupier and the Vichy government. After the war, Havas was nationalized, with the state taking control of the shares previously held by the Germans.

In 1947, the agency was several million francs in debt and faced increasing competition from a renascent Publicis. But at least the division between its advertising and its news arms was now clear, with the press agency operating under the new banner of Agence France Presse. Havas diversified into tourism, setting up a number of travel agencies. Advertising revenues picked up and by 1957 more than 80 per cent of its income came from advertising sales (WARC profile in association with AdBrands, October 2006). It was during this period that Havas and Publicis – ostensibly arch-rivals – are said to have entered into a tacit agreement to divide the country's advertising spoils evenly between them in order to ward off international competition. This has never been officially acknowledged, but it seems plausible given their vast web of business and political contacts.

In 1959, Jacques Douce was named commercial publicity director, and he slowly began to shape Havas into something resembling the organization we know today. As a second string to the agency's existing creative arm, Havas Conseil, he founded the spin-off agency Bélier, in which he took a stake. In 1972 all of Havas's advertising-related operations were combined under the new name Eurocom. This entity began tentative explorations abroad, acquiring minor agencies in the United

States and entering into a joint venture agreement with Marsteller Advertising, a subsidiary of Young & Rubicam (a partnership that would unravel in the early 1990s).

In 1989, under newly appointed CEO Alain de Pouzilhac, Eurocom took a 60 per cent stake in UK advertising group WCRS. This was later increased to full ownership. Then, as we've heard, Eurocom acquired RSCG, eventually fusing all of its creative agency units under the Euro RSCG banner. By now Eurocom was operating virtually independently from Havas – which had become an unwieldy collection of businesses embracing television (it had launched Canal Plus in 1984), media sales, publishing and tourism.

In 1997, the structure was subsumed into the Compagnie Générale des Eaux (CGE), a former French utilities company that chairman Jean-Marie Messier was busy transforming into a media conglomerate, soon to be re-branded Vivendi. As the Vivendi saga unfolded, the empire once known as Havas was dismantled and sold off. Although it had been unthinkable only a few years previously, all that remained of the giant organization founded by Charles Louis Havas was the advertising division – now renamed Havas and functioning as an independent entity.

But the drama was by no means over. At the turn of the millennium Havas made two important purchases. In 1999 it merged its lacklustre media capabilities with those of Spain's giant Media Planning Group and the veteran New York media buyer SFM (which you may recall from the previous chapter). And in 2000 it bought the US group Snyder for US$2.1 billion, instantly propelling it into the prized top tier of communications groups.

Then the bad news began. A tentative bid for the British-based Tempus Group in 2001 was trumped by WPP. Economic turmoil, combined with restructuring costs, resulted in a loss for that year of 58 million euros. The company seesawed between profit and loss over the next couple of years. Its fragility attracted the attention of French businessman Vincent Bolloré, who built up a 20 per cent stake in the company. An urbane Breton with a wide range of interests, including paper, cotton, shipping and media, Bolloré was portrayed by the press as a corporate raider. Havas CEO Alain de Pouzilhac made no secret of the fact that he was violently opposed to what he described as a 'creeping takeover' of the group.

In early 2004, Havas confirmed that it was considering making a bid for Grey Global Group. This worried some shareholders, who felt that the company might be overstretching itself. The situation was resolved when Havas was once again beaten to its prey by Martin Sorrell and WPP.

Meanwhile, the antagonism between de Pouzilhac and Bolloré had escalated into a battle – magnified and encouraged by the media. Bolloré had demanded four seats on the Havas board, which de Pouzilhac was ill-inclined to give him. The Havas CEO feared for the future of the company – was it to be pillaged and sold on for profit by the Breton buccaneer? Why hadn't Bolloré clearly stated his intentions? The scene was set for a showdown at the Annual General Meeting of 9 June 2005. As shareholders and reporters filed into the auditorium at the Maison de la Chimie – an 18th-century mansion on the Left Bank – there was a sense of anticipation rarely present at such dry gatherings.

Taking the stage, Bolloré assured shareholders that he was not 'Darth Vader' and that this was not a corporate raid: he had plans for the future of Havas. 'I have invested in [the company] in order to develop it and I intend to remain for the long term. I'm committing myself here, before you... My only wish is to regain some of the ground that it has lost over the last two years.'

When the votes came in, Bolloré won his seats on the board. Two weeks later, Alain de Pouzilhac resigned as CEO. In July 2005, Vincent Bolloré was appointed chairman of Havas. When the dust settled, Havas remained the world's sixth largest marketing communications group.

So now you're asking yourself: 'The sixth? What happened to the fifth?'

Well, the fifth has certain idiosyncrasies that set it apart from the other organizations in the top tier, so it deserves special treatment.

It's called Dentsu.

# Japanese giants

## 12

*'Fifteen seconds and counting'*

The 47-storey Dentsu building slices through the Tokyo skyline like a shark's fin swathed in glass. Every day, around 6,000 people come to work here for the world's fifth largest advertising organization, whose net income of more than 40 billion yen (US$453 million) is largely generated in Japan. Entering the building – which was designed by the French architect Jean Nouvel – is like stepping into the first-class lounge of a spaceport. The lobby is an infinite ballroom lined in marble and steel. The round reception desk seems to hover silently, cradled by softly glowing panels. Glossy-haired receptionists in silver-grey uniforms beam immaculate Shiseido smiles. An exposed glass elevator threads through a mesh of steel as your stomach plunges into the receding city.

I spent almost a week visiting Dentsu and I never got a handle on the geography. Perspectives seemed to warp and elide. There were entire floors of restaurants. The executive floor looked more like a museum, with priceless works of art on the walls. On other floors, rows of desks tapered into the middle distance. To get an idea of the organization's bustle and hum, I was encouraged to visit its website, where vertical multicoloured columns tracked the elevator movements in real time.

I was an honoured guest of Dentsu, which was an extremely useful position to be in. The Japanese know how to take care of visitors. There was no way I'd be allowed to leave before I knew everything there was to know about the company. But first, I was given a little background.

## A short history of Dentsu

It's easy to find out about the history of Japanese advertising while you're visiting Dentsu, because the Advertising Museum of Tokyo is located right next door to the agency's headquarters in Shiodome. The museum was established in 2002 to commemorate the centennial of the birth of Dentsu's fourth president, Hideo Yoshida, who is widely regarded as the father of modern Japanese advertising. We'll get to him shortly.

Although the company that became Dentsu was founded in 1901 – and its rival, Hakuhodo, in 1895 – forms of advertising existed in Japan long before then. From the earliest days of the Edo period (starting in 1603) advertising flyers were posted on the pillars of Shinto shrines and Buddhist temples, as well as on fences and gateposts. Japanese newspapers had yet to appear, so ads were often inserted into books. Owing to the shogun rulers' policy of *sakoku* or 'isolation' – under which no Japanese was allowed out of the country and foreign entry was strictly controlled – news of the outside world came in the form of Dutch newspapers, the Dutch East India Company being the only overseas organization permitted to trade with the country.

During the *Meiji* period (1868–1912) under the Emperor Meiji (meaning 'enlightened ruler' – his given name was Mutsuhito), the country opened up to foreign influence. Along with other trappings of Western-style civilization – from the telegraph and the railway to certain styles of dress – newspapers and magazines finally arrived. Modernization further accelerated after the end of the Sino-Japanese War in 1895. As the press became increasingly dependent on advertising for revenue, the first advertising agencies were founded to trade in media space.

In 1901 a journalist named Hoshiro Mitsunaga laid the foundations of Dentsu by creating the news agency Telegraph Service Co. to cover the stormy political events of the day. In a barter-style arrangement, many newspapers paid for his stories by donating advertising space, which he sold on through a subsidiary company, Japan Advertising. In 1907 these two units were merged under the name Nippon Denpo-Tsushin Sha, eventually shortened to Dentsu. The company won exclusive rights to distribute the United Press wire service in Japan – and it used this monopoly to negotiate even cheaper rates for advertising space. Advertising itself was becoming increasingly prominent, with the emergence of full-page spreads and a significant rise in the number of women's magazines. In the run-up to the First World War, Dentsu was already a force to be reckoned with, operating out of offices in the Ginza district.

Advertising spend slowed during the harsh inter-war years. In 1936 Dentsu's news service was nationalized and the company now concentrated exclusively on advertising. Although the industry assumed its inevitable wartime role as a diffuser of propaganda, its income was severely restricted. At the end of what must have been the most sombre period for the company, Dentsu founder Hoshiro Mitsunaga died in 1945.

The arrival of Hideo Yoshida as the company's fourth president in 1947 was a turning point for Dentsu. It coincided with the rise of the Japanese middle class and the emergence of mass consumption, eagerly supported by advertising. Yoshida became known as 'the big demon' and his hardworking staff as 'little demons'. He took advantage of the post-war period by recruiting former army officers and bureaucrats with useful government connections. Senior executives were expected to report for duty an hour earlier than the rest of the staff – and to provide daily reports on the progress of their departments. The annual team-building trip was a bracing climb up Mount Fuji.

Seeing the future and liking the look of it, in the 1950s Yoshida became Japan's greatest advocate for the launch of commercial broadcasting. After investing in radio, Dentsu practically underwrote the introduction of television, as well as guaranteeing advertising support. The very first TV spot broadcast in Japan was a time check sponsored by Seiko watches. It was, naturally, a Dentsu creation. The agency's symbiotic relationship with the media meant it was soon able to grab the lion's share of television advertising space – up to 60 per cent of primetime – making it impossible to ignore for the country's largest advertisers. Dentsu had also invested heavily in the press and forged agreements to buy newspaper space in bulk. By the 1960s Dentsu pretty much had the lock on media in Japan. In 1974 it was named the largest advertising agency in the world by *Advertising Age*.

Although the Japanese economy experienced severe dips in the seventies – the fallout of the Vietnam War and two oil crises – advertising expenditure continued to rise. A trade imbalance caused by the growth of exports to the United States caused further economic instability in the early 1980s. By the middle of the decade, however, driven by the development of satellite TV, advertising spend was climbing again. During a 10-year period from 1981, total expenditure more than doubled.

Dentsu has remained reliant on Japanese billings for much of its history, but it has also acknowledged that this is a potential weakness and has fought insularity. In 1981 it established a joint venture with Young & Rubicam called DYR. This allowed the US agency to enter the Japanese market while giving Dentsu access to the United States and Europe.

Dentsu also showed considerable foresight by opening a branch in Shanghai that same year. It has since become one of the most prominent overseas agencies in China. It has a strong network of subsidiaries throughout Asia, with a more muted presence in Europe and North America. It acquired the UK's Collett Dickenson Pearce in 1990.

The collapse of Japan's 'bubble economy' in 1991 and the subsequent lapse in consumer spending heralded a change in the way that Japanese agencies did business. At that point they were essentially media brokers. Although they developed creative product, the spots were compressed to 15 seconds in order to cram as many as possible into a break. But Japan's newly cash-strapped consumers now required a bit more persuasion before they reached for their wallets. In order to convince them, advertisers would have to build attractive brands, which meant paying more attention to creativity – an area in which the agencies were weak. Their evolution from commodity providers to creative resources is still ongoing. In addition, the arrival of satellite TV and the internet threatened Dentsu's dominance of the media market and offered new avenues for advertisers – as well as a way for smaller, nimbler agencies to break through the blockade.

Dentsu established partnerships to accelerate its advance into overseas markets. In 2000 it invested in the Bcom3 group of agencies, which included Leo Burnett. The following year it went public, with a listing on the Tokyo Stock Exchange. The acquisition of Bcom3 by Publicis gave Dentsu a 15 per cent stake in the French advertising group. That relationship ended in 2012 – when Publicis bought back its stake – and Dentsu shocked the industry by then announcing a £3.2 billion cash deal to buy UK-based group Aegis, owner of media buying and planning entity Carat, along with several other operations. This consolidated Dentsu's status as a member of the Big Five and put it more squarely in competition with Omnicom, WPP and Interpublic.

Dentsu is the world's largest single advertising agency, with more than 20,000 employees worldwide. Far larger than its closest rivals in Japan, it dominates advertising spend in the country, particularly on television where it is responsible for almost a third of all spending.

## Advertising haiku-style

Slashed to only a few seconds, Japanese ads blurt from the screen like noisy, incandescent fireworks. But while Western creatives reared on 'mini movie' commercials might sneer at this pared-down format, it slots perfectly into Japanese culture.

Dentsu chief creative officer Kunihiko Tainaka says, 'TV commercials in Japan try to place an emphasis on fast, emotional impact. You'll often find simple words and phrases, songs, jingles and highly memorable characters. The aim is to stand out from the other commercials. We have the feeling that Western advertising is very rational: it's marketing oriented and strategic. Our advertising is media oriented and instinctive.'

The compressed format springs partly from tradition. In the early days, running a TV ad conveyed such high status on a brand that 15 seconds sufficed to make the point. But it transpired that viewers were predisposed to swallow these bite-sized spots. Tainaka explains that Japanese advertising has clear links with another, much older aspect of the country's culture: *haiku*, the beautiful one-line poetry whose best-known proponent among Westerners is probably Bashō. 'This is an art form entirely based on symbolism. The Japanese are skilled at reading between the lines so the audience can extrapolate from a single image.'

The ability to appreciate a self-contained world without insisting on narrative may explain Japan's pre-eminence in the field of video games. Even its famous Manga comics demonstrate a non-linear approach to storytelling. Executive creative director Akira Kagami says, 'Outside Japan, comic books are generally story oriented. Manga tend to be situation oriented. Once again, the approach is more abstract. You can see Manga strips with just four panels. Even two is occasionally enough.'

He points out that accusations of lack of creativity based on the brevity of Japanese commercials is unfair. Selling a product in 15 seconds is a skill in itself – and when you have only a few words to play with, precision is everything.

'Strangely enough,' he adds, 'as digital media take hold and attention spans become shorter, I have the feeling that advertising in other markets is becoming more like our own. In the seventies and eighties, there was a much bigger gap in comprehension between Western and Asian audiences, which was reflected in our performance at international creative competitions. But since the 1990s, Asian creativity has been welcomed and admired.'

In any case, Japanese advertising cannot be approached in a simplistic, catch-all fashion. There are regional styles. Advertising for a metropolitan, Tokyoite audience – the heartland of the Kantō region – is glossy and modern. But there's also work aimed at the south-central Kansai region, whose capital is Osaka. The region is considered more cultural and idiosyncratic than businesslike Tokyo. The advertising crafted for its citizens is more cynical – and often does better at Cannes.

The need to make an instant impact explains another well-known aspect of Japanese advertising: the use of Hollywood stars to sell beer, whisky, soft drinks and cars. But Kagami suggests this kind of advertising might be evolving. 'Japanese audiences are becoming far more sophisticated and well travelled – and Western stars don't have the exotic appeal they once did. In fact, I'd say there's a swing towards Japanese icons. When you only have 15 seconds to play with, celebrities make an instant connection. Their background is established. You don't have to develop the character.'

Not surprisingly, given its past, Dentsu has never given a moment's thought to separating media from creative. Indeed, the media drives the creative, not the other way around. The agency says this has made it easier to devise 'through the line' campaigns, with a single idea developed for several different media, especially the internet and mobile phones. 'The line has vanished. We believe that you may have made a big mistake by unbundling media from creative in the West,' says Kagami. 'Our creatives can consider different media choices right from the start of the process.'

A unique employee within Dentsu is the TVC planner, also known as the 'TV specialist'. This discipline is not analogous with media planning. The TV specialist's role involves coming up with the original idea for a TV commercial and overseeing the entire production process.

At Dentsu it doesn't matter where a creative comes from. People from a wide variety of backgrounds are recruited because the agency has a sophisticated internal education system to support their development.

So what's it like to be a creative at a Japanese giant?

## Soccer and Shiseido

As well as being one of Japan's creative stars, Masako Okamura was one of the first female creative directors at Dentsu. 'Maybe that's why people sometimes mistook me for a boy,' jokes this willowy, gamine woman. It could also have something to do with the fact that she is a devoted soccer fan, and is often clad in Chelsea or Real Madrid team shirts. (She even admits to watching tapes of spectacular soccer goals to ease stress.) 'When I have an important meeting I change into a Prada dress and people say, "Oh, she's a girl after all!"'

After starting out in the PR division, Okamura became a copywriter in 1992. She is proud to have worked with Akira Odagiri, considered one of the masters of Japanese creativity, who now heads the creative department at Ogilvy & Mather Japan. She was promoted to creative director in 2001, making her one of the most senior members of Dentsu's approximately 800-strong creative staff. Although Dentsu politely declines to name its clients, a little research reveals that its biggest accounts include Shiseido cosmetics and Toyota.

Okamura's working day begins at around nine and can end at any time from four in the afternoon to four in the morning, 'as is the case for most creative people around the world'. Although the agency's creative directors are assigned identical booths, she has a view of Mount Fuji from her desk. 'On the desk are all kinds of funny toys from around the world, as well as various stock images sent from overseas production companies, so the younger staff members often drop by to see if anything inspires them.'

The creative process is a team effort that requires regular brainstorming sessions. 'In my team the one hard and fast rule is that meetings are limited to 90 minutes – just like soccer games.'

Okamura acknowledges that some aspects of Japanese advertising may appear to be barriers to creativity – for instance, the reliance on celebrities. Yet she feels there are ways of being creative within these constraints. For example, in the middle of a recent stand-up comedy boom, a campaign for Shiseido's male grooming range Uno featured 50 hip young comedians in individual 15-second spots – a feat that got the brand into the *Guinness Book of Records*. As for the brevity of Japanese spots, she points out, 'Young people in their teens and twenties can grasp a visual idea in a few seconds. This kind of advertising works very well on mobile phones. It is now being adopted in the West, but it was pioneered here.'

But as the drive towards creativity continues, an alternative approach is emerging. A 2005 spot called 'Husky Girl' might be considered something of a pivotal work. The ad promoting the giant Ajinomoto Stadium in the suburbs of Tokyo was no less than 90 seconds long. It featured a series of beautiful young girls – with the voices of chain-smoking truck drivers. The payoff shot revealed that their vocal cords had been shredded by all the shouting and cheering they'd been doing at the stadium's football matches. The gently humorous ad hinted at a new direction in Japanese advertising.

Although longer spots and Western-style, story-driven ads are beginning to make an appearance, the more caustic tone of British advertising is unlikely to reach Japanese screens. Sex, politics and religion are strictly taboo. Political correctness is the rule.

The spots that survive are greatly appreciated. Okamura observes that while in other markets consumers might be suspicious of advertising, the Japanese are fans. There's even a consumer magazine devoted to the subject, called *CM Now* (CM being shorthand for 'commercial'). To an Anglo-Saxon viewer the ads have an optimism and exuberance – an almost childlike innocence – that our own irony-heavy, 'seen it all before, wasn't impressed the first time', media culture seems to have lost.

Japanese society is changing – and consumer responses along with it. As a woman in a predominantly male environment, Okamura is aware of the progress that is being made. 'After the collapse of the bubble economy in the 1990s, the modes of behaviour that defined men and women became blurred. Men have become less career-obsessed, more spiritual. And women have become more independent. They have their own money and they spend it more freely. So women in advertising are portrayed as independent, both emotionally and economically.'

Viewing habits in Japan are also changing. Almost everyone has internet access and a fully interactive mobile phone. Understandably, although TV is still the leading medium, the grip of the home screen has slackened slightly. 'Over the past 10 years, I think there's been a decrease in the tendency to watch TV every evening,' says Okamura. 'But that's because the nature of TV has changed. Now you can watch TV on your laptop or on your mobile phone. So we have seen the shift of commercials onto these new media.'

And Japanese consumers don't feel hunted by the agencies, Okamura insists. 'Advertising is a form of culture among the younger generation. Today, they barely differentiate it from any other form of entertainment.'

## The challenger agency

Dentsu's dominance of the Japanese media has made life difficult for other agencies. The second largest agency is Hakuhodo, with revenues of some US $1.4 billion. It was founded in 1895 by an entrepreneur called Hironao Seki as a provider of advertising space in educational publications. There was a glut of these during the *Meiji* period as the country rushed to modernize, slavering for knowledge. Soon Hakuhodo became the exclusive provider of book advertisements for leading newspapers, which made it the country's biggest agency. But the publishing sector declined with the arrival of television after the Second World War, allowing Dentsu to stride into first place. The organizations have remained arch rivals ever since.

Nonetheless, Hakuhodo has pressed a couple of advantages. It was the first agency in Japan to develop US-style research techniques, which led in 1981 to the creation of the Hakuhodo Institute of Life & Living, which provides in-depth insights into Japanese consumer trends. It was also swifter than its rival to explore opportunities abroad, forming an alliance with McCann Erickson in 1960. Although McCann bought its way out of the agreement in the early nineties, Hakuhodo formed another joint venture, this time with TBWA, which handled the Nissan account outside Japan. The alliance was formalized under the name G1 Worldwide in 2000.

Although a number of Western agencies have entered Japan – either as joint ventures or, more recently, solo entities – they've generally had a tough time of it. They bring clients with them into the market, but they struggle to win significant Japanese accounts and their billings remain unimpressive compared to those of Hakuhodo and Dentsu. Most sources agree that the top 10 agencies in the country remain Japanese. Small, switched-on Western networks like Fallon, Wieden & Kennedy and BBH are present, however, and have a subtle influence on the creative output of the domestic giants.

Japanese-owned independent boutiques are few and far between. But one that's worth taking a closer look at is called Tugboat.

There could not be a greater contrast between Dentsu and this tiny creative agency of half-a-dozen people. Its small but cool offices are located on the ground floor of a discreet building in Omotesando – one of the hippest districts in the city, where young Japanese preen on café terraces before strolling along to the distorted glass Rubik's cube that is the local Prada store.

Ironically, Tugboat boss Yasumichi Oka learned his trade at Dentsu, which he left in 1999 after 19 years to start his fledgling agency – taking three members of his creative team with him. 'To say that Dentsu were annoyed is not entirely accurate,' says Oka today. 'They were perplexed. Nobody leaves their job in Japan, especially if they work at the country's biggest advertising agency.'

But Dentsu itself had lit the fuse that sparked Oka's departure. The agency sent him to Britain and Sweden with a brief to see how small creative hot shops worked and come back with a full report. Instead, he returned to Japan with a new vision of how advertising could be done. 'The very fact that Dentsu sent me on the trip indicates that it is tentatively exploring new forms of creativity. But I wanted to be a pioneer.'

The agency's name is a reflection of his philosophy: like the country, Japanese advertising is an island. Oka wants to haul it towards new ideas and influences.

'The main danger was that clients would not support our philosophy,' he admits. 'But in fact, our clients are self-selecting. Those that seek a traditional approach go to the big agencies. Those that are willing to take risks and explore new avenues come to us.'

Since its launch, the agency has worked for advertisers such as tele-coms giant NTT, beverage behemoth Suntory, Japanese Railways, Fuji Xerox, Sky PerfecTV! and even Burberry. It has made pop promos, designed packaging and organized events. It has also racked up a stack of awards at international advertising competitions. And it does not hesitate to make TV ads that are 30 seconds or even one minute long. (One ad, for the TV station Star Channel, weighed in at a colossal two minutes.)

Oka believes advertising should stir viewers' emotions and cling to their brains for hours after the spot has screened. The Tugboat style is bold, optimistic and often faintly trashy, mashing Manga elements with surreal Anglo-Saxon humour. For instance, an ad to promote Japanese Railways' express service to the ski slopes featured a skiing ostrich. And the agency's visceral 'Ronin Pitcher' spot, to promote base-ball coverage on PerfecTV!, was a John Woo-like explosion of slow motion violence. Viewers got a gory close-up of the pitcher's fingernail shredding as he hurled the ball at supersonic speed. To promote Fuji Xerox photocopiers, a series of ads depicted a pushy salesman surprising people in their baths or accosting them outside public toilets. All this is risky stuff for taboo-ridden Japan.

'You can tell how straight-laced clients are by looking at how many agencies have followed in our footsteps,' says Oka. 'The sum total is zero. We're the only ones doing the kind of advertising we do. I expected to start a revolution, but so far it hasn't happened.'

Because of this, the agency has turned its attention abroad. It has begun pitching seriously for business outside Japan and building informal links with other hot shops in Europe and the United States. 'My goal now is to be the first small Japanese agency to have a credible international reputation,' Oka says. 'I want to be mentioned alongside agencies like [the UK's] Mother or [Amsterdam agency] 180.'

Oka may just have the talent and determination to succeed. Forget the *ronin* pitcher – meet the *ronin* ad man.

## Think small.

Our little car isn't so much of a novelty any more.

A couple of dozen college kids don't try to squeeze inside it.

The guy at the gas station doesn't ask where the gas goes.

Nobody even stares at our shape.

In fact, some people who drive our little flivver don't even think 32 miles to the gallon is going any great guns.

Or using five pints of oil instead of five quarts.

Or never needing anti-freeze.

Or racking up 40,000 miles on a set of tires.

That's because once you get used to some of our economies, you don't even think about them any more.

Except when you squeeze into a small parking spot. Or renew your small insurance. Or pay a small repair bill. Or trade in your old VW for a new one.

Think it over.

*'Think small.' The most admired print ad of all time.*

(By kind permission of DDB and Volkswagen)

'A British agency in New York.' David Ogilvy in the 1950s,
when he started his own agency.

*David Ogilvy with two of the advertising icons he created: the man in the Hathaway shirt and Commander Whitehead of Schweppes.*

*'A powerful presence.' Bill Bernbach's agency
sparked a creative revolution.*

'I knew damn well I could make ads better.' Leo Burnett on
his way to a pitch, clutching his trusty portfolio.

'In a way, Madison Avenue was advertising.' BBDO creative legend
Phil Dusenberry, who helped mould today's ad industry.

*Pioneering British adman John Hegarty of BBH.*

*'We didn't know what we sold more of: jeans or boxer shorts.'*
*The trendsetting 'Launderette' commercial by BBH for Levi's.*

*Economist ad: one of the first in a long-running series and a testament to David Abbott's copywriting skills.*

*Italian graphics and advertising genius Armando Testa.*

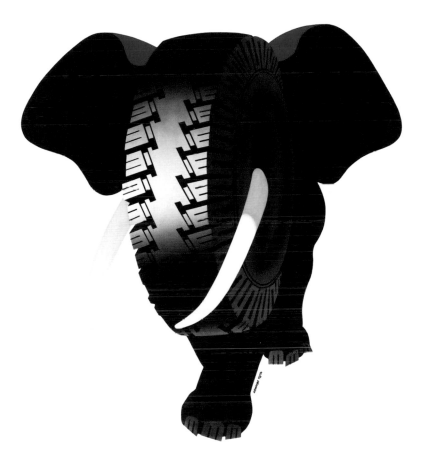

*Testa's groundbreaking ad for Pirelli tyres.*

*Dentsu building exterior.*

*A view of Toyko from the top of the Dentsu building*

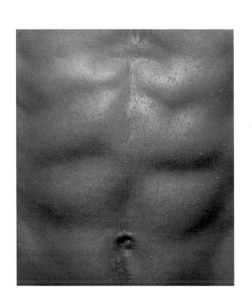

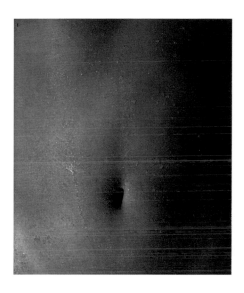 

*Marcello Serpa's poster campaign for soft drink Guarana reaped Latin America's first Grand Prix at Cannes.*

*'Advertainment' of the highest order. Audiences lapped up director Jonathan Glazer's 'Surfer' spot for Guinness.*

# The alternatives 13

*'Exiles from the mainstream'*

The tall narrow building on Herengracht in Amsterdam may once have been the home of a wealthy merchant. Like many of the houses along this picturesque canal-side street, it is approached via an imposing stone staircase. On entering, you half expect a butler to materialize and take your coat before ushering you into a book-lined room, perhaps with a fire blazing in the grate. But this is a 21st-century advertising agency: the butler has been replaced by a brisk receptionist; the fire with a plasma screen and a crescent-shaped leather sofa.

Welcome to the headquarters of 180, one of the most successful of a group of super-hip agencies that have clustered in Amsterdam. Some, like KesselsKramer, have Dutch roots; others, like 180, Wieden & Kennedy, BSUR and Amsterdam Worldwide, are tribes of expatriates who have deliberately exiled themselves from the mainstream.

On the metaphorical map of advertising, the Amsterdam crowd is out on the edge. But it also forms part of a larger grouping that might be referred to as 'the alternatives'. These are the boutiques, the micro-networks – the agencies that offer a divergent path to the big global ideas factories. Some of them emerged in the eighties, still more in the nineties. Armed with an enviable reputation for creativity, they are also known for their early adoption of the internet. A few of them even managed to drop the surnames and think up brand names for themselves.

One of the peculiarities of the Amsterdam clique is that it tends to specialize in sports shoe brands. 180 handles Adidas, Wieden & Kennedy works for Nike and Amsterdam Worldwide is contracted by Asics. This partly relates to the old axiom about keeping your friends close but your enemies closer: the European headquarters of Nike had been located near Amsterdam for some time before Adidas moved its communications department into the same orbit; a trick it had also pulled on Nike's home turf in Portland, Oregon.

But the links between the agencies are even closer than that.

## Amsterbrand

Back in 1992, Scottish adman Alex Melvin had spent 10 years working as a strategic planner for various London ad agencies. He'd handled big accounts such as Guinness, British Rail and Midland Bank. But Melvin was also a sportsman with two great passions: soccer and sailing. That year he decided to devote more time to the latter – a lot more time. He left advertising to set up a racing team in Stockholm with round-the-world yachtsman Ludde Ingvall.

That took care of the sailing. Soccer was next on the agenda.

The following year, Melvin wasn't expecting much when he took a call from a headhunter. But his attention snapped into focus when he heard that the post in question was with the agency Wieden & Kennedy, which had set up shop in Amsterdam to service the Nike account. 'They need someone who knows a bit about football,' the headhunter told him.

Based in Portland, Oregon, Wieden & Kennedy had been founded 10 years earlier by Dan Wieden and David Kennedy. The pair had worked together at McCann Erickson's Portland office, but it was during a stint at a smaller agency called William Cain that they met Phil Knight, owner of an obscure sports shoe brand called Nike. He became the duo's first client when they decided to go it alone. The agency thrived on the back of its close partnership with Nike, for whom Wieden penned the 'Just Do It' slogan. It helped that Knight disapproved of most advertising. Innovative and exigent, he challenged the agency to impress him. 'Nike constantly wants us to surprise and amaze them,' Wieden said, defining in fewer than 10 words the only client relationship that can lead to great advertising ('What makes Nike's advertising tick', *The Guardian*, 17 June 2003).

The ads ranged from gritty and dramatic to elemental and human. A spot for Nike's Air Revolution shoe featured muddy Super 8 images of athletes, both professional and amateur, over the Beatles song 'Revolution'. The Beatles took legal action over the use of the track, resulting in some useful additional press coverage. But even without the surrounding furore, it was one of the most effective uses of rock music in advertising.

Another commercial, for the 'Just Do It' campaign in 1988, starred an 80-year-old San Francisco runner, who said, 'I run 17 miles every morning. People ask me how I keep my teeth from chattering in the wintertime. I leave them in my locker.'

Wieden & Kennedy was the first agency to challenge the hegemony of Madison Avenue. And now it was moving into Europe.

Alex Melvin thought he'd better just do it.

He joined W&K in 1993 as its first European planning director. He then embarked on what he describes as 'the best five years of my life, personally and professionally'. As well as being a key figure in the development of Nike's global football strategy, he worked with Microsoft (on the launch of Windows 95) and Coca-Cola. He also found himself surrounded by a highly unusual group of people: 'The agency was populated by creative refugees from all over the world of advertising. In my opinion, that one office of Wieden & Kennedy changed the way international advertising was done. Micro-networks, the use of digital media – we were experimenting with all that stuff.'

But the problem with the overseas branches of US agencies, in Melvin's view, is that they can't help importing an American style of advertising, 'in this case, West Coast cool'. With a couple of colleagues – Guy Hayward and Chris Mendola – he began wondering what a purely international agency would look like. After all, global brands required advertising with no cultural baggage. 'This would be an agency with absolutely no affiliation – zero cultural heritage. And as none of us spoke Dutch, it might as well be based in Amsterdam.'

Unfortunately, Wieden & Kennedy got wind of the fact that the three were planning to leave – as well as a scurrilous rumour that they were pitching for the Adidas account. Melvin insists that, although they were aware of the Adidas pitch, they were innocent of contacting the company. (They were later officially cleared of the charge after a legal wrangle.) Nevertheless, they were tossed out on their ears. The intensity of the rivalry between Nike and Adidas can scarcely be imagined. 'Since we found ourselves on the street in a strange city where we didn't speak the language, the decision was made for us. We decided we'd pitch for Adidas anyway.'

A brief phone call to Adidas turned up the helpful information that one of the agencies on the pitch-list had dropped out – as well as the slightly less encouraging news that the embryonic 180 had only 48 hours to convince Adidas that it deserved to be heard. Enlisting the help of creative director Larry Frey, who had worked with Wieden & Kennedy in the United States and Japan, they 'sat in a small apartment and plastered the walls with ideas,' says Melvin.

An analysis of the Adidas brand revealed that it was undergoing a major resurgence thanks to two things: the introduction of the Predator football boot and the growing street-wear phenomenon driven by Adidas Originals. Partly as a result of the latter, a whole generation of young consumers regarded Adidas as much as a street fashion brand as a performance sports brand. 'Our pitch to Adidas,' Melvin continues, 'involved an approach that clearly grounded Adidas in the world of performance sport, to avoid it becoming subject to the fickleness of fashion. We distilled our thinking down to two words: "Forever Sport". That line ran on all Adidas communication for four years until the job was done in consumers' minds.'

The pitch took place in London. Obviously they won the business – that much you know – but it was a slight case of 'be careful what you wish for'. Melvin says, '[Adidas] wanted a commercial on the air in 35 countries within three months – when we didn't even have an agency.'

180 went on to produce years of eye-popping advertising. And unlike many of the traditional agencies, it had a handle on the digital environment from the very start. In 1999, in the run-up to the 2000 Olympic Games in Sydney, the agency hired comedian Lee Evans for a series of short films. The 12 two-minute vignettes showed Evans visiting various athletes, trying out their equipment and generally playing the clown. The athletes were all sponsored by Adidas and the films were lightly but noticeably branded. They were designed to be shown on the internet – but TV stations demanded to air them and the vignettes even ended up getting screened in the UK on the BBC, a resolutely commercial-free environment. 'We got in a bit of trouble for that one,' chuckles Melvin. 'The spots were so entertaining that they just didn't look like advertising.'

A highlight of the 'Impossible is Nothing' campaign in 2004 was a special effects extravaganza that depicted a miraculously rejuvenated Muhammad Ali in the boxing ring with his *daughter*, Laila.

'There's no magic formula for making great advertising,' says Melvin, 'but the first ingredient is world-class talent. And that's the great thing about Amsterdam: it's a city that's easy to attract talent to. It's easygoing, it's multicultural, it has a reputation for creativity and it is at the heart of Europe.'

There are many parallels between 180 and another Amsterdam agency: StrawberryFrog. The agency rebranded itself Amsterdam Worldwide in 2008 when its founders parted ways, but it remains historically important as one of the agencies that put the city on the international advertising map.

Born on Valentine's Day 1999, the agency fitted into a late nineties context in which the 'virtual network' suddenly became possible. Globalization was proceeding apace, the European telecommunications industry was deregulating, internet penetration was rising and mobile phones were about to become ubiquitous.

Founders Scott Goodson and Brian Elliott were both nomadic Canadians. Goodson saw the potential of the wired world in Sweden, where he initially went to visit his future wife – and ended up co-owner of a creative agency called Welinder, whose biggest account was Ericsson. The Swedes being the most techno-literate people in Europe, Goodson had a mobile phone in 1989 and was developing internet advertising in 1992. He met Elliott, a strategic planner, at the same agency.

A couple of years later, Welinder was bought by Publicis and Goodson moved on, accepting a job with J Walter Thompson in Toronto. The atmosphere wasn't quite the same, as he related in telephone conversations with Elliott, who had moved to a small agency in Amsterdam. Elliott recalls, 'The problem was that, at Welinder, we'd seen that a different kind of agency was do-able. Scott was frustrated because… well, you know what it's like at a big international agency: a conference call can never involve too many people. But the web had made size irrelevant. A small number of people could communicate with the world. So we thought, "Enough – we can do this."'

Amsterdam was chosen because it was cheap, groovy and connected. Apart from the tax advantages, it was a mercantile city and a cultural crossroads. Goodson stumbled on the name StrawberryFrog when he was looking for the opposite of a 'dinosaur', which is how he'd begun to view the traditional Madison Avenue agencies. He started out with 'lizard', but then somebody suggested the amphibian. 'But we didn't want to just call ourselves "Frog" because that's kind of boring. So we did some research and found… the strawberry frog, which is from the

Amazon. It's actually red with blue legs. It's kind of a funky little red, blue-jeaned frog… I also think it does a good job of explaining what we do. We're a small, highly-focused, passionate group of people that moves very fast and efficiently' ('Ready, set, leap!', *Reveries* magazine, October 2002).

At the beginning, the agency was viewed as intriguing but quirky. Elliott says, 'We'd get invited to big pitches as the wild card. It was, "Let's get those crazy StrawberryFrog guys in here." We were the comic relief. But then we would win the pitch.'

## Professional radicals

At the end of the 1990s, *Campaign* chose an outfit called Howell Henry Chaldecott & Lury as its Agency of the Decade. Founded in 1987, HHCL was the British template for the alternative agency – the hot shop that everyone else wanted to emulate. For a while, it seemed as revolutionary in nineties London as Doyle Dane Bernbach had been in fifties New York.

The founders of HHCL were Robert Howell, Steve Henry, Axel Chaldecott and Adam Lury. Howell had been an account handler at Young & Rubicam's London office, Lury a planner at BMP and Henry and Chaldecott a respected creative team at WCRS.

The agency's opening salvo was to run a trade press ad showing a couple making love on a sofa in front of the telly. Aimed at clients, it read: 'According to current audience research, this couple are watching your ad. So who's really getting screwed?' As a result, the agency got sacked by one of its first clients, Thames Television. But it was a hell of a debut.

HHCL staff carried business cards identifying themselves as 'professional radicals'. The agency scrapped the old-fashioned advertising notions of 'creatives' and 'suits' and challenged everyone in the agency to come up with ideas. It encouraged clients to become involved in the creative process during 'tissue meetings' (in which the agency presented them with rough drafts, or 'tissues', of potential solutions).

HHCL made fresh, funny, low-budget TV spots that were a marked contrast to the overblown epics of the eighties. Although the agency came up with many innovative campaigns, its most enduring contribution to the TV advertising archives was probably its work for Tango, the fizzy drink. The first spots were simple: somebody would take a sip of Tango and a fat, bald man, entirely painted orange, would spring out of nowhere and slap their face. It was surprising, absurd and very English.

But HHCL was not just about absurdist humour. Its ads for Fuji camera film were black-and-white portraits of people excluded from mainstream society owing to race, disability or age. And the multiracial cast of the agency's TV commercials – black and Asian actors with regional accents – showed a realistic Britain for perhaps the first time in advertising.

The real significance of HHCL was as a laboratory for advertising techniques that would become familiar after the turn of the millennium. Its aim was to offer '3D marketing' – now more often referred to as 'integrated' or '360 degree' marketing. It considered design and public relations central to its remit. It acquired a sales promotion company and merged it with the main agency. It was home to a host of dotcom advertisers, and in 1994 it was the first agency to include a website address in a TV spot. It also pioneered the branding of 'idents', sponsoring the brief flashes that identify programmes at the beginning and end of ad breaks. HHCL no longer exists, but it remains a shining moment in British advertising.

Among its many fans were the founders of another London agency that set out to transform the business: Mother. It remains highly influential at the time of writing, although it seems slightly more establishment these days.

Mother was founded in December 1996 to handle the launch of Channel 5, the UK's fifth terrestrial television channel. It broke with the traditions of the eighties in many ways, starting with its location. It was one of the first creative concerns to set up shop in the east of London, in Clerkenwell, rather than in Soho or Covent Garden. Its headquarters resembled an artist's atelier, with staff ranged along workbenches in the same open-plan room. Once again, the 'suits' were ditched: instead of account planners and handlers, figures called 'strategists' were a combination of the two. Overseeing all this were the 'mothers', who played the coordination role normally handled by the traffic department. Meanwhile, staff had pictures of their actual mothers on the backs of their business cards. The ground floor was 'dominated by a giant kitsch caravan... the lighting is by chandelier' ('Mother loves you', *Creativity*,

1 March 2002). The agency has since moved to sleek, shiny offices up the road in Shoreditch, but the collaborative look of its space remains intact.

The agency's name is said to have been chosen because your mother is someone you can rely on. Coincidentally, it was also the codename of the male government official who gave the orders in the cult TV series *The Avengers*, which rather chimes in with the kitsch quality of some of Mother's work. Many of the agency's early spots were drenched with references to the look of 1970s television. As might have been expected in fad-prone London, the style was aped by other agencies, with the result that Mother moved away from it.

Mother believes that the key to effective advertising is simply to tell the truth. The most obvious example was a campaign for a brand of instant noodles, Super Noodles. The TV spots portrayed consumers as lazy, inept slobs – although with a modicum of oafish charm. In its Mother Bible – an insight into its philosophy – the agency explained that, let's be honest, a pot of Super Noodles was unlikely to become 'the reason Mum's kids love her'. 'So a pack of Super Noodles becomes a packet of nosh for when you are too lazy, rushed or, more likely, drunk to prepare proper food. In this instance, the customer recognizes themselves and gives the advertiser the benefit of the doubt.'

As this book went to press, Mother had stubbornly resisted selling even a tiny sliver to one of the international giants, insisting that it wanted to stay 'pure'. Small, flexible, honest and determinedly independent – how much more radical can you get?

## Far from the Madison crowd

Lest I be accused of giving the Brits too much coverage, I had better turn my attention to the United States. The world's largest advertising market is by no means bereft of fleet-footed agencies offering an alternative approach (although many of them have forged alliances with the giants).

It's difficult to pick a favourite. How about Goodby, Silverstein & Partners in San Francisco? Headed by Jeff Goodby and Rich Silverstein, the agency was founded in 1983 and has successfully retooled itself for the digital age. It has been described by *Creativity* magazine as 'a creative hothouse' that helped to 'define modern advertising' ('The

Creativity 50', 1 March 2006). In the same article, creative director Gerry Graf – who worked there before moving on to TBWA in New York – summarized the role of an alternative agency when he said: 'They were simply smarter and funnier than everyone else; they made the big New York agencies look old and stupid.'

Don't know their work? Got to be kidding… this is the agency behind 'Got milk?' It all began in 1993 when Jeff Manning, then executive director of the California Milk Processor Board, hired Goodby, Silverstein to turn a drink with a dull image into something resembling Coke or Sprite. The agency's research revealed that milk was so closely associated with certain granular snacks – like cookies or brownies – that consumers could barely imagine swallowing them without the appropriate liquid accompaniment.

This was the trigger for the first TV spot, 'Aaron Burr'. It featured a history buff called at random by a radio quiz show host. Suddenly finding himself live on air, he was unable to answer the $10,000 trivia question – to which he clearly knew the answer – because he'd just taken an enormous bite of peanut butter sandwich. His eyes goggled as he realized that the carton of milk at his elbow was empty, preventing him from washing down the cloying ball of food. Unable to understand his mouth-stuffed mumbling, the DJ hung up on him. The ad's offbeat humour made milk seem fun; and the slogan was stickier than peanut butter.

Since that award-winning spot, the 'Got milk?' campaigns have taken on myriad forms, including that of a milk-starved planet in a distant galaxy. For the latter, the agency literally created an entire world – faintly inspired by old episodes of *Star Trek* – with interactive web experiences that blended seamlessly with the print and TV work.

Our tour of creative outposts would not be complete without a visit to Crispin, Porter + Bogusky, which single-handedly turned Miami into a creative advertising capital. The agency was founded in 1965 by Sam Crispin, but it remained stubbornly out of the limelight until 1987, when Chuck Porter was brought in to transform its creative fortunes. Two years later, he recruited Alex Bogusky as creative director. Around the same time that, in faraway Amsterdam, 180 and StrawberryFrog were insisting that they didn't need a worldwide network to do international business, the Miami-based duo realized that they could stay put and still make a global impact. To an extent, they created the agency of the future before others were even aware that the future was happening.

Porter told *Adweek*: 'We always had virtually the exact vision of what the agency would be – we wanted to build a world-class agency in Miami. And we made all of our decisions based on that… If you did terrific, interesting work, everything else would work itself out. We always thought that way, and we still do' ('How the little creative shop in Miami grew up, but refuses to grow old', 9 January 2006).

The agency first got itself noticed with the 'Truth' campaign – an antismoking drive. Using non-preachy tactics to reach a youth audience, it hilariously exposed the tactics used by big tobacco companies to hook youngsters on cigarettes. One of the ads depicted a mock awards show in hell, with awards handed out to tobacco executives for the Greatest Number of Deaths in a Single Year.

Having unsold cigarettes, Crispin Porter went on to successfully re-launch the Mini Cooper – a dinky little car with a British heritage that had attracted little interest in the United States in its earlier incarnations. The agency captured the car's plucky Brit appeal with the slogan 'Let's motor' and some equally nifty stunts – like parking one atop a gas-guzzling sports utility vehicle.

For my money, however, the most extraordinary 'off Madison Avenue' agency is based in Minneapolis, and its name is Fallon.

## Driving branded content

The agency had a long gestation period. It started out as an informal out-of-hours partnership between Pat Fallon, who worked at an agency called Martin/Williams, and Thomas McElligott, then creative director at Bozell & Jacobs. The pair had worked together on private projects for seven years before deciding to open their own agency in 1981. They were joined by Fred Senn, Irv Fish and Nancy Rice.

Right from the start, Fallon McElligott Rice – to give it its original name – wanted to offer an alternative to Madison Avenue. In their book about the agency's work, *Juicing the Orange* (2006), Pat Fallon and Fred Senn evoke the ghost of Bill Bernbach when they write: 'Even though research showed that people develop a psychological resistance to repeated exposure to a single ad, Madison Avenue was bombarding consumers and calling it success.' They imagined 'a new kind of agency that would communicate with consumers in fresh, intelligent and engaging ways'. Above all, it would be about creativity: not 'self-indulgent…

art for art's sake ads that win awards but don't affect the client's bottom line', but the kind of hardworking creativity that people like Bernbach and David Ogilvy produced.

It had been said before and it could easily have been dismissed with a yawn – but Fallon actually delivered. Its very first client was a tiny local barbershop with no budget. Fallon's posters featured 'famous people with bad haircuts'. An image of the wild-haired Albert Einstein was headlined: 'A bad haircut can make anyone look dumb.' Other eccentrically coiffed individuals, from Betty Boop to Moe Howard, followed. 'The barbershop's target market loved the campaign so much that people were stealing the posters from bus stops,' Fallon and Senn report.

Although it started out with small, local clients, Fallon eventually attracted national advertisers such as *Rolling Stone* magazine, *The Wall Street Journal* and Lee Jeans. After a series of mergers and takeovers it found itself in the midst of the WPP group. But the agency entered a creative depression and in 1992 Pat Fallon bought it back from WPP for US\$14 million (WARC profile in association with AdBrands, December 2005) and began to turn it around. A return to form was confirmed with the win of the BMW account in 1995.

It was for BMW that Fallon created what is undoubtedly its most influential campaign: 'The Hire', a series of short action movies, shot by top Hollywood directors, and run exclusively on the internet. In 2001, this was an extremely risky option for a mainstream brand. But BMW had been inspired by its product placement deal with the Bond movie *GoldenEye*, and research showed that luxury car customers were using the internet to research vehicles that interested them. In addition, it was known that young men aged 25 to 35 were already online in a big way.

In their book, Fallon and Senn explain: 'We believed that the best way to signal that these short movies were legitimate was to get famous directors. With the help of Hollywood screenwriters, we created about 15 scripts and asked A-list directors to pick one.'

Intrigued by the possibilities of the web and keen to experiment, a clutch of top directors came on board, including John Frankenheimer (*Ronin*), Ang Lee (*Crouching Tiger, Hidden Dragon*), Wong Kar-wai (*In The Mood For Love*) and Guy Ritchie (*Lock, Stock and Two Smoking Barrels*). Clive Owen, a newly hot actor after his performance in the film *Croupier*, was signed up to play the films' protagonist, an unnamed driver who is hired by various individuals and inevitably steered into danger, with only his nerve and his BMW to get him out.

The movies were promoted like genuine blockbusters, with giant posters in the streets and TV spots that looked like trailers. The agency even ran ads in industry trade magazines like *Variety* and the *Hollywood Reporter*. The first film went online on 25 April 2001. Nine months later, bmwfilms.com had logged more than 10 million film views by 2.13 million people. It was hardly surprising: with their heavyweight directors, starry casts (Madonna, Mickey Rourke, Forest Whitaker) and Hollywood production values, the films signalled the future of advertising – provided you had the budget.

According to BMW's corporate website (bmwusa.com), the eight films garnered almost 100 million views before the site was finally closed down in October 2005. (They can still be found on YouTube.) It was a triumph for Fallon and BMW – but it was much more significant than that. The internet had finally been established as a legitimate medium for mainstream brands – and 'branded content' had arrived.

In the meantime, Fallon had been acquired again – this time by Publicis Groupe. Although it had been forced to close its New York office, which was effectively competing with the Minneapolis agency, Fallon had opened a London branch in 1998 and was keen to develop a small international network. Backing from the French group gave it the clout to do so. Soon, additional offices had opened in Singapore, São Paulo, Hong Kong and Tokyo.

The London office was behind another groundbreaking campaign, this time for the Sony Bravia LCD TV. To get across its idea of 'colour, like no other', the agency released 250,000 brightly coloured rubber balls into the hilly streets of San Francisco and stood back to film the results. Bouncing and tumbling down the sharp inclines, the balls resembled multicoloured hail. An anecdote from creative director Juan Cabral illustrated the direction the media – and advertising – were heading in. 'During the shoot I got an email from someone who said they'd already seen our idea online. It turned out to be a film that someone had shot from their window on their mobile phone while we were making the ad. It had gone all the way round the world and come back to me' (*Shots* conference, London, 21 March 2006).

This was not the last time the film was appropriated by enthusiastic amateurs. Reliant on a neat idea rather than special effects, the charming spot was appreciated by viewers for its 'authenticity'. The ad took on a life of its own, generating a hit song and numerous spoofs. More interestingly, unofficial new versions began cropping up on the web, edited to different music. Juan Cabral pointed out: 'Media is global now. It's not just me any more – it's me plus everyone.'

Like the BMW campaign before it, the Sony commercial offered an insight into the way consumers interacted with brands on the web. Agencies were slowly beginning to tame the internet, even though many of them still bore the scars of their earlier over-hasty efforts.

# Dotcom boom and bust

## 14

*'We just wasted two million dollars'*

In December 1999 I was holed up in a hotel in New York City, idly zapping through TV channels while I waited for the streets to thaw. Dotcom advertising was everywhere that winter: I remember stumbling across a spot for Amazon.com featuring a motley group of employees in Santa hats singing carols. Other dotcoms followed the same 'wacky' route, while similarly failing to explain exactly what they were trying to sell. When I returned to New York a year later, most of them had vanished from the screen forever.

Were advertising agencies to blame for the dotcom bust? There are certainly grounds for arguing that they hastened the implosion. Hypnotized by the venture capital cash being waved in their faces, they agreed to shelve everything they'd learned about building brands in order to produce shallow, only occasionally witty advertising whose sole aim was to generate hyper-rapid awareness for their clients. Meanwhile, traditional advertisers rushed online with clunky banners and pop-ups.

It was fun while it lasted. On 10 September 1999 *Campaign* magazine ran an article headlined 'The dotcom wars'. Its first sentence read: 'If somebody were to make a billboard for the dotcom age, it would be several hundred feet high and sprawl across Highway 101 in Silicon Valley, reading "Welcome to the new gold rush".'

In 1998, the top 50 internet advertisers in the United States had spent only US\$420 million on offline advertising. In the first two months of the following year, the dotcoms increased their ad spend by more than 280 per cent. On the other side of the pond, the UK was experiencing a similar boom. By the end of 1999, total spend on advertising had passed the £15 billion barrier for the first time. A spokesman from the Advertising Association said that dotcom advertising activity was bolstering the success of traditional media. 'It's difficult to see any clouds on the horizon,' he added ('Dotcom boom helps propel UK ad spend beyond £15 billion mark', 26 May 2000).

The outdoor industry was one of the greatest beneficiaries of this largesse, as dotcom companies plastered their incomprehensible logos all over town. Billboards did indeed clutter Highway 101. In the UK, spend on outdoor advertising by dotcoms rocketed from £1 million in 1998 to an implausible £23 million by the end of the following year. Rather than building brands, many of these posters were aimed at attracting investors. There were reports of British dotcoms asking their media buyers to concentrate on sites in the City in order to raise their profile among the financial community.

There were occasional voices of reason. Stevie Spring, chief executive of the poster contractor More, told *Marketing* magazine: 'What we've seen is the dotcom companies needing fast fame, and spending lots of money to do it. Most have yet to get to the next stage, where they have to really build brands as well' ('Dotcoms gain real presence outdoors', 30 March 2000).

The dotcom frenzy reached its height during the last half of 1999 and the first weeks of the following year. Agencies in the United States reported fielding five calls a day from dotcoms who wanted to get campaigns off the ground by the fourth quarter. Some agencies warned that brand-building took time, while others admitted that it was difficult to turn down multi-million-dollar clients.

An article in *New Media Age* summed it up rather well: 'Bewildered middle-aged agency suits sat open-mouthed as teams of idiots in three-quarter length trousers and Japanese trainers hosed backers' money at them... They took briefs from 26-year-old marketing directors whose sole previous experience had been the production of club fliers...' ('How dotcoms killed off the ad agencies', 13 September 2001).

Even when the teams behind them were reasonably experienced, the ads were nothing if not eccentric. In the UK the faces behind ready2shop.com – fashion experts Trinny Woodall and Susannah Constantine – also turned out to be the bodies behind the site, appearing naked in a print ad. Others resorted to the emerging 'guerrilla' style of advertising. The women's site Hangbag.com projected its logo and URL onto the side of the Natural History Museum, which was hosting a London Fashion Week event. A spokesman said: 'We wanted to bring the Handbag brand out of the ether and inject it with an urban, streetwise personality.' It may have been the first and last appearance of the words 'handbag' and 'streetwise' in the same sentence.

The apotheosis of the dotcom boom was the Super Bowl of 2000. Dozens of dotcoms blew millions of dollars on dizzyingly expensive and mostly dreadful 30-second spots. Top prize for hubris went to E-Trade.com, which ran a loony ad featuring a dancing monkey. The endline said: 'We just wasted US $2 million. What are you doing with your money?'

And what exactly did the dotcoms get for their money? As Salon.com pointed out in its after-match report, 'the bottom line looks like a bit of gawking press coverage and a temporary [surge] in site traffic, but nothing so lasting that it could be called "brand building", and nothing so irrefutably valuable... that it could possibly justify the huge expense for a whole batch of unprofitable companies' ('Fumble.com', 3 May 2000).

One Super Bowl advertiser was to become the symbol of the dotcom bust: Pets.com, whose jaunty sock puppet mascot charmed a nation, but utterly failed to save a company. 'What bell-bottoms were to the 70s, the sock puppet was to the dotcom era,' commented *Wired* magazine ('1999 – What were they thinking?', August 2005).

Pets.com burned through millions of dollars in two years. Like another famous dotcom casualty, the fashion site Boo.com, it found that the cost of administration, storage, shipping and marketing greatly outstripped income. As it prepared its Super Bowl ad, it had already lost US $61.8 million on sales of US $5.8 million to the end of December ('Pets.com to put puppet on Bowl', *USA Today*, 25 January 2000).

The sock puppet was created by TBWA/Chiat/Day in San Francisco. It was basically a fuzzy white sports sock with mismatched felt eyes, brown markings, a red tongue and ears tagged on with safety pins. Its collar was a wristwatch and it carried a microphone. The ads were knowingly amateurish and the puppet's wisecracking style appealed to consumers. (In one Christmastime ad, the puppet stared at the row of stockings hanging on the fireplace, turned to the camera and intoned, 'The horror!') Each spot ended with the line, '... because pets can't drive'.

The sock puppet generated articles in the press and was invited onto talk shows. A range of merchandise was launched to capitalize on its popularity. Despite the success of the advertising, customers failed to bite, believing they were better off going to the pet store than waiting to receive dog food and cat litter they'd ordered online. While Pets.com went under, the sock puppet remained its most valuable asset, and was eventually sold on to a licensing company. The advertising agency had done a brilliant job of selling the mascot, but had been unable to raise enthusiasm for the site.

Pets.com was the perfect case study of dotcom fever. As the *Financial Times* explained, investors had 'dared to dream of new internet-based commercial markets with instant worldwide reach'. In the first flush of enthusiasm, the dotcom companies 'did not need to prove that their ideas would work, only that they had a compelling vision' ('Tech stocks in turmoil', 23 December 2000).

When investors realized that it would be years before most dotcoms went into profit – if indeed, they ever did – they cooled off fast. By the winter of 2000, the temperature was glacial. The *FT* article reported that the Nasdaq market, home to the biggest tech companies, had lost more than US$3,000 *billion* in value since its peak the previous March. 'This will go down as the year in which more stock market wealth has been destroyed than ever before.'

As traditional advertising felt the icy blast, online spending froze. In the United States, the Internet Advertising Bureau confirmed that after growing at rates of 150 per cent year on year, spend in the third quarter had fallen by 6.5 per cent – the first decline since the IAB began issuing figures in 1996. Ironically, this was partly due to the success of the internet as a medium – the number of website pages was growing as fast as the number of advertisers shrank. Many of the departed were bust dotcoms; but traditional brands were also wearying of the web.

An article in *The Economist* summarized the situation nicely. It pointed out that in print advertising there was a high level of wastage – advertisers in newspapers and magazines paid the same price for a space regardless of whether readers looked at their ads or not. But on the internet they were paying for page views or clicks on their banners. In other words, unlike their deal with magazines, they weren't forced to pay for people who didn't notice their ads. 'Online publishers are, in effect, punished for the efficiency of their medium' ('Banner ad blues', 24 February 2001).

When the situation normalized, everyone seemed vaguely surprised that the internet had not vanished in a puff of smoke. In fact, the web continued its rise as a powerful medium for information and entertainment, but advertising on it required a more sophisticated approach. Increasingly it became deployed as one element of a multimedia campaign. Banners began to look as outmoded as lead type. The emerging social networks offered the chance not just to advertise to consumers, but also to converse with them.

The one thing everybody accepts is that the digital explosion has changed the advertising equation forever. Even 15 years ago, it was difficult to imagine a scenario in which the TV set gathered dust in the corner of the room while people consumed entertainment on ever smaller, more portable devices. But now it seems very plausible indeed.

# Latin spirit

## 15

*'Football fans chant advertising jingles on the terraces'*

'**I**f you want to find Spanish agency people in Cannes,' somebody advised me, shortly before I set off for the annual advertising jamboree, 'first look for the South Americans. They're always swapping countries with one another.'

This insight not only turned out to be entirely accurate – as we're about to discover – it also prompted me to cover Spain and Latin America in the same chapter. As well as having strong historic, cultural and mercantile links, the Spanish and the South Americans make a similar kind of advertising. Jacques Séguéla would call it 'the advertising of the heart'. In other words, it has a certain warmth and sensuality that the work produced by the droll Brits, the wisecracking Americans and the suave French often lacks.

As luck would have it, the first Latin American agency types I ran into were two Argentine guys from Publicis Lado C, a Madrid outfit. Creative duo Fabio Mazia and Marcelo Vergara were working at the famous Argentine agency Agulla y Baccetti – one of the biggest names of the eighties in that market – when they were lured to Spain by BBDO, which wanted them to work on the Renault account. Later, when Renault shifted its business to Publicis, they were asked to set up a spin-off agency to handle the client.

'We'd never considered changing countries before, but the shared language made the decision easier,' confirms Mazia, as he and his colleague relax in a hotel bar in the scruffily trendy way that only creatives can pull off. 'Of course, it's still 12 hours away by plane and another continent, and there are as many differences as there are similarities. But Agulla y Baccetti has fathered a generation of Argentine advertising people who are now gaining international recognition. Juan Cabral [of Fallon] is the perfect example.'

Other Argentine agencies are also considered influential: in particular Savaglio/TBWA. Ernesto Savaglio is one of the country's best-known admen, having repositioned supermarket brand Carrefour in the early 1990s with a populist campaign that doubled as a protest against hyper-inflation. He specialized in satire, controversy and adopting 'the voice of the people'; an unfamiliar tone in advertising at the time.

I ask Mazia if he feels that there is an Argentine 'style' of advertising. 'The country is such a mixture of cultures that the result is highly idio-syncratic,' he replies. 'For example, there is an ironic sense of humour, which contrasts with a strong love of sentimentality. I'd say it's a blend of Spanish culture, Italian culture, American culture, and a melancholy sensibility that is often associated with the tango. I also think people admire the fact that we have Third World budgets, yet we manage to do First World advertising. Having to be creative on a small budget forces you to stretch your talent.'

Vergara adds, 'One of the main differences [from Europe] is that Argentine people love advertising. Football fans chant advertising jingles on the terraces and sitcoms refer to popular campaigns.'

A mention of football leads us neatly on to a country that has had a disproportional impact on global advertising – and especially on Cannes, where it has reaped an impressive pile of awards over the years. It is, of course, Brazil.

# The boys from Brazil 1: Washington Olivetto

'In the sixties, Argentine advertising was better than ours,' considers Brazilian advertising guru Washington Olivetto. 'Several leading Argen-tine creatives moved here, which contributed to the development of our own advertising. After the eighties, Brazil greatly outdistanced Argentina in creative terms. More recently the gap has closed again.'

Olivetto is the superstar of Brazilian advertising – as famous there as any rock musician. This high profile led to him being kidnapped in 2001 and held for 53 days before he was released in a police raid. But Olivetto had already generated many more – and more cheerful – column inches before that incident. For a start, he is listed in the *Guinness Book of Records* as the creator of the longest-running advertising cam-paign with the same leading character, for household cleaning product

Bombril. The simple but highly effective idea has comedian Carlos Moreno impersonating various unlikely figures – from Che Guevara to the Mona Lisa, but more often contemporary politicians – in amusing print and TV ads. It has racked up more than 300 versions.

Olivetto launched the campaign in 1978, when you'd have been hard pressed to find another image of a Brazilian man who was willing to do the housework. Traditional male/female stereotypes were only just beginning to break down – and Olivetto's campaign struck a chord with consumers. Research showed that 90 per cent of those who'd seen one of the ads couldn't wait to find out who Moreno would be impersonating next. At one point the spots were so popular that they appeared in the TV listings.

'The campaign was actually dropped in 2004, but it was brought back by public demand in May 2006,' says Olivetto. 'The characters tend to be topical, so the blend of advertising with news and satire means that the campaign never goes out of date. Moreover, the talent of the protagonist, Carlos Moreno, is awesome, making our job much easier.'

Olivetto has a writer's soul and a salesman's charm. He was, he says, reading and writing prodigiously at the age of five. Growing up, he imagined a future in journalism. But he also admired his salesman father, and was delighted to discover 'that I could blend the style in which I wanted to write with the style of selling that I most admired – ie advertising. I decided to become a copywriter.'

Modern Brazilian advertising began in the 1960s, says Olivetto, but 'it gained visibility and strength in my generation – in the seventies and particularly the eighties, when we began to get noticed internationally. The strength and quality of Brazilian television, in particular TV Globo, was undoubtedly fundamental.' Launched in 1965, the Globo network is one of the world's most popular TV channels, with 80 million viewers every day. It is famous for its prime-time soap operas, or *telenovelas*. Its parent company beams Portuguese language satellite programming around the world.

Olivetto started out as a trainee at a small agency called HGP. But it was with his next agency, Lince Propaganda, that he won a Bronze Lion at Cannes, for an ad for a brand of designer bathroom fittings called Deca. He was only 19 years old. 'The award gave me a lot of visibility and I was invited to work for DPZ, which at the time was the most brilliant Brazilian agency. I became creative director and stayed there for 15 years.'

In 1986 he was invited by the Swiss advertising group GGK (see Chapter 9, European icons) to set up its Brazilian outpost, originally to handle the Volkswagen account. Dubbed W/GGK, the outfit's billings increased eightfold in three years; in July 1989 Olivetto and his business partners bought the Swiss shares in the agency with Brazilian capital and renamed it W/Brasil.

The agency developed a reputation for eye-catching TV advertising in a market where airtime was actually cheaper than magazine space. Brazilians were gluttonous TV viewers: a *telenovela* was capable of pulling in 90 per cent of all households. For the price of a double-page spread in an upmarket magazine, the agency could place a 30-second spot during the news and reach 45 million people. Olivetto admitted at the time that, owing to the country's schizoid economy and supersonic inflation, only a fraction of that number was likely to buy the products he was promoting. But, rather like Argentine viewers, 'Brazilian people love to be entertained by the television and are very receptive to advertising.'

When then President Fernando Collor de Mello froze a large chunk of personal and corporate savings as an anti-inflationary measure in 1990, Olivetto acted quickly. For a tyre retailer called Zacharias – whose customers had evaporated overnight – his agency created an ad reading, 'If you have anything which needs doing but no money, come in and we'll find a way.' It put into practice, in extreme circumstances, the theory that brands should continue advertising during a recession, so they can emerge in a stronger position when the economy recovers. Olivetto did not suggest this approach to all his clients, however. 'We concentrated on clients selling [fast-moving] consumer products and advised others not to advertise. People just won't buy new washing machines in a climate like this,' he told the *Financial Times*. 'We want our clients' business for 20 years, not three months, so we were totally fair in giving our views of their prospects' ('Finest moment of adland's rock star', *Financial Times*, 19 July 1990).

Even in that harsh environment, the *FT* seemed to approve of the flamboyant Olivetto style. 'He regularly sends flowers to the female staff, the day's work is celebrated with drinks all round and every other Friday, stars are brought in ranging from TV personalities to footballers, artists to singers,' the newspaper enthused.

Today, of course, Brazil is one of the promising BRIC economies, along with Russia, India and China. And although the country has not quite delivered the boom that some analysts predicted, the fact remains that W/Brasil now has a far larger pool of consumers to reach with its warm and witty advertising. And Brazil itself continues to do well in international advertising competitions. How does Olivetto explain this success?

'What makes Brazil an extraordinarily creative country in advertising and in other areas – such as music, soccer, architecture and fashion – is the miscegenation factor. We are a blend of many races and that makes us creative, sensual, musical, talented and good-humoured.'

Despite his appreciation of this cultural *métissage*, Olivetto is one person who won't appreciate my linking Spain with South America – or indeed Brazil with the rest of the region. According to him, Brazil should have a chapter to itself. 'Brazil is not situated in Latin America. It is a continent apart, with a different language, different features and its own personality. Obviously, our Latin-American, Italian and Spanish brothers influence us. However, our personality is absolutely distinct, which is neither a quality nor a shortcoming. It is just our way of being and this reflects itself in our behaviour and in our advertising.'

## The boys from Brazil 2: Marcello Serpa

One of the agencies Olivetto commends is Almap/BBDO, which regularly spearheads Brazil's assaults on Cannes. The creative force behind the agency is Marcello Serpa, who in his early forties is already something of an adland legend, with truckloads of awards to his name. As approachable as he is physically imposing, he is also credited with having pioneered a new kind of print advertising.

While he is, as he puts it, '100 per cent Brazilian', Serpa began his career in Germany, where he studied graphic design and commercial art in Munich from the age of 18. He then worked at GGK in Düsseldorf – which, as we've already established, was the top German creative agency of its day. In 1987 he finally returned to Brazil, where he worked for the agency DPZ in Rio de Janeiro and then São Paulo. His next stop was DM9, part of the DDB Worldwide network. It was here that he won Latin America's first Grand Prix at Cannes, in 1993, with a campaign for the diet soft drink Guarana. It simply showed two perfectly toned, tanned and slender torsos, with bottle caps covering their taut navels. No further explanation was necessary.

'The approach came out of my education in Germany,' Serpa explains. 'Brazilians are very anarchistic in their approach to creativity, while Germans are far more disciplined. They gave me the concept of reduction, by which I mean expressing an idea in the simplest possible terms. Every inessential element must be removed. At that time, straightforward, purely visual ideas were still unusual.' He chuckles. '[Famed copywriter] Neil French says I was responsible for killing long copy in advertising, though of course it never entirely went away.'

Serpa's approach was illuminating in that it showed the direction advertising would take in the new era of globalization. Multinational youth-oriented brands needed campaigns that could run across many markets with minimal adaptation, so heavy copy and wordplay were out.

A minimalist approach also suits the Brazilian market, suggests Serpa. 'We don't always have very big budgets to play with in Brazil,' he says. 'Sometimes we're expected to make a TV commercial for one hundred thousand dollars, which is a drop in the ocean compared to an American super-production. And simple ideas are often inexpensive ideas.'

The year 1993 turned out to be a pivotal one for Serpa, because he also joined Almap BBDO as joint CEO with José Luiz Madeira – who came from a planning background – and the pair proceeded to transform the agency. Founded in the 1960s by Alex Periscinoto and Alcantara Machado, Almap had been acquired by Omnicom in 1988 and attached to the BBDO network. Considered lugubriously traditional at that point, it was rejuvenated by the appointment of Serpa and Madeira. They produced award-winning work for Audi, Volkswagen, Pepsi and Bayer, among others, and the agency topped lists of the most awarded in the world. From then on, there could be no doubt that Brazil was firmly on the creative map.

Serpa claims Brazilian clients have become 'a bit less brave' in the face of a sluggish economy, but he tempers this with the observation that they benefit from the country's pro-advertising culture. 'In Brazil, clients are consumers too. They don't sit in their ivory towers adding up figures – they actually watch advertising at home with their families. And they care about what people think. They want a spot that's going to stand out and impress their kids. Clients say to me, "Can't you give me a commercial that everyone will be taking about?" That's a very refreshing approach.'

# The reign of Spain

To find out about Spanish advertising, I turned to Manuel Valmorisco, a friendly bear of a man and one of the country's leading creative talents (who made his mark at the head of his own agency and as executive creative director at Lowe in Madrid and Paris). He confirmed my tentative theory that there was a Hispanic advertising culture, with links as far-flung as Argentina, Miami and Cuba.

'Many Cuban creatives arrived here after the revolution and brought an American marketing style with them. But we have also had a long relationship with Argentina. During the dictatorship and the various financial crises that followed, a steady tide of Argentine talent flowed across the Atlantic to nourish Spanish creative work.'

Domestically, the history of Spanish advertising has centred on the battle for creative supremacy between Barcelona and Madrid. 'There's no doubt that in the seventies, eighties and even the early nineties, Barcelona was more innovative than Madrid,' Valmorisco opines. 'It had developed a film production industry with many good directors. Lots of people started their own hot shops. The style was freer than in Madrid, which was where all the multinational agencies [and clients] were based. The Barcelona agencies had a closer relationship with cutting-edge designers and art directors. But today the size of billings in Madrid is perhaps twice that of Barcelona – and the creative work has caught up.'

Spain's creative revolution is associated with the Barcelona agency MMLB. Founded in the mid-1970s by Marçal Moliné, Miguel Montfort, Joaquín Lorente and Eddy Borsten, MMLB was to Spain what DDB had been to the United States and what CDP was becoming – at roughly the same time – to London. In a newly democratic market with a flourishing media, it was the first purely creative boutique, operating without a media department. 'MMLB was an agency with a distinct positioning, a different image,' recalled Marçal Moliné. 'In all those years we never had to chase clients or struggle to get on pitch lists. They came on their own and growth was continuous' (*Anuncios Online*, 11 December 2001).

MMLB devised its media plans with an independent shop called Tecnimedia. This outsourced approach is said to have inspired the creation of Spain's successful Media Planning group in 1978. Later one of

Europe's largest media planning and buying concerns, it eventually merged with the media arm of France's Havas in 1999.

On the creative front, MMLB copywriter Joaquin Lorenté is the father (as we've established, every country needs one) of modern Spanish advertising. He provided a contemporary link back to figures such as Pedro Prat Gaballí, who had developed scientific theories of advertising akin to those of Claude Hopkins in the 1930s. 'Lorente *is* advertising,' said the publicity blurb for an exhibition devoted to him at the Generalitat de Catalunya in 2006. 'MMLB was the school and Lorente was the teacher, gathering pupils around him like a master with his apprentices.'

More to the point, MMLB can be said to have created a Barcelona school of advertising, when a warm Catalan style became fused with a revolution in music, fashion and design. The Spanish public, which had previously tended to associate it with propaganda, began to appreciate advertising for the first time.

As we've already been told, one agency does not make a revolution – but two graduates of MMLB took care of that problem by setting up their own shop. In 1977 creatives Ernesto Rilova and Luis Casadevall teamed up with account handler and strategist Salvador Pedreño, who had worked with big clients such as Heinkel and Braun at the more conservative Unitros agency. Together they formed RCP. The idea was to combine creativity with hard-nosed marketing strategy. And it worked. In the summer of 1981, RCP won Gold at Cannes for its spot for Ambi Pur room deodorizer. It showed a blindfolded cat ignoring a dead fish right under its nose. Next to the fish sat a container of Ambi Pur. As soon as the container was removed, the cat pounced on the fish.

RCP's minimalist style – which owing to budget constraints hung on simple ideas rather than high production values – established a template for a decade of Spanish advertising. In 1987 Saatchi & Saatchi acquired RCP. But two of its founders re-emerged three years later with a new agency. And they hadn't lost their touch: in 1992 Casadevall Pedreño won the Grand Prix at Cannes with a spot called 'Nuns'. This promoted a brand of extra-strong glue. Two nuns passed a stone statue of a cherub at their convent, noting with alarm that his penis had broken off. They wrapped the little organ in a handkerchief and took it to their reverend mother. In the next shot, we saw her gingerly gluing it on – upside down. When she'd gone, a younger nun rectified the situation. The ad was held up as an example of Spanish advertising's 'beautiful simplicity'.

Another respected figure to emerge from the Barcelona advertising scene of the 1970s is Luis Bassat. After starting out as a salesman – initially to pay his way through university – Bassat founded an advertising agency, Venditor, in 1965. He sold that operation in 1973, convinced that he could build another, better agency with a more international image. At that point he was already casting around for an international partner – and having read David Ogilvy's *Confessions of an Advertising Man*, he'd set his heart on working with O&M. In 1975, with his new outfit Bassat Associados flourishing, he approached O&M and offered to sell half the agency to the network. 'We don't accept presents,' its then president, Jock Elliott, reportedly told him ('Olympic feats of the Barcelona boy turned O&M maestro', *Campaign*, 30 January 1998).

Five years later, however, O&M changed its mind. It acquired 25 per cent of the agency, giving Bassat a seat on the board. In 1992, he organized the opening and closing ceremonies of the Olympic Games in Barcelona. Many admen in Spain claim to have been involved in the Games in one way or another, but Bassat played a key role.

The period between Spain's entry to the Common Market in 1986 and the Barcelona Games in 1992 saw the second wave of its creative revolution. 'I never got as many phone calls from multinational groups asking for advice on what company to buy as I did this year,' Luis Bassat told the *Financial Times* in 1989 ('Riding high on an economic surge', 28 December). And surfing the crest of the wave was a Madrid agency: Contrapunto.

The outfit was founded in 1974 by a band of six agency professionals, including its first creative director Jose Luis Zamorano. Although it was one of the most creative agencies of the seventies, it gained international recognition only at the beginning of the next decade, with the arrival of a new generation of creatives in the form of Juan Mariano Mancebo and José Maria Lapeña. Indeed, Contrapunto became the first ever Spanish agency to win the Grand Prix at Cannes in 1989, a full two years before its Barcelona rivals Casadevall Pedreño took the prize.

The winning ad was considered another example of Spanish advertising's ability to keep things simple while hitting a heart-warming note. Promoting TV channel TVE, it showed a small dog – his name was Pippin, we later learned – doing everything in his power to distract his young owner from the TV screen. But nothing would budge the hypnotized boy from TVE's array of entertainment. Finally, after regretfully touching a photo of his master on the mantel, the dog picked up a suit-case in his teeth and left home. (A later sequel showed Pippin sitting alone in a bar on Christmas Eve, his suitcase by his side.)

Now part of the BBDO network, Contrapunto continues to produce strong work, under a third generation of creative talent.

And it is not alone. Take SCPF in Barcelona, for example. In 1996, it was started by four leading members of the agency Delvico Bates: creative director Tony Segarra and managing executives Luis Cuesta, Ignasi Puig and Félix Fernández de Castro. They've done great work for Ikea, Vodafone, BMW – and even the über-hip restaurant El Bulli. They have also established an office in Madrid and another in Miami, which acts as a jumping-off point for both the US Hispanic market and Latin America.

In Madrid, the creative torch has been passed on to Señora Rushmore, created in 2000 by former executives from Tiempo BBDO: Miguel García Vizcaíno, Marta Rico and Roberto Lara. The agency was named after a character in an interactive advertising campaign the trio once ran (her real identity is that of Dolores Goodman, better known for her role as Miss Blanche in the movie *Grease*) and its extraordinary website is designed to resemble her fusty apartment. Señora Rushmore's very first account was the football team Atlético de Madrid. The team was going through a particularly bad patch at the time, hence the tagline, 'A year of hell'.

The lure of Buenos Aires may be strong, but Spain still has plenty of dynamism to spare.

# International outposts

## 16

*'If you stay in the middle of the road,
you get run over both ways'*

**A**dvertising agencies are often involved in election campaigns. Few
have had the opportunity to work for Nelson Mandela, which is
one of the numerous reasons that TBWA\Hunt Lascaris stands out from
the crowd. The agency resembles a book or a movie that surpasses its
genre to become a cultural phenomenon. In the 1990s, Hunt Lascaris
burst out of South Africa to impress the whole of adland.

'From the very start, our mission was to be the first world-class agency
out of Africa,' says John Hunt, who founded the Johannesburg operation with Reg Lascaris in 1983. 'Everyone was trying to be the best on
the block, but we had international ambitions which we articulated very
clearly.'

Hunt and Lascaris initially crossed paths at a local agency. Lascaris
was an account man and Hunt a copywriter. He'd started out as an
aspiring writer and occasional journalist, but when an acquaintance
working in advertising saw one of his articles in a newspaper, she suggested he might make a good copywriter. (He's kept up writing as a
'parallel career', however, and one of his plays, an anti-censorship drama,
won a prestigious award.) By the time he went into business with
Lascaris, he'd 'worked for two or three local agencies before going off
to backpack around the world for a couple of years'. He adds, 'It may
not have been the best pedigree for working for agencies in South
Africa, but I have a feeling it was probably an advantage, because it
meant I didn't have to unlearn too much.'

Hunt and Lascaris started literally from scratch. 'We sold our first
campaigns from the boot of a car. It took four or five years for us to
really get traction with local clients. In 1985 we signed an affiliation

agreement with TBWA. That meant we could attend the agency's international conferences and measure our work alongside spots from all over the network. People were saying, "This is great stuff," which gave us a lot of confidence.'

The agency's breakthrough account was BMW, which it won in 1990. Two spots in particular caught the attention of the media. The first mocked a well-known Mercedes Benz commercial, which showed a driver emerging unscathed from the wreckage of his Merc after a smash on the notoriously sinuous Chapman's Peak coast road near Cape Town. The ad was apparently based on a real-life incident. The Hunt Lascaris version featured a BMW effortlessly racing around the same hairpin curves, with the tagline 'Beat the bends': say it aloud and the provocation becomes obvious. The spot sparked a debate about comparative advertising and got the agency into the public eye.

Another spot for BMW demonstrated power steering. It showed a mouse running across the dashboard and jumping onto the steering wheel. By scampering across the wheel from left to right, the tiny creature managed to steer the car. At the end, the mouse stood up and took a bow.

'Suddenly, journalists were calling us up and asking, "Have you got any more ads like this?"' says Hunt. 'We won accounts like the Seychelles tourism board and found that we were becoming more of a regional player than a purely South African one. It was confirmation that our global ambitions were not out of place.'

In late 1992, however, Hunt Lascaris won the ultimate South African advertising task: to run the campaign for Nelson Mandela's African National Congress during the run-up to the country's first multiracial elections. This did not require any change of political views on the part of the founders – they had always been liberals and reformers. In the early 1980s, Lascaris wrote a book called *Third World Destiny*, which challenged the racial segregation of markets and insisted that advertising had to be aimed at people, not colours. While Lascaris certainly found apartheid repugnant, his argument was in part pragmatic. 'The bottom line for me was, when 80 per cent of your market is black, you can't fiddle around talking about racial differences' ('The world's hottest shops', *Campaign*, 25 September 1992). The book became a bestseller.

At the time of its appointment by the ANC, around 30 per cent of the agency's employees were black. In addition, it would make ads showing, for example, black and white people drinking together in a pub. These spots did not reflect reality – but they portrayed South Africa as the agency felt it should have been. In another book, *Communications in the Third World*, published in 1990, Lascaris had written that advertising 'reflects dreams and longings' and suggested that effective communication could 'accelerate these wished-for realities'. Now this desired future suddenly seemed within reach, and Hunt Lascaris was to play a crucial role in making it a reality. The ANC brief ranged the agency against the local branch of Saatchi & Saatchi, which was handling the campaign for FW de Klerk's ruling National Party.

At the beginning of 1993, Hunt Lascaris transformed a through-the-line division called Applied Marketing and Communications into a dedicated ANC unit, which would be on duty 24 hours a day in shifts. The agency started by attacking the opposition with tactical ads. For instance, when the National Party put up the price of petrol, Hunt Lascaris created a poster showing a petrol gauge at empty, with the line, 'This is what the NP thinks of your brains'. In the run-up to the election, the agency switched to a massive radio campaign, as this was the best means of reaching the largest percentage of the population. Of the 23 million people eligible to vote, 18 million had never voted before, as many as half were illiterate, and the geographical coverage was vast. TV was considered expensive and not as widespread as radio.

Campaign slogans included a reworking of Abraham Lincoln's 'A government of the people, by the people, for the people', with its underlying reference to the abolition of slavery, and the more direct, 'The ANC for jobs, peace and freedom'. Working for Mandela did not make the agency popular with everyone in South Africa: Hunt's phone was tapped and the agency received a number of bomb threats. At the height of the campaign, the building was ringed by a barbed-wire fence.

At the same time, Hunt says, 'our ads were being discussed on CNN and our profile shot through the roof'. He recalls that Mandela was 'even more impressive in reality than his PR might lead you to believe'. 'Working with him changed me as a person. It put things in perspective. I met him six months after he'd been in prison for 28 years, yet he showed no bitterness. When he was briefing us on the campaign, he insisted that we avoid referring to the past. "Let's turn our mind to the future," he'd say. He also understood the value of cutting through the complications of politics and getting to the point, which made our job easier.'

Mandela invited the agency to the post-election celebrations, which Hunt describes as 'a most wonderful time'. At the end of it all, although 19 parties contested the election, the three main parties – the ANC, the National Party and the Democratic Party – had accounted for 90 per cent of the estimated US $40 million spent on advertising during the elections ('Ads bonanza in South Africa poll', *Campaign*, 29 April 1994).

Away from politics, Hunt considers that South Africa's particular mix has driven the agency's trenchant, humorous approach to advertising. With so many cultures, attitudes and education levels, there's little room for complexity. Local budgets also tend to argue for a more direct approach. Hunt's favourite phrase is, 'Life is too short to be mediocre'. He's also been known to say, 'If you stay in the middle of the road, you get run over both ways.' At the same time, the agency's ads retain a certain subtlety. 'A lot of our work has a sort of wry smile,' he suggests. 'It's not as "in" as English humour, and not as "pie-in-the-face" as the American variety.'

Looking back at the agency's rise to prominence in the mid 1990s, he observes: 'After the elections, South Africa went from being the poisonous country to the prodigal country. It was in a transitional phase and that made it seem very sexy to outsiders. It was strange, edgy and fun.'

In 1994 – the year after the elections – the agency's ad for soluble headache tablet Aspro Clear won gold at Cannes. It featured a man offering a glass of dissolved Aspro Clear to a woman, presumably his wife, in bed beside him. 'But... I don't have a headache,' said the woman. 'Excellent,' replied the man, grinning lasciviously. For advertising people around the world, it was one of those 'Why didn't I think of that?' moments.

The agency's new-found fame had its downsides – like other South African operations, it began losing home-grown talent to Britain and the United States. It also had to balance the needs of international and domestic clients. Today, the key advantage of TBWA\South Africa – as it is now known – is that it remains African first and global second. The continent and its consumers represent considerable potential for ambitious advertisers – and the agency is perfectly positioned to show them around.

# Australia's favourite admen

While South Africa should seem impossibly remote from a European perspective, its regular appearance on the evening news gives it an odd familiarity. Australia, on the other hand, feels considerably further flung.

Australia's king of advertising, John Singleton, specializes in a no-nonsense brand of charm that has endeared him to the media and the public alike. Referred to as 'Singo' by the press, Singleton is regarded as a talented copywriter and born rebel with an irrepressibly irreverent spirit.

When he floated John Singleton Advertising on the Australian Stock Exchange in 1993, journalists gleefully related examples of his unapologetically sexist campaign for Eagle Beer. Featuring a couple of macho characters known as 'Beer Men', the TV spots showed, for example, a dog tearing off a young woman's jeans. When feminists complained, Singleton replied, 'I don't care. There's only about eight of them and they don't drink beer anyway' ('Australia's biggest shop goes public', *Adweek*, 6 December 1993). He developed the Beer Man's Philosophy, one of the tenets of which was: 'Beer Man realizes women are no longer to be regarded as sex objects. These days they have to be able to cook as well.' As you'll have gathered, Singleton's comments come with a knowing, if barely perceptible, wink.

Singleton was born in 1941 in a tough inner city area of Sydney. But he was bright and gifted and enjoyed a good education at the respectable Fort Street High School. He started out in advertising in the 1960s, founding the Sydney agency Strauss, Palmer and Singleton, McAllan (SPASM), which he later sold to DDB. The agency was one of the first to stop aping the style of American commercials and use convincingly Australian characters in TV spots.

After leaving the DDB network, Singleton started his eponymous agency in the 1980s. It swelled into the giant STW Group, which owns more than 50 marketing services operations, including Singleton Ogilvy & Mather and a stake in J Walter Thompson's Australian operations.

But while he remains the adman that every Australian knows, Singleton cannot claim to have been the country's advertising pioneer. That title goes to George Herbert Patterson.

The man himself died in 1968, but his legacy lives on as George Patterson Y&R. Patterson was already 44 and had been in advertising for more than 20 years by the time he launched the agency that bears his name in 1934. He was born in South Melbourne on 24 August 1890, the fourth child and only son of a comedian and an actress (*Australian Dictionary of Biography – Online Edition*). When their mother died in 1905, the children were sent to stay with relatives and George quickly got a job in order to support his sisters. He started as an office boy with the machinery merchants Thomas McPherson & Sons, but his theatrical background and aptitude for selling steered him in the direction of marketing, and by 1908 he had risen to advertising manager of the firm.

Patterson led a somewhat picaresque life and in 1912 he departed for Britain and the United States, where he worked for a while in New York. He returned to Australia with the outbreak of the First World War. After initially being rejected for enlistment on medical grounds, he eventually joined the Australian Imperial Force, serving in Egypt and on the Western Front.

In 1920, Patterson joined forces with Norman Catts to form a Sydney advertising agency called Catts-Patterson Co Ltd. Their clients included Palmolive, Ford, Dunlop, Pepsodent and Gillette. But the two men later fell out and Patterson resigned. In 1934 he acquired an almost bankrupt agency and turned it into George Patterson Ltd. Although he had pledged not to swipe any accounts from his previous operation, Colgate-Palmolive and Gillette insisted on following him. In an unusual twist, Patterson was rewarded with a place on the boards of many of his most loyal clients – including Colgate-Palmolive and Gillette – virtually guaranteeing that his agency hung on to their business. To overcome newsprint shortages in the Second World War, Patterson's agency became the first in Australia to set up a radio production department. It was also the first to build a national network of offices, and the first to establish a research department. It was Australia's leading agency in billings for decades.

In 2005, when 'Patts' – as it was nicknamed – became part of the WPP empire, the Australian press lamented the end of an era. 'Just about every brand of note has at some stage in its life been handled by Patts,' noted an article in *The Australian* ('Industry benchmark bites the dust', 25 August 2005). 'Such was Patts' power it could dump clients when a bigger, juicier deal came along.' Yet the article added admiringly that when Patts won an account, the client rarely left without the agency's permission.

In the 1960s the agency had become part of the Ted Bates network, which turned out to be the wrong choice of international partner. Bates was weaker globally than many of its competitors and Patts remained largely reliant on local business. Having said that, it hung on to its position as Australia's number one agency until 2002, when it was knocked off the top slot by rival Clemenger. (Started by tennis player Jack Clemenger in 1946, this powerful marketing services group is best known in adland as the Australian outpost of the BBDO network.) As the misfortunes of Bates came home to roost, the network was swallowed up by the WPP group – and Patts with it.

But admired brands are as resistant in Australia as they are everywhere else. A little while later, George Patterson Y&R bobbed to the surface, promoting itself as 'Australia's newest (and oldest) agency'.

# Shooting stars

## 17

*'We work for the directors and they work for us'*

In Paris, even the world's most glamorous industries amount to the same thing: a warren of offices at the top of an elegantly crumbling apartment building, accessed by a narrow curving staircase or a clanking cage elevator. Partizan, the highly respected film and commercial production company, is no different.

I'm here because I'm a fan of Michel Gondry, the mind-bendingly talented movie director who honed his skills on music videos and commercials produced by Partizan. The company's website calls him 'the director whose work makes other directors cry,' and points out that he made it into the *Guinness Book of Records* as the director of the most award-winning commercial ever: the 1995 Levi's 'Drugstore' (the last time I looked you could see it at **www.partizan.com**).

But I won't meet Gondry today. My appointment is with the man who gets the work of people like Gondry onto the screen: Georges Bermann, the executive producer of Partizan. I want to ask him about the delicate relationship between advertising agencies and production houses; or perhaps more to the point, between creative directors and film directors.

From a public relations point of view, directing ads is the polar opposite of directing movies. Everybody knows who directs films – few people know who shoots ads. In most advertising trade magazines the client, the agency and its creative director get star billing when a new ad is launched. The director and the production house appear further down the page – if at all. As for the public, unless curiosity drives them to scour the internet, they are unlikely to learn the identities of the people who direct the extravagant sales pitches they see on their televisions every night.

This is a great shame, because some of the most talented directors of all time have worked in advertising.

Let's name names. Close to the top of my personal list is Tony Kaye, whose no-holds-barred artistry for clients such as Volvo, Guinness and

Sears, among others, has been making the ad break a more exciting place since the 1980s. A controversial, outspoken figure, he continues to intrigue rivals, viewers and the media. If you have to watch only one spot on his production company's website (**www.supplyanddemand.tv**), make it Volvo 'Twister', made for AMV BBDO in 1995, in which a meteorologist drives his car into the path of a tornado – although that stark description hardly does the ad justice. My bet is that you'll then go ahead and watch all the other spots on Kaye's reel. In 2002, the Clios advertising festival presented him with a Lifetime Achievement Award for his contribution to advertising.

And then there's Frank Budgen, co-founder of the London production company Gorgeous Enterprises (its receptionists chirrup, 'Hello, Gorgeous!' when you call them up) and director of many advertising blockbusters: remember the Sony PlayStation ad featuring the crowds who clamber on top of one another to form a giant, squirming human mountain?

Anybody who has seen his chilling British gangster flick *Sexy Beast* (2000) needs no introduction to Jonathan Glazer, another admired commercials director. He shot the fantastic Guinness 'Surfer' spot, which first aired in 1999: a black-and-white mini-masterpiece in which the power of crashing waves was symbolized by charging white horses.

Impossible to talk about directors without mentioning Joe Pytka, the prolific American film-maker who has been shooting commercials for more than 30 years for iconic brands such as IBM, McDonald's and Pepsi. According to the Directors' Guild of America, Pytka has directed more than 5,000 spots. With a background in documentary film-making in the sixties and seventies, he brought a gritty new reality to commercials.

More than six feet tall, with a mane of white hair, Pytka is famous for telling it like it is. He first got noticed when, making ads to pay for his documentaries, he shot some spots for Iron City Beer in real taverns, with genuine customers. Recalling his debut for the DGA's magazine, he said: 'I had done these documentaries that were fairly emotional, but which I had to manipulate to get my point across. I wanted to get to that point in my commercial work, working with real people in real situations. At the time, no one was doing it. Commercials were real theatrical... For about two or three years in Pittsburgh, I was doing these commercials for a local brewery where we'd go somewhere with real people – and they were very successful' ('Joe Pytka, King of the Commercial World', *DGA Monthly*, September 2002).

On the subject of unconventionality, I'd like to put a word in here for Traktor, the Swedish collective that brought a surreal new twist to advertising with its Jukka Brothers films for MTV – the content of which can only be summarized as 'Scandinavian redneck morons discover music television' – followed by similarly warped material for the likes of Nike, Levi's and Miller Lite. Evil beavers, mad chickens, savage dogs and seriously bad dancing: find them all at **www.traktor.com**.

Other names, such as Spike Jonze and David Fincher, are cult film-makers who have – unbeknown to the public and even to some fans of their movies – had an indelible impact on the advertising industry.

All of which brings us back to Michel Gondry, Partizan – and Georges Bermann, *ici présent*.

## From pop to soda

'I didn't start out wanting to make ads,' says Bermann, as we sip coffee in his Spartan office. On the wall is a poster for Michel Gondry's film, *The Science of Sleep*, which Partizan also produced. 'The company was founded in 1986, during the grand époque of the music video. That's what I wanted to do and that's what we were initially known for. Even today, if somebody asks you what you do and you say, "I produce advertising films", they'll probably ask you to explain what you mean. It's not a metier most people are aware of.'

Partizan's success as a producer of rock videos got it noticed by the advertising community. Controversially, Bermann suggests that advertising is always a step behind other creative professions. 'Advertising has rarely invented anything. Artistically, it recycles. It's something I've noticed with videos: we'll do something and the idea will find its way into an ad about three years later.' He points out that this is logical, given that television advertising is mass communication. 'A new form needs to penetrate the consciousness of the public before it can be used effectively in an ad.'

Partizan made its first commercials in the United Kingdom in the mid 1990s, putting its roster of rock video pioneers at the disposal of brands. This turned out to be a wise decision, as the golden age of the video has passed, largely thanks to the internet. Today, Partizan makes more advertisements than it does videos, although the latter remain an important element of its offering.

Partizan, like other large production companies, works with a stable of directors who are contractually bound to it. The production house acts as both agent and manager for its directors, promoting them to the advertising agencies and matching them with suitable film projects. 'It's a reciprocal engagement: we work for the directors and they work for us,' Bermann explains. 'It's not just the simple fact that we introduce them to the advertising agencies. We nurture their careers. We give them the opportunity to work in France, Britain and the United States, on commercials, videos and full-length films. And the difference between ourselves and a conventional talent agency is that we take a risk – as a producer of films, we have to deliver a result.'

For the record, Partizan has a stable of around 70 directors and offices in nine cities including Paris, London, Berlin, Beirut, Mumbai, New York and Los Angeles. 'Michel Gondry is one of the best known to the general public because he's made feature films,' says Bermann, adding with a smile: 'But don't worry: in the narrower sphere of the industry, we are known to have access to other geniuses too.'

He disagrees, however, with my theory that advertising is a breeding ground for talent. He considers it an applied art. 'Occasionally it gives directors a chance to experiment and to try different things. More often, it enables them to make a living while they are waiting for a chance to make a feature film. In terms of innovation, I believe music videos are still in advance.'

He accepts that the likes of Alan Parker and Ridley Scott emerged from the advertising industry – but the past is another country. 'That was before the era of the music video. And it was in England, where the film industry was very small. If you were a director there, making commercials was a way of getting behind the camera. I don't think the directors of the future will come from a purely advertising background, although the industry is certainly capable of producing arresting images.'

How much freedom, anyway, does a director have on an advertising shoot? Some creative directors suggest that the hand-holding is almost total. For example, by using sample clips from other films, an agency can make a rough mock-up of a spot and give it to the director as a template. Not all directors are equal – I'd be very nervous about telling a Joe Pytka or a Tony Kaye to leave their creative impulses at home – but one gets the impression that the creative agency cracks the whip.

Certainly, the production company is not encouraged to interfere. 'In practice, we have little power. Our role is on the one hand to choose the director, and on the other to respond to the demands that are made by the agency. The skill, of course, is in suggesting the right director for the project. Afterwards, once the agency is convinced that it has the right person to interpret the script, our role is marginal. We enable the process from a technical point of view, but we keep a professional distance. In fact, it would be seen as extremely bad form if we started giving our opinion. Of course,' he chuckles, 'if anything goes wrong on the shoot, it's invariably the production company's fault.'

And looming over the ensemble, naturally, is the client. In an interview with *Boards* magazine, Frank Budgen once expressed frustration at the gulf between director and client. 'I wish the clients were involved more up-front. The way it is now, weeks of pre-pro[duction] can be canned because the client doesn't like something... Clients see us as guns for hire, but the truth is that you do everything to a standard. I'd like the chance to say to the client, "This is the way I work, and this is what I want from this project"' ('The year of Frank', 2 December 2002). Nevertheless, Budgen admits that the work, while often frustrating and exhausting, can also be immensely satisfying.

So how do young tyros break into the industry? Encouragingly, Georges Bermann says there is no rule about where a director comes from. They can emerge from the world's finest film schools, or graduate from shooting experimental Super 8 (or more likely digital) films in their backyards. Former design student Michel Gondry, for example, started out making animated videos for a rock band in which he was the drummer. One of the videos was spotted on MTV by Björk.

Bermann concurs that young directors can get exposure making TV commercials, but it rather depends on the agency. He quietly despairs at the advertising industry's lack of willingness to take risks. 'In the United States, it's practically a zero risk environment,' he says. 'They accept that they're not making ads to explore the possibilities of film, but to sell products. That's why a large percentage of their advertising is based on humour, which is highly effective. But there's not a great deal of room for manoeuvre in the comedy register. The United Kingdom is a more audacious market. Agencies are keen to engage young directors because they bring with them the latest trends. British agencies are interested in the wider culture, so their advertising reflects that.'

He believes those who aspire to making great ads should embrace influences from art, literature, theatre, dance – but not the work of other directors. 'The most creative advertising is inspired by everything apart from advertising. Whether creativity is necessary when your main aim is to sell things is another debate.'

# Controversy in Cannes

## 18

*'It's not just about fun in the sun'*

Nights in Cannes always end in the gutter. That's to say in the Gutter Bar, a hole-in-the-wall joint opposite the delectably euro-trashy Martinez Hotel. The drill is this: you wallow in the Martinez until the bartender turns you out, and then you sashay across the road to the Gutter. The bar's real name is 72 Croisette, but nobody ever calls it that. Its Anglo-Saxon sobriquet is descriptive rather than metaphorical: until the late hours of the morning, drinks are served through a side hatch, so you knock back your poison al fresco, standing in the street. For a journalist covering the festival the place is a key axis: hang around long enough and you're guaranteed to either rub up against an advertising industry luminary, or hear some useful gossip about one.

Rather like the film festival – a less glamorous and more restrained affair – the annual advertising industry gathering at Cannes is officially about handing out awards, attending seminars and soaking up the best films from around the world, but some would say it's *actually* about networking, necking, swigging champagne, doing recreational drugs and falling asleep on the beach. One of the finest things about socializing with advertising people is that they do it so well.

The event takes place in mid-June and is properly called The Cannes Lions International Festival of Creativity: the significance of the 'lions' will become clear in a moment. The 'Creativity' tag was added in 2011, replacing the word 'Advertising' – either to reflect the changing nature of the business or to open the way for even more entries from a wider selection of categories, depending on your level of cynicism.

It attracts up to 11,000 delegates a year. In competition are over 30,000 pieces of communication: films, press, outdoor, radio, interactive, direct marketing and so on. Each discipline has a team of international jurors. The hub of the occasion is the Palais des Festivals, a giant waterfront building that looks like a clump of ice-cubes swamped in concrete. Here you can pick up your accreditation, leaf through magazines, drink coffee, check out exhibitors' stands and attend seminars in darkened theatres. If you're committed to your work, you can watch reels of commercials in neighbouring darkened theatres.

Alternatively, you can spend your time schmoozing with your fellow advertising types over breakfast, coffee, lunch, tea, cocktails and dinner. And after dinner, there's always an agency party or three to attend at the beach clubs along La Croisette. Followed by drinks at the Martinez, followed by more drinks at the Gutter Bar – followed by oblivion.

There are a number of prize-giving ceremonies throughout the week, but the hottest ticket is still the film awards bash on the last night. The winning ads are awarded Gold, Silver and Bronze Lions. The best of the Gold Lions is awarded the Grand Prix. It has become a tradition that if the audience disagrees with one of the jury's decisions, it whistles discordantly during the screening of the winning ad. This merely proves that many advertising people are very young; and that some of them are far from polite. When the ceremony is over there is a closing party on the beach.

Cannes is not the only awards ceremony on the advertising calendar – far from it. Others include the D&AD Awards, the IPA (Institute of Practitioners in Advertising) Awards, the Clio Awards, the Cresta Awards, Eurobest, the Epica Awards, The London International Advertising Awards, the New York Festivals and The One Show. Then there are numerous regional and local events. At the end of it all an influential publication called *The Gunn Report* (compiled by former Leo Burnett creative chief Donald Gunn) tots up all the major awards the leading agencies have won during the year and provides a ranking. Advertising agencies love receiving awards because these shiny hunks of metal and glass are tangible proof of their most ephemeral asset – creativity.

There's something special about Cannes. It's big, glossy and a bit over the top. And it can afford to be – although the organizers decline to provide an official figure, it is said to make a profit of €10 million a year on an income of €20 million. This is hardly surprising with entry fees of between €430 and €1,275 for each piece of work (depending on the category) and an individual delegate fee of €2,550. The event is currently run by the British publisher and events organizer EMAP, which acquired it in 2004 for a reported £52 million.

But to uncover the history of the Cannes Lions, we must visit an elegant art-filled apartment in the sedate 16th arrondissement of Paris, and take tea with the man who transformed the festival.

## The man behind Cannes

Roger Hatchuel was the figurehead of Cannes for almost 20 years. EMAP bought the event from an offshore trust, but it was Hatchuel's name that appeared in headlines when the deal was announced. As he recounts, the week-long festival began as a subdued occasion run by an intimate circle of cinema advertising contractors. And every other year, it took place in Venice.

'The story started in 1953,' explains Hatchuel, who is trim, dapper and polite, with a hint of steely determination that has no doubt served him well. 'At that time the only audiovisual medium available to advertisers outside the United States was cinema – commercial TV had not yet begun in Europe. Investment in cinema advertising was nonetheless very low, which is why you had this small group of independent contractors who all knew one another. They banded together to form an industry association.'

In order to promote themselves, the contractors decided to hold an annual festival to which they would invite potential clients. And as they were closely linked to the cinema industry, they decided to stage the event in the two European cities associated with film festivals: Cannes and Venice. The Venice link explains the adoption of the lion as the form and name of the award. (A winged lion is the symbol of the city's patron saint, St Mark.) The first winner was apparently an Italian spot for Chlorodont toothpaste.

The Screen Advertising World Association was based in London, largely owing to the prominence of the contractor Pearl & Dean. Hatchuel, who had previously been head of advertising at Procter & Gamble France, came across it when he was hired to run the French cinema advertising contractor Mediavision. Reluctantly, he allowed his boss – Mediavision co-founder Jean Mineur – to talk him into becoming chairman of the association. 'I felt it would be terrible for my personal image, because as far as I was concerned the association was run very unprofessionally by a bunch of old guys. But I respected Monsieur Mineur so I went along with him. This was in 1985. A year later, I told them, "Look, I'm not going to stay involved in this festival if it's run in an unprofessional way as a non-profit organization. We need investment, marketing and manpower so we can turn it into a real business." Bear in mind that, until the early eighties, they had refused to accept entries that had been shown only on television, because they saw themselves as a cinema advertising organization.'

By then Venice had been dropped as a location owing to the frequent transport strikes and lack of affordable, central accommodation for delegates. From 1987, Hatchuel took a financial stake in the Cannes festival and began to develop its activities. 'I wanted to turn it into the Olympics of advertising as far as awards were concerned, the Davos in terms of networking and seminars, and the Harvard in terms of opportunities to learn.'

Progress was slow: Cannes did not accept print entries until 1992. (Internet, media strategy, direct marketing and radio categories have been added over the years.) Hatchuel tried to steer the image of the festival away from sun, sea and sex towards something more serious. In 1991 he established a slogan: 'Less beach, more work.' This later became: 'No beach, all work.' 'The strategy was not 100 per cent successful,' he says, with a twinkle in his eye, 'but I was able to convince people that the festival had genuine value – that it was not just about having fun in the sun.'

For Hatchuel, at least, the festival was often a source of stress. There were accusations of underhand voting tactics and 'ghost' ads – those that had been created purely for the festival and never run in reality – and the clash of egos among the highly strung creatives on the jury could be spectacular. Their decisions were never less than controversial. Hatchuel still shudders at the memory of 1995, when a jury chaired by the combative Frank Lowe considered that none of the work merited a Grand Prix, to the extremely vocal displeasure of the awards night audience.

In 2004, when it became clear that his son Romain did not want to take over the running of the festival, Hatchuel decided it was time to bow out at the age of 71. And so EMAP stepped in. Delegates who returned to the festival under its new ownership noticed little difference – a few more seminars, perhaps, a few bigger names in the lecture halls, an earnest air of professionalism. But the Gutter Bar appeared entirely unchanged.

# Counting the cost

Agencies spend thousands of dollars entering work for Cannes and then going along to see how it does. An article in *Creative Review* reported that in 2001, one agency spent US$500,000 entering awards ('What's Cannes worth?', 1 July 2003). Occasionally, agency people suggest that the Effie Awards – a rival prize-giving event that judges campaigns on sales effectiveness rather than on creativity – is more relevant to the industry. But despite this occasional grouching, most advertising heavy-weights defend creative awards.

'Ideally you want to be top of the creative awards and top of the effectiveness awards,' says WPP supremo Sir Martin Sorrell. 'But I certainly don't think the two are mutually exclusive.'

Phil Dusenberry, the BBDO creative legend who drove home the mantra 'the work, the work, the work' during his career at the agency, said: 'Creative awards are your report card – they enable you to keep track of how you're doing. But you can't let them become your goal. The best reward is making the cash registers ring.'

But these days, big clients such as Procter & Gamble go to Cannes too. 'Award shows are an important part of the advertising industry culture,' a P&G spokeswoman told *Advertising Age*. 'We are delighted to see our agency partners recognized for the work they do in industry forums.' Marlena Peleo-Lazar, vice president and chief creative officer for McDonald's USA, added, 'Between the movies and luncheons that people think happen at Cannes, there is an ongoing dialogue about work... This really reminds you of the brilliance that does happen in the business' ('Are advertising creative awards really worth the cost?', 15 June 2006).

Erik Vervroegen, the multi-award-winning international creative director at Publicis, believes that attitudes to the festival are changing. 'In a world where millions of pieces of communication are screaming for attention, clients realize that creativity is the only thing that makes a difference. When you consider the amount of work the judges have to look at, they are in an even more extreme position than the public, because they are obliged to make a decision based on what they see. Any piece of creative work that emerges from the pile is obviously effective.'

He adds that an agency that wins awards has no problem attracting bright young creative talent. 'If you're not winning, you're considered insipid.'

Kevin Roberts, worldwide chief of Saatchi & Saatchi, would agree. 'The people who complain about Cannes are the people who never win,' he says. 'Creative people generally need to be liked and recognized. In my view awards have nothing to do with clients or new business – they're about inspiring your creative talent. At Saatchi, we're only as good as our creative talent. So when Saatchi wins a lot of awards, guess what happens? Our creative people want to stay, and other creative people want to come and join us. We're in the ideas business, ideas come from creative people, and creative people need to be motivated by recognition. Simple.'

Cilla Snowball, the boss of much-awarded London agency AMV BBDO, says, 'It's important for us to feel as though we're punching above our weight in creative terms. But how do you measure creativity? Cannes is one of the ways of doing that… Awards are a measurement, a beacon, a stimulus, they give people a sense of achievement, and everybody wants to win one.'

And there's no doubt that Cannes is incredibly influential. The creative reputation of not just an agency, but also an entire country can be boosted by a good run at Cannes. Such was the case in the mid-1990s, when Stockholm agency Paradiset DDB won a string of awards for its off-the-wall advertising for jeans brand Diesel, culminating in its client being named Advertiser of the Year in 1998. For a while, it seemed as though Sweden was the new hotbed of creativity. The spotlight has since moved on – although the Swedes still make pretty sharp advertising. Spain, Brazil and Thailand have all benefited from this halo effect at one stage or another.

So how do you win an award at Cannes? One of the criticisms levelled at the festival is that specific cultural references are unlikely to make it past the international juries: what may seem like a terrific joke in your domestic market will probably leave the rest of the world cold. Wordplay in any language other than English is clearly out. You need a big, crowd-pleasing visual idea that expresses what advertising people invariably call 'a universal truth'.

Richard Bullock of production company Hungry Man advises: 'Cannes is a good way of seeing new work and measuring yourself against your peers, but there's no shortcut to winning. On a day-to-day basis, you focus on solving the problem you've been given. If you try and win an award, the chances are you won't.'

# New frontiers

## 19

*'The future is being invented in Beijing or Shanghai'*

There have been promised lands before. In the early 1990s, after the fall of the Berlin Wall, advertising agencies scrambled into Central and Eastern Europe at the behest of their impatient masters. General Electric, Colgate, Procter & Gamble, Unilever and RJ Reynolds were among the clients keen to exploit this virgin territory. The death of socialism brought into the world millions of potential customers – almost 40 million in Poland alone – some of whom had been clamouring for years for access to Western goods. Philip Morris and Gillette had been probing the region for more than a decade. McDonald's opened its first branch in Hungary as early as 1989; so did Ikea. *Playboy* was equally keen on Hungary, and quickly signed a licensing deal for a local language edition. Cigarettes, scented soap, expensive toothpaste, cheap furniture and glossy sex: welcome to the free world.

But it was not easy going. In 1991, food was still being rationed in Moscow. Advertising executives from the West found themselves grappling with antediluvian telephone systems and sophisticated corruption. Gillette struggled to translate 'The best a man can get' into Czech. Agencies discovered that Eastern audiences did not respond well to one of the basic standbys of advertising: authority figures such as dentists and scientists explaining the benefits of fluoride or biological washing powder. Specially tailored advertising was required, but Western clients were uneasy about devoting large budgets to markets where they were unlikely to see big profits. The concept of branding was largely unknown and local companies tended to think in terms of one-off ads rather than long-term strategies.

'There has been a lot of ad agency over-enthusiasm about Eastern Europe,' a Young & Rubicam executive admitted to *Marketing* magazine. 'Anyone going into the Soviet Union… needs a lot of patience and deep pockets… Russians tend to think that if a product needs advertising it's either substandard or there's an oversupply' ('Ignorance blunts ad firms' forays in East', 12 July 1990).

Years later, agencies were still struggling to get it right. *The Wall Street Journal* reported that 'cultural gaffes' were common and that adapted Western commercials showed 'scenes and products irrelevant to the everyday lives of Central European consumers'. Even worse, there was a consumer backlash against expensive Western goods and nostalgia for defunct local brands ('Ad agencies are stumbling in East Europe', 10 May 1996).

One of the more promising markets was the Czech Republic. The aspic-preserved old town of Prague attracted so many tourists that an article in *Adweek* described it as 'the ultimate theme park… a real Magic Kingdom'. It added: 'And those millions in Western currencies pouring into the country can't hurt, either.' Finally, it seemed, the cash registers were beginning to ring. Local adman Jiri Kartena commented: 'Around the time of the revolution, we went through the seventies. Now the eighties have begun. Everybody wants to be in business. Everybody wants to make money. Everything is fast, fast, fast' ('Let the 80s begin', 23 May 1994).

Having been classed for more than a decade as 'an emerging market', at least half of Eastern and Central Europe has now gone ahead and emerged, although ad spend is only a quarter of that of the West. The Czech Republic and Hungary are considered mid-sized European markets. Russia, we're told, is experiencing a genuine boom. 'There are more Rolls-Royces on the streets of Moscow than there are in London,' says Perry Valkenburg, European president of TBWA, who built the agency's network in Eastern Europe. Agencies have set their sights on smaller markets like Romania, which still fit into the 'emerging' category. But even in Poland, salaries remain low, unemployment high and agencies continue to struggle. Despite the large population that made it look so promising, it has yet to live up to its potential.

## Asian creativity

Thanks to cultural differences and the economic turmoil of the 1990s, the Western advertising networks have hardly enjoyed a smoother ride in Asia. Since 2000, however, their attitude to the region has remounted from a steady simmer to bubbling enthusiasm. China gets them excited the most, but the country is expected to tug smaller markets such as Vietnam and Indonesia along in its slipstream. Vietnam, certainly, has a growing economy and clutches of young, brand-hungry young consumers in Ho Chi Minh City and Hanoi. Mature markets such as Japan and South Korea are recovering from their economic travails. India is the world's largest democracy, with a growing middle class spurred by technology expertise.

The big agencies have been in Asia for many years now. J Walter Thompson opened an office in India in 1920 – a fact that is likely to be a source of pride for Sir Martin Sorrell, the boss of its parent company WPP and a confirmed Asia enthusiast. McCann-Erickson opened an office in Tokyo in 1960. Other networks moved into the region in the seventies and eighties.

One old Asia hand is Neil French, the former WPP 'creative godfather' who is often credited with having brought the creative revolution to the Far East in the 1980s. French began his advertising career in Birmingham (which he describes as 'a splendid place to come *from*') before moving to London in the late 1970s. In 1983 he arrived in Singapore as a creative director of Ogilvy & Mather. After spells at Batey Advertising and the Ball Partnership, he rejoined O&M as regional creative director. He was eventually made worldwide creative chief of the WPP group, but left in 2005 after making controversial remarks at a conference about women in the advertising industry, which caused a stir in the trade press. (He suggested in blunt terms that their maternal instincts tended to get in the way of their careers.)

Recalling his arrival in Singapore, French says the market was unsophisticated – almost a blank canvas for somebody steeped in the creative ambience of 1970s London. 'There was no distinct style when I rocked up. All I had to do was mimic my betters in London, and bingo. After a year or so, I realized that if they'd buy rip-offs, they might buy something a bit original.'

One of the agencies on French's CV had a considerable impact on the advertising output of South-East Asia. The Ball Partnership was established by Michael Ball in 1986 and had no qualms about shaking up the scene. 'Don't you wish your ads stood out like Ball's?' read one of its promotional posters. At the time, said Ball, 'Singapore had the ugliest advertising outside Africa. It was hideous, dominated by reversed type in which the ink invariably ran into the letters, making them barely visible'

('The world's hottest shops', *Campaign*, 22 January 1993). Whether it was working for big overseas clients like Mitsubishi or small local firms like the Yet Kon chop shop, the agency injected drama and quirkiness into Singapore advertising.

Risky ads didn't always go down well with authorities, however. The Singapore government cracked down on posters that it felt introduced inappropriate Western sentiments to its citizens: images of youthful rebellion were received particularly badly. But this was the natural by-product of cultural colonialism. Western agencies in Asia employed large numbers of expatriates, and few of them were as talented as French. Fewer still had a detailed understanding of the cultures they were attempting to infiltrate. But that, too, began to change with the turn of the millennium. As the old guard drifted back to senior roles in London and New York, young local executives were placed in top slots. And in 2004, Cannes finally got its first Asian jury president in the form of Piyush Pandey, head of Ogilvy & Mather India.

In terms of creativity, however, Thailand still outshines the whole of Asia. The country scores extremely well at Cannes – and Neil French thinks he knows why: 'What appeals to the better judges also appeals to real people: humour and the ability to put on screen what those same real people are thinking, in an engaging way.'

Thailand needs to look in the rear view mirror, however, because another Asian market is making creative inroads at Cannes. It's still early days, but industry leaders have little doubt about where the future lies.

## And so to China

In 1918, an American former journalist and pioneering adman put his name on the door of Carl Crow Inc, 'the largest organization in the Far East devoted exclusively to advertising'. The story of Crow's Shanghai outpost is colourfully told in Paul French's excellent book *Carl Crow – A Tough Old China Hand*.

As French recounts, Shanghai after the First World War was booming as trade picked up. 'Europe needed just about everything China could produce – rubber, coal, soybean oil, cotton and silk, as well as other goods such as cigarettes...' Well-heeled Western visitors mingled with an emerging Chinese nouveau riche. The Bund became a showcase for corporate architecture; fine department stores sprang up and Nanking

Road was nicknamed 'the Oxford Street of the Orient'. Foreign brands 'were attracted by low import tariffs as much as the dream of a seemingly limitless consumer market'. Indeed, Crow's adventures in advertising later formed the basis of his own bestselling book, *Four Hundred Million Customers*, published in the 1930s.

Overseas brands and local merchants clearly needed to advertise, and Crow was in the perfect position to help them do so. Having already worked in China for many years, he could do business with both domestic clients and newcomers from Europe and the United States. As described by French, the Crow operation sounds conspicuously modern. He bought space in newspapers and magazines all over China, and compiled the first guide to the country's publications. He engaged in market research, studying consumer behaviour and spending habits and providing intelligence on competing clients. He employed teams of billposters in 60 cities. When the authorities cracked down on fly-posting, he leased official poster sites across the country – 'at one point he had 15,000 of these locations'.

Carl Crow Inc was in the creative avant-garde, too. Crow commissioned some of Shanghai's leading cartoonists and illustrators. The most important of these was TK Zia, also known as Xie Zhiguang, whose illustrations of spirited, seductive, yet distinctly Chinese young women contributed to the mythology of wicked Shanghai. 'Xie's sexual messages became… explicit and his models wore ruby red lipstick and transparent *qipaos* [mandarin-collared sheath dresses] with high slits up the legs, and had the artist's trademark penetrating eyes that drew the consumer's attention.' An ad for Pond's Vanishing Cream in the *Shenbao* newspaper in March 1920 is believed to have 'heralded the modern girl image in Shanghai advertising that was to become ubiquitous throughout the 1920s and 1930s', writes French. Other sources suggest that Xie's advertising images revolutionized women's dress styles in China, encouraging them out of trousers and into skirts.

But Crow had more than sex to sell. He believed that the Chinese consumer was distrustful of advertising, so he insisted that his illustrations of cigarette packs and soap bars should be as accurate as possible.

Nor was his the only international advertising agency in Shanghai. Advertising and the media in China were largely the creation of Westerners: the first modern newspapers and magazines had been established by expatriates in the 19th century. In 1921, a British agency called Millington Ltd was founded. Advertising continued to grow until the

Sino-Japanese War in 1937, when the overseas shops pulled out. Local agencies continued operating until the 1960s, but after being brought into state ownership they eventually became a casualty of the Cultural Revolution (1966–76).

Overseas agencies returned with China's 'Open Door' policy of the late 1970s. Dentsu was first into the market, in 1979, followed by McCann-Erickson, which was able to establish a representative office thanks to its joint venture with Jardine Matheson, the famous Hong Kong trading company. Having been rendered irrelevant by the Cultural Revolution, advertising was politically correct again. In 1987, then-premier Wan Li stated: 'Advertising links production and consumption. It is an important part of the economic activities of modern society. It has become an indispensable element in the promotion of economic prosperity' ('400 million to more than 1 billion consumers: a brief history of the foreign advertising industry in China', *International Journal of Advertising*, vol 16, no 4, 1997).

This vast market was once again open for business.

The parallels between Carl Crow's Shanghai and the booming China of today are striking. China is now the world's third largest advertising market, according to ZenithOptimedia, which means that Asia-Pacific is poised to overtake North America as the world's biggest advertising spender in the very near future – if it hasn't done so by the time you pick up this book. The region's advertising expenditure currently stands at more than US $140 billion.

Sir Martin Sorrell is well aware of the importance of China. And he suggests that it would be foolish to underestimate Chinese creative talent. With their vast heritage in the fields of luxury craftsmanship and the arts, these people have creativity in their genes. 'The future is probably being invented by a bunch of young graduates in a shed in Beijing or Shanghai,' Sorrell says. Kevin Roberts, the worldwide boss of Saatchi & Saatchi, states: 'The most important market for advertising over the next 10 years is going to be China. And after that, it will still be China.'

One man who knows China well is Arto Hampartsoumian, who has headed the BBH office in Shanghai since it opened there in November 2006. Changes to World Trade Organization rules the previous year allowed foreign agencies to enter the market without having to form a joint venture with a local partner. BBH got off the ground with an 18-strong operation, handling clients such as Johnnie Walker, Bailey's, Bose audio equipment and the World Gold Council.

'The most extraordinary thing you feel here is the enormous sense of optimism,' Hampartsoumian says. 'While in the West there is an underlying anxiety about the future, here there is a conviction, particularly among the young, that things are going to get better and better. And let's face it – if you were born in China in the early eighties, you've witnessed unprecedented growth in wealth and opportunities. India is a far more mature market in comparison, and its relationship with Western brands goes back much longer.'

China's questionable human rights record is certainly not perceived as a barrier to entry by foreign brands. As they have demonstrated in the past, they are insensible to local politics if the economic conditions are favourable and the media accessible. Hampartsoumian accepts, 'This is still the Wild East – it's the last frontier. I realize that living in Shanghai is not living in China. There's no doubt that the disparity between rich and poor will continue to be a problem, and the social implications of the speed of development here are enormous. But this generation is very different and far harder to control. I believe that for China, there is no going back.'

# The agency of the future

## 20

*'Brands can no longer force themselves on an unwilling public'*

For almost 30 years, the advertising landscape evolved remarkably slowly. Anybody who had worked with Bill Bernbach in the early 1950s would not have felt out of place at an agency in the late 1970s. About the only technological innovation of any note had been the adoption of FM radio by rock stations. Only when cable and satellite emerged in the 1980s did tectonic shifts in media consumption habits begin to occur. By the early 1990s, it was clear that fragmenting TV audiences and the rise of the internet were going to change everything. It seemed likely that, at some point in the near future, computers and television sets would merge. 'Convergence' became the new buzzword.

In May 1994, Edwin L Artzt, chairman and CEO of Procter & Gamble, told the American Association of Advertising Agencies: 'The advertising business may be heading for trouble – or it may be heading for a new age of glory. Believe it or not, the direction... is in our hands. The reason: our most important advertising medium – television – is about to change big-time... From where we stand today, we can't be sure that ad-supported TV programming will have a future in the world being created – a world of video-on-demand, pay-per-view and subscription television. Within the next few years... consumers will be choosing among hundreds of shows and pay-per-view movies. They'll have dozens of home shopping channels. They'll play hours of interactive videogames. And for many of these [there will be] no advertising at all. If that happens, if advertising is no longer needed to pay most of the cost of home entertainment, then advertisers like us will have a hard time achieving the reach and frequency we need to support our brands' ('P&G's Artzt: TV advertising is in danger', *Advertising Age*, 23 May 1994).

The advertising agencies agreed that he was probably right, scurried off to write white papers on the issue, and did relatively little. This was not the first time they had been warned. Way back in the early 1960s, a West Coast adman named Howard Gossage had pinpointed everything that could go wrong with advertising. Known as The Socrates of San Francisco, he was uncommonly lucid about his own trade. Advertising, he considered, was 'thoughtless, boring and there is simply too much of it'. He was opposed to repetition, suggesting that it took only one direct hit to kill an elephant. Although he was not lacking in cynicism regarding consumers, he at least argued for the involvement of audiences in advertising, citing the old proverb that when you bait a trap, you should always leave room for the mouse. He believed that an ad 'should be like one end of an interesting conversation'.

But it is the following quote that is often highlighted by Gossage fans for its relevance today: 'Advertising may seem like shooting fish in a barrel, but there is some evidence that the fish don't hold still as well as they used to and they are developing armour plate. They have control over what type of ammo you have, when the trigger gets pulled, and how fast your shot moves. Oh, and they're not all in the same barrel anymore' ('Rich media, online ads and Howard Gossage', Clickz.com, 8 November 2004).

The arrival of the digital video recorder in 1999 chilled agencies to the marrow. Allowing the viewer to 'time shift' viewing and skip commercial breaks, it represented the slow death of scheduled television and, potentially, the 30-second advertising spot. And then there were all the other distractions available to audiences: video games, blogs, social networks, phones that were becoming entertainment centres… suddenly, the agencies didn't know which way was up. The advertising industry resembled one of those cartoon characters frantically plugging leaks in a rowboat, only to find more fountains of water springing up around them.

Even Kevin Roberts, the worldwide CEO of Saatchi & Saatchi, suggests that consumers are, on average, less confused than advertisers. 'Consumers know exactly what they want,' he says. 'They want it all. They want to read their news in the newspaper. They want a weekly magazine to give them a bit of perspective. They want updates on their mobile phones. They want to check stuff out on the internet. They want to listen to the radio in their cars. They want big pictures on their TVs in the evening. They're not remotely confused.'

For Roberts, this is a bonanza for brands. In the future there will be more screens, not fewer. In our homes, at work, in supermarkets, on mobile phones... all the world's a screen. 'Our job is to create emotional connections with people, wherever they may be,' he says.

An early, courageous attempt to create a new model for this environment was the London-based agency Naked Communications, founded in 2000. Naked did not have a creative department. Or a media department, or planners, or account handlers. It didn't believe in traditional media, or alternative media. It believed in looking at its clients' needs and coming up with innovative solutions – which may or may not have anything to do with conventional advertising.

The three founders of the agency – Will Collin, Jon Wilkins and John Harlow – met at London media specialist PHD. Their backgrounds were in strategic planning, research and media planning. Collin told me at the time that, for him, one of the drivers behind the creation of Naked was disillusionment with the existing industry model. 'While I was at PHD we pitched for a number of big, centralized media [planning and buying] accounts. But I quickly realized that what these big clients wanted was to get the cheapest possible price for the media, with the agency fee ratcheted down to the lowest possible level. It was depressing enough that we couldn't compete on those terms – but what was worse was that, in that context, our strategy, ideas and thinking didn't seem to matter. When push came to shove, what the client really wanted was cheap media. In other words, you had to buy lots and lots of telly so you could get a big discount.'

Collin, Wilkins and Harlow inferred that the thing they were really passionate about – finding creative ways of connecting with consumers – wasn't what clients primarily went to media agencies for. 'Although some clients seemed highly motivated and engaged by what we were telling them, we had the impression we were telling them in the wrong place. Trading sits at the heart of the media planning and buying agency.'

The trio decided to take away the creative thinking element and sell it by itself. They would unhook strategy from execution and implementation and sell raw ideas – hence the name of the agency. 'It comes back to the old aphorism that you only respect what you pay for. What traditional agencies actually charge for is execution: making commercials, building websites, sending out mail shots... they give the strategy away for free.'

Being an ideas merchant would give Naked absolute freedom when it comes to solving marketing problems. Traditional advertising agencies with large creative teams are inevitably going to argue for advertising as the ideal solution to a client's problem. Digital agencies are similarly biased. 'We've always said that we don't want to own the means of production. One of our favourite quotes is, "You wouldn't ask a fish monger what to have for dinner," which goes to the heart of what we're trying to do.'

Eschewing the term 'media neutral', Naked preferred to describe itself as 'communications agnostic'. 'After all, if you are a retailer, your most important means of communication is your store. If you are an automotive manufacturer, actually having your cars on the streets probably does more for your brand than advertising. But we're not discounting advertising as a potential solution. We don't exist merely because the power of television is being eroded. We exist because the industry is built to 1950s specifications.'

Naked has since expanded worldwide, with 16 branches at the time of writing. When the agency made its debut in New York, there were sceptical mutterings from some corners of Madison Avenue. But the futuristic agencies kept coming. Take Anomaly, for example. The agency opened in 2004 – four years later *Fast Company* included it in a list of the world's most innovative companies, along with the likes of Google, Apple and Facebook. Anomaly sells ideas, which could just as easily be products as advertising campaigns. Or it might create the product and the packaging and the launch campaign as well. It creates intellectual property that it then licenses to clients in return for a share of revenue. As partner Carl Johnson said, 'We would rather invent the next Vitamin-Water than do the ads for VitaminWater.'

One thing it did create was a line of luggage for Virgin America. 'Richard Branson's new airline hired the team in 2005 to feed ideas into every part of its operations. Anomaly realized it could use the crew's luggage as a branding medium and brought in snowboard company Burton to help craft an edgy black suitcase with skateboard wheels and a removable cosmetics pouch. Sales from the luggage... will be shared three ways among the companies' ('The world's most innovative companies', 1 March 2008).

Around the same time, Australian creative director Dave Droga expressed similar ambitions for his new agency, Droga5, which he founded as an idea generator. 'I want clients to give us the freedom to come back with a myriad of communications solutions,' Droga told *Campaign*.

'That may involve entertainment, architecture, community and online… I haven't reinvented the wheel; I just want to take that wheel off-road and everywhere' ('Why Droga enjoys being in control of his destiny', 4 August 2006).

Droga's viral internet campaign for the clothing designer Marc Ecko won the Cyber Grand Prix at Cannes that year. It showed grainy footage of a graffiti artist apparently tagging Air Force One with the words 'Still free'. Such films – which can be diffused via the internet to a few and circulated by many – have become common. Even conventional spots, instead of beginning and ending their lives on television, now enjoy a parallel existence on YouTube. Ads also make perfect mobile snacks.

French creative director Rémi Babinet of the agency BETC says: 'Advertising agencies are the specialists of the short film. With the multiplication of screens, our expertise is likely to become even more relevant. Mobile media offer a particular opportunity, because the smaller the screens are, the more attractive short films become.'

The challenge is that successful viral spots are self-selecting: if they're not entertaining enough, nobody passes them on. This means that brands are often forced to disguise the 'selling' aspect of their advertising. But they stand to gain in the long term, because once they've established their credentials as entertainers, consumers will be keener to hear from them in the future.

## Content providers and inventors

Branded entertainment is the talk of Cannes these days. There is some debate about what it actually is, but Richard Armstrong, a partner at Kameleon, an agency specializing in the field, told me in an interview for Stylus.com: 'It's about creating ideas people want to spend time with.' In a world of unlimited choices, this is essential. 'Branded entertainment encourages consumers to seek you out, rather than requiring you to interrupt them.'

It's now common for brands to have their own 'channels' on YouTube, where they launch new videos and archive older material. There is plenty of evidence to suggest that viewers will respond to quality branded content. When energy drink Red Bull sponsored Austrian daredevil Felix Baumgartner's free fall from the stratosphere on 14

October 2012, 8 million viewers watched a live stream of the event online. At heart it was a conventional sports sponsorship; but the activation of digital media turned it into a global phenomenon. The highlights video on Red Bull's YouTube channel had garnered more than 32 million views at the time of writing.

A more conventional form of online branded content is the web series: short 'webisodes' that mimic some of the conventions of traditional TV, along the lines of the BMW film extravaganza mentioned earlier. During the 2012 Olympic Games, Kameleon made a series of short documentaries for Procter & Gamble's YouTube channel, telling the stories of athletes from the point of view of their mothers. Asian agency Fuse (part of the Omnicom group) created an online branded drama in China for a Unilever anti-dandruff shampoo brand called Clear. Not very alluring, you might think. But the story of a group of young friends battling career and life challenges became a huge hit, running on prime-time TV as well as online. The third series in 2012 attracted a total of 1.3 billion views online, according to the agency.

Because branded content frees its creators from the constraints of the 30-second spot, the storytelling can be richer and more engaging. Perhaps that's why it's attracting the attention of major established talents: David Lynch has directed an online film for Dior; Roman Polanski helmed one for Prada. The films are languorous, glossy and expensive, which luxury brands love, as do their consumers.

Facebook has given agencies another platform to play with. And it has upped the ante even further: social networks, as you know, are all about 'liking' and 'sharing' content. The better the content, the more likes. Brands rushed to establish fan pages on Facebook, relished all the likes, but then realized they needed content to lure new fans and keep old ones coming back. Some of the things they've come up with are pretty straightforward: in 2011 Heineken began posting fans' photos of its cans, in amusing or unexpected locations, on its Facebook page. Agencies (in Heineken's case it was AKQA) love coming up with ideas for consumer-generated content because it reinforces a sense of community for the brand and reaps plenty of likes.

But far more extravagant things can be done on social networks. Nike's 'Write the Future' campaign in 2010 – linked to the World Cup – included a spectacular commercial made by Wieden & Kennedy. A Facebook and Twitter element encouraged consumers to 'write the future' of their favourite players with a witty line or two. The best lines were then written in giant LED letters on the Life Centre building in Johannesburg.

Campaigns that play on Facebook's tendency to encourage narcissism always work well. In 2011 the Japanese agency Projector created the brilliant Museum of Me for Intel. This gathered personal information from your Facebook page and turned it into what looked like an online trailer for an art exhibition – except the pictures in the virtual gallery were of you and your friends. 'A soaring soundtrack turns the sentimentality to max. The experience is a cross between a photo album, a phone book and a funeral. Not until the very end do you realize that it was all just an ad: "Intel Core i5. Visibly Smart"' ('Robot cleaners and the Museum of Me', *The Guardian*, 24 January 2012).

Facebook, Twitter, Pinterest, Instagram... every social network is of interest to agencies, because it offers them the chance to get closer to consumers, engaging them on an active basis in a way traditional TV never could.

Following in the footsteps of Anomaly, agencies have realized that they can create things other than advertising. Designing apps for mobile phones and tablets is one thing – but how about making gadgets? Nike already dominated the social running space thanks to its Nike+ and Nike Personal Trainer social apps (essentially: get off your butt and do some exercise so you can show off to your friends). In 2012 it pushed the idea further with the Nike+ Fuel Band, created in collaboration with its digital agency R/GA. The plastic wristband (technically called an 'accelerometer') tracked physical movements and turned them into points – the more you move, the more points you get. These can be shared over social networks. The Nike+ Fuel Band turned exercise into a 24/7 social one-upmanship game – and it won the Cyber Grand Prix at Cannes.

Great though it was, the Fuel Band was made for just one client. Agencies have since latched on to the fact that if they design the technology first, without the prompting of a client brief, they can patent it and license it. For example, TBWA created an interactive window-shopping platform called Wi\Sh, which it showcased at the adidas NEO store in Nürnberg, Germany. Arriving at the window, shoppers saw a digital version of the store, with life-sized items on virtual shelves. A sign invited them to visit the Adidas e-commerce site on their phones and enter a code. From that moment, items that they dragged and dropped into the basket on the interactive glass of the shop window would also appear on their phones. They could save products for later purchase, share them with friends – and of course pay for them right away.

Although TBWA's Helsinki office developed the experience in partnership with Adidas, the agency retained the intellectual property rights. Creative director Martin Mohr says: 'We can "skin" the platform any way we like. It's a bit like a blog, where you have a basic framework that you can personalize. We can adapt this system to any brand's window.'

Mohr admits that patenting an invention was a strange new experience. 'But it illustrates the changing nature of agencies and what they do for clients. It's not about creating advertising – it's about creating new channels. It's about building stuff.'

## Shape-shifting giants

TBWA Helsinki was also behind the creation of a unit called Gamelab, which attempts to place brands in an environment that has been surprisingly resistant to them – video games. It's a vexing problem for agencies: their research shows that players actively dislike advertising in games. But Gamelab founder and agency vice-president Väinö Leskinen thinks he has the answer: 'The brand needs to be an integral part of the game… it has to add value to the players' experience.'

The first example was a partnership in China between McDonald's and Rovio, creator of the wildly successful smartphone game Angry Birds. While dining at McDonald's, players could unlock hidden game modes and get free power-ups. It was a perfect match of gaming and location-based marketing. And it was backed by a TV spot.

Innovation is often identified with smaller, more nimble shops. But the TBWA example shows that the big, traditional agency networks won't go away – and they're all grappling with this new universe. In 2012, Sir Martin Sorrell's WPP acquired AKQA, 'one of the last big independent digital specialists', for a reported US$540 million ('WPP acquires AKQA to beef up digital marketing', *The New York Times*, 20 June 2012).

The advertising giants understand that they must help their clients thrive in the multi-screen world – or face uncomfortable questions about their utility. Happily, the key to successful advertising remains unchanged.

Andrew Robertson is the worldwide CEO of BBDO. An Englishman in New York, Robertson has taken a leaf out of David Ogilvy's book and branded himself as such in his striped shirts and brightly coloured braces. But despite his somewhat traditional dress code, he is enthusiastic about technology. 'If I could have carried my entire record collection around with me when I was a teenager, I would have done,' he says. 'Today, that's no problem. What consumers want is access to everything, all the time. They don't even have to pay for it: you can download a two-hour movie for less than the price of a postage stamp. On the one hand, that's the single biggest threat to us as an industry, because people are no longer waiting around to hear what we've got to say. The opportunity is that if you can create content that's good enough, you can obtain face-time with consumers that money can't buy. Not only will they watch it, but they'll encourage others to watch it too.'

The answer to all this, say Robertson and his peers, is good, old-fashioned creativity. 'Our job is to create content that captures and holds consumers long enough to provide them with a message, a demonstration or an experience that changes what they think, feel and most importantly do concerning a product.'

The most awe-inspiring medium in the world is rendered banal by content that lacks magic. For advertising agencies, then, the question is the same as it ever was: what's the big idea?

# Conclusion

*'Advertising by invitation only'*

This is the most exciting time to be working in advertising since the 1950s. During my global tour of the business, more than one person told me that the industry had experienced three revolutions: the invention of the printing press, the creative revolution – and the digital one that is happening right now.

In fact it seems to me that the creative revolution was a rather prolonged affair. After the explosion of creativity at Doyle Dane Bernbach in the fifties, the shockwave rippled across Manhattan, finally making landfall in the United Kingdom in the early 1970s. From there it travelled on to Western Europe, arriving in Latin America and Asia in the 1980s and doubling back to Eastern Europe in the 1990s. By then, the technology that is powering today's revolution had already begun to emerge. China may be the first economy to feel the brunt of two revolutions at once.

What makes advertising so fascinating right now is that nobody really knows how it will evolve. Many of the agencies described in these pages can still be looked upon as role models; others are museum pieces. Advertising's future will not resemble its past. Experts are busy tracking increasingly slippery consumers and mapping their behaviour, but their findings always come with a question mark attached. For sure there are smartphones and social media and screens everywhere, but how do these intersect and interact? The picture is still far from clear.

Agencies have accepted that they must look beyond the trusted combination of TV, print, outdoor and radio, but the range of alternatives is scarily huge. After all, a new media vehicle seems to emerge every week. A few more probably have arrived on the scene since I wrote that last sentence. Today's media landscape is not one of convergence, but of diffraction: an ever-expanding number of media options competing for consumer attention. The advertising industry is in danger of looking like a fat kid playing tag with a group of nimbler opponents who remain tantalizingly out of reach. It will end up red-faced, exhausted and undignified. What it needs to do is sit back, open its bag of candy, and wait for its prey to come creeping back into range.

The good news for those of you who wish to work in the industry is that the collapse of old certainties has given rise to new opportunities. The word 'communication' now covers such a vast territory that it almost defies definition. Psychologists, sociologists, anthropologists, musicologists, technology wizards and gaming enthusiasts... any or all of them might have a role to play at a modern agency.

But those with the most to gain from today's multi-channel revolution are undoubtedly the consumers. In France, 'publiphobes' wish to rid the world of advertising. But their quixotic mission has been rendered almost irrelevant by the manifold nature of media. Advertisers can pump out as many messages as they want – we don't have to pay attention. Even better, we can invite them to send us a CV and decide whether or not we wish to interview them.

The truth is that few people expect to rid their lives of advertising entirely. A good sales pitch for a useful or attractive product will always grab our attention. But now the pitch has to be spectacularly good, relevant to our particular situation, and delivered in the appropriate way, at the right moment. It's enough to make you sympathize with the agencies.

One thing is certain: advertising is not going away. As long as somebody has something to sell, adland will always have a place on the map.

# REFERENCES

## Books

Brierly, Sean (1995) *The Advertising Handbook*, Routledge, Abingdon

Bullmore, Jeremy (1991) *Behind the Scenes in Advertising*, WARC, London

Challis, Clive (2005) *Helmut Krone. The Book*, Cambridge Enchorial Press, Cambridge, UK

Douglas, Torin (1984) *The Complete Guide to Advertising*, Chartwell Books, New Jersey

Fallon, Pat and Senn, Fred (2006) *Juicing the Orange*, Harvard Business School Press, Boston

Fendley, Alison (1995) *Saatchi & Saatchi: The Inside Story*, Arcade Publishing, New York

Fox, Stephen (1984) *The Mirror Makers*, William Morrow & Company, New York

French, Paul (2006) *Carl Crow – A Tough Old China Hand*, Hong Kong University Press, Hong Kong

Heller, Stephen (2000) *Paul Rand*, Phaidon, London

Hopkins, Claude C (new edition, 1998) *My Life in Advertising/Scientific Advertising*, NTC Business Books, Lincolnwood, Chicago

Kufrin, Joan (1995) *Leo Burnett, Star Reacher*, Leo Burnett Company, Inc, Chicago

Lawrence, Mary Wells (2002) *A Big Life (in Advertising)*, Knopf, New York

Levenson, Bob (1987) *Bill Bernbach's Book*, Villard Books, New York

Loiseau, Marc and Pincas, Stéphane (eds) (2006) *Born in 1842, A History of Advertising*, Publicis Groupe

Lorin, Philippe (1991) *Cinq Géants de la Publicité*, Assouline, Paris

Marcantonio, Alfredo (2000) *Remember Those Great Volkswagen Ads?*, Dakini, London

Mayer, Martin (1958) *Madison Avenue, USA*, Harper, New York

Myerson, Jeremy and Vickers, Graham (2002) *Rewind: Forty Years of Design & Advertising*, Phaidon, London

Ogilvy, David (1963) *Confessions of an Advertising Man*, Southbank Publishing, London

Ogilvy, David (1985) *Ogilvy on Advertising*, Vintage, London

Packard, Vance (1957) *The Hidden Persuaders*, Cardinal, New York

Pirella, Emanuele (2001) *Il Copywriter, Mestiere D'Arte*, Il Sagiattore, Milan

Pollitt, Stanley and Feldwick, Paul (eds) (2000) *Pollitt On Planning*, Admap Publications, Henley-on-Thames

Raphaelson, Joel (ed) (1986) *The Unpublished David Ogilvy*, The Ogilvy Group, Inc

Ritchie, John and Salmon, John (2000) *CDP: Inside Collett Dickenson Pearce*, B.T. Batsford, London

Scott, Jeremy (2002) *Fast and Louche*, Profile Books, London

Séguéla, Jacques (1979) *Ne Dites Pas à Ma Mère Que Je Suis Dans la Publicité… Elle Me Croit Pianiste Dans un Bordel*, Flammarion, Paris

Séguéla, Jacques (2005) *Tous Ego: Havas, Moi et les Autres*, Editions Gawsewitch, Paris

Souter, Nick and Newman, Stuart (1988) *Creative Director's Sourcebook*, MacDonald, London

Stabiner, Karen (1993) *Inventing Desire*, Simon & Schuster, New York

Testa, Armando and Tsiaras, Philip (1987) *Armando Testa* (exhibition catalogue) Parsons School of Design, New York

## Online resources

AdBrands (www.adbrands.net)
Advertising Age (www.adage.com)
Brand Republic (www.brandrepublic.com)
Clickz (www.clickz.com)
LexisNexis (www.lexisnexis.com)
Musée de la Publicité (www.museedelapub.org)
Shots (www.shots.net)
Stocks and News (www.stocksandnews.com)
Stratégies (www.strategies.fr)
World Advertising Research Centre (www.warc.com)

# INDEX